DISCIPLINING DEMOCRACY

A volume in the series

Histories of American Education

Edited by Jonathan Zimmerman and Tracy L. Steffes

A list of titles in this series is available at cornellpress.cornell.edu.

DISCIPLINING DEMOCRACY

HOW THE MODERN
AMERICAN UNIVERSITY
TRANSFORMED
STUDENT ACTIVISM

DAVID S. BUSCH

CORNELL UNIVERSITY PRESS
Ithaca and London

First published 2025 by Cornell University Press

Library of Congress Cataloging-in-Publication Data

Names: Busch, David S., 1986- author.
Title: Disciplining democracy : how the modern American university transformed student activism / David S. Busch.
Description: Ithaca : Cornell University Press, 2025. | Series: Histories of American education | Includes bibliographical references and index.
Identifiers: LCCN 2024029689 (print) | LCCN 2024029690 (ebook) | ISBN 9781501779961 (hardcover) | ISBN 9781501780127 (epub) | ISBN 9781501780110 (pdf)
Subjects: LCSH: Service learning—United States—History—20th century. | Student movements—United States—History—20th century. | College students—Political activity—United States. | Education, Higher—Political aspects—United States. | Education, Higher—Aims and objectives—United States. | Education, Higher—Social aspects—United States. | Civics—Study and teaching (Higher)—United States.
Classification: LCC LC220.5 .B87 2025 (print) | LCC LC220.5 (ebook) | DDC 378.1/9810973—dc23/eng/20240725
LC record available at https://lccn.loc.gov/2024029689
LC ebook record available at https://lccn.loc.gov/2024029690

For A & J

When I feed the poor, they call me a saint. When I ask why the poor have no food, they call me a communist.

—Archbishop Dom Hélder

Contents

ACKNOWLEDGMENTS

In late August 2013, I sat down in Nico Slate's office for the first time. But we did not stay in his office long. Like we did during many of our meetings, we ended up outside as we discussed my research and teaching. Throughout the many stages of this book, those walking discussions sustained me through the various trials and tribulations of writing, challenged me to ask more critical questions of my historical actors and myself, and, perhaps most importantly, provided me a model of what it means to be a scholar, mentor, and friend. Thank you, Nico.

I also want to take a moment to express my gratitude to my other mentors and friends at Carnegie Mellon University, when this book was an unwieldy idea. Thank you to Jay Aronson, Wendy Goldman, Christopher Phillips, Scott Sandage, Lisa Tetrault, and Joe Trotter, all of whom helped me grow as a scholar and thinker. A special thanks goes to Judith Schachter, who always willingly put aside time to read my work. I am grateful for having had the chance to learn with a group of supportive peers, including Christine Grant, Susan Grunewald, Mark Hauser, and Clayton Vaughn-Robertson.

Many of these discussions would never have happened without the influence of Ken Bindas. In 2010, after taking over a year off to travel, I returned to the classroom and had the fortunate opportunity to take Bindas's course on modern American history at Kent State University. His approach—one that invited students to be coauthors and co-collaborators in the classroom—illuminated the richness and intellectual commitment of historical scholarship. I will always remember his class.

Over the course of writing this book, I have had the privilege of being able to discuss my work with service learning practitioners and former student activists. In particular, I am grateful for my discussions with Timothy Stanton, both on the sunny day in Palo Alto, California, and the gray midwinter day in South Bend, Indiana. And a big thank-you to the many individuals who willingly opened up their schedules to talk with me about their experiences, including Keith Archuletta, Heather Booth, Gail Falk, Marguerite Fletcher, Jimmy Garrett, Allan Guskin, Judy Guskin, Hillary Thomas-Lake, Harris Wofford, and many others.

I also want to thank Jonathan Zimmerman, who saw promise in this book even when I doubted it. I was especially grateful that he took the time to meet with me at the History of Education Conference in Arkansas, where we split a not very good quiche and a key lime pie but had a rich discussion on the multiple meanings of *service* in American higher education. That conversation—and the many emails and exchanges since—proved immensely valuable to the ways I thought about this book and how I developed as a historian of education. Thank you, Jon. Additionally, I received pointed feedback from Tracy L. Steffes and two anonymous reviewers, all of whom further developed this book. At Cornell University Press, I had the honor of working with Sarah Grossman, whose humor, empathy, and support were invaluable as I moved this from a rough manuscript to a final book during what was a very difficult personal time in my life. Just as importantly, Sarah's early advice proved instrumental in providing structure and clarity to the work.

Every historian should thank the numerous archivists and grant funders. For this book, I traversed many states and cities. I would like to thank Sarah Hutcheon at the Schlesinger Library; Michael Edmonds at the Wisconsin Historical Society; Meredith Eliassen at San Francisco State; Sonja N. Woods at Howard; Lynn Conway at Georgetown; Jennifer Betts at Brown; and the amazing staff at both the John F. Kennedy Library and the National Archives and Records Administration. Without your work and insight, this book would still be lost in the archives. Just as importantly, I would not have been able to visit the archives without the support of fellowships and funding. I am grateful for fellowships from the Social Science Research Council, Radcliffe Institute for Advanced Study, and Carnegie Mellon's Center for Africanamerican Urban Studies and the Economy (CAUSE). These fellowships enabled me to do a deep dive into all these archives very early in my research.

Finally, thank you to my personal community of support. To my family, who never stopped believing in me and supporting me, even when I might not have deserved such faith in my youth. And, to my best friend and partner, Alli: In ways that I cannot put into words, you have sustained, motivated, and inspired me. Thank you for all the times you put aside your work to not only listen to me as I vented about writing blocks, phrasing, and arguments but also to read my work and offer your own critiques. Without your support, I am not sure if I would have completed this book. In the two years that I revised and finished this book, we welcomed our first son, who has shown strength, courage, and wisdom well beyond his years. I can only hope that he applies such courage to making our institutions more responsive and more just in the ways that many young people sought to do in the pages of this book.

ABBREVIATIONS

A3M   April 3rd Movement (Stanford)
CAC   Community Action Coalition (Georgetown)
COOL   Campus Outreach Opportunity League
CSI   Community Service Institute (SFSC)
E4A   Education for Action (Harvard-Radcliffe)
HUSA   Howard University Student Association (Howard)
MSU   Michigan State University
NAACP   National Association for the Advancement of Colored People
NAG   Nonviolent Action Group (Howard)
PBH   Phillips Brooks House (Harvard-Radcliffe)
SASC   Southern Africa Solidarity Committee (Brown)
SCAR   DC Student Coalition Against Apartheid and Racism
           (Georgetown)
SCLC   Southern Christian Leadership Conference
SDS   Students for a Democratic Society
SEC   Student Education Corps (Michigan State)
SEI   Students for an Educational Institution (Howard)
SFSC   San Francisco State College
SMART   Silent Majority Against Revolutionary Tactics (SFSC)
SNCC   Student Nonviolent Coordinating Committee
SOSA   Stanford Out of South Africa (Stanford)
SRA   Students for Rational Action (Brown)
STEP   Student Tutorial Education Project (Michigan State)
SWOPSI   Stanford Workshop on Political and Social Issues (Stanford)
UYA   University Year of Action
VISTA   Volunteers in Service to America

Introduction
Disciplining

Mario Savio is best remembered for his impassioned speech on the steps of Sproul Hall at the University of California, Berkeley, in 1964. The speech serves as a symbol of the movement he is commonly associated with: the Free Speech Movement. But the name of the movement is misleading. The motivating issue on campus was more than just the right to free *speech*. It was also the right to *act* on ideas. As Savio explained during the first sit-in at Sproul Hall, "free expression, for the university, means that you can talk about lots of things," but "those things you can't do are the taking of action on various ideas that you discuss."[1] The institutional division between thought and political action, Savio believed, set limits on a student's pursuit of knowledge. He argued that "you can't separate knowledge from action."[2] Clark Kerr, the president of the University of California, disagreed. "I don't think you have to have action to have intellectual opportunity," Kerr argued amid the campus sit-in. "Their actions—collecting money and picketing—aren't high intellectual activity," he noted. "These actions are not necessary for the intellectual development of the students."[3]

Between the stances of Savio and Kerr, what emerged from the campus movement at Berkeley was an institutional and educational compromise. In 1965, Martin Meyerson, acting chancellor, and William K. Coblenz, university regent, convened a committee to rethink general education. One area they focused on was how to link curricular content to forms of social action in civic and public life. "Students attending Universities should receive some credit toward a degree for work done in the community," explained Coblenz, whether in "social work, or in business or labor, whichever is their choice."[4] Academic leaders supported student demands for action, seeing such appeals as part of a larger project of expanding the educational and civic mission of the modern American university. But institutional legitimacy came with a caveat. They emphasized in the proposal that the university could only support "non-political social action." The programs that gained institutional support promoted volunteerism and community service. Meyerson's committee was aptly named the Chancellor's Committee for Community Service.[5]

The educational and institutional compromise at the University of California became the model for the modern American university's new civic and educational mission. Between the first programs established in the 1960s and those promoted by academic leaders across American higher education in the 1980s, what came to dominate as the new civics was "service learning"— a particular model of civic education that added on experiences for students in the form of volunteer and public service but discarded other forms of political activism. Reflecting on the university's response to the campus sit-in in 1964, Savio concluded, "We've been disciplined for insisting on being citizens *all the time*, whether we're on campus or off."[6] Savio's word choice — *disciplined*—is instructive. The verb *to discipline* and the noun *discipline* evoke a set of ideas and practices that are considered fundamental to the modern university's educational mission. The disciplining of the mind connotes the rigorous training needed to shape the mental functions of critical analysis. A discipline provides a demarcated intellectual and methodological space to train an individual with the ability to explore a particular branch of knowledge. When applied to the sphere of political participation, the core principles of disciplining have the same effect: they create a set of rules and boundaries for appropriate types of behaviors and actions.[7] Through service learning programs, academic leaders encouraged the active involvement of the student in a democracy in a way that avoided political conflict and controversy. In other words, the university *disciplined democracy*.

I argue that service learning triumphed as the dominant model of the new civics because it fit a particular type of disciplining culture in the modern American university. Two intersecting ideas of the university informed the institution's mode of disciplining. The first was the university's historical development. America's educational development, whether at elite institutions like Harvard or land grant colleges like Michigan State University, was always tied to the development of the nation as a whole. Although taking different forms, the primary educational goal of the university was to develop citizens in service of the nation.[8] The second was the modern university's technocratic and value-neutralist model of research that came to dominate mid-century American intellectual life.[9] The value-neutralist model of research rested upon a division between empirical research and moral judgment. In the post–World War II university, the combination of service to the nation and a value-neutralist model of research produced a distinct disciplining cultural outlook that shaped how academic leaders responded to student activists. University leaders supported student engagement off campus, but only if the actions fell within the realm of national service. They also believed that such programs had to be separate from the regular curriculum, otherwise such activities would affect the perceived neutral pursuit of knowledge. Modes of action that questioned prevailing American political institutions and systems—that is, those models that went beyond national service—fell outside the disciplinary boundaries of good citizenship in the American university. In contrast, a service learning model of civic education—with an emphasis on public and volunteer service within existing political arrangements—more easily fit the national and technocratic disciplinary culture of the modern American university. In promoting service learning as the new civics, academic leaders made social action and institutional neutrality compatible.

Historians have contributed to an extensive literature on student activism and the university, with a particular focus on the 1960s. They have illuminated the tactics, demands, and intellectual foundations while also highlighting student political successes both on and off campus. But focusing only on the politics of activists—especially those with left or progressive leanings—plays into the hands of conservative critics who believe colleges and universities have too easily succumbed to progressive protest and ideology. The focus on the institutional success of student activists has also led to a persistent belief that the university represents a source of social and political transformation.[10] Neither view holds up to the historical record. Progressive student activists did bring about important reforms, but the reforms were largely on the periphery of the university, either as marginal disciplines or in the realm of student affairs. Moreover, the outcome of reform efforts—in this case, service learning programs—reflects the conservative nature of the university itself. What we are missing is a better understanding of the cultural and political logic of the modern American university. Examining the rise of service learning thus opens up a different way to consider the university's mode of disciplining—how the university system more broadly adopts, reconstructs, and redistributes political challenges.

The institutional compromise and programs created a basic template—with a normative political logic—for how university leaders respond to political and epistemic challenges to their authority after the long 1960s. The process of disciplining democracy that took shape during the 1960s mediated politics in three overlapping ways. The first is disciplining as a *regulating* force that determines what appropriate forms of civic action in the public sphere are. The second is disciplining as an *epistemological* force that defines whose knowledge takes precedence. And the third is disciplining as an *ideological* force that governs what the necessary political beliefs for "good" citizenship are. Underlying each institutional mode of disciplining democracy was an added financial constraint that concerned the type of civic activity a university could support without threatening its financial solvency.

The programmatic product of disciplining democracy—service learning programs—contains all three forms. The programs engage students in volunteerism or public service as the primary mode of action, maintain the epistemic authority of the expert, and promote loyalty to American political ideals. Service learning programs were also linked to and dependent upon federal, foundational, and corporate revenue streams, providing students and academic leaders alike with the requisite financial support for the programs. The programs have ebbed and flowed in size and capacity with the ebb and flow of student politics more generally, demonstrating the persistent use of disciplining democracy to exert influence on how student activists have conceived of their political roles since the 1960s. The programs created a release valve for students to engage in politics in a more controlled way that served to support rather than challenge existing political structures within and beyond the university.

This book locates the ideas of student activists and academic leaders within the intellectual and institutional culture of the modern American university. Whether critiquing or affirming aspects of the university, the ideas and programs of student activists and academic leaders alike were always inflected with prevailing assumptions of good citizenship within the modern American university. The challenge student activists, faculty supporters, and academic leaders faced was how to integrate formal education and expert knowledge with social action. The ideological sticking point was what type of action the university could support as part of its education and research mission. In the context of the university, service learning proved to be politically convenient and ambidextrous; it provided a model that linked formal study with community engagement while gaining support across partisan lines due to its emphasis on "nonpolitical" community development. Thus, on multiple levels, efforts to change the American higher education system took place within the logic and function of the system itself.[11] Rather than being a concerted effort by academic leaders and policy makers to intentionally redirect student activism and politics, service learning triumphed as a political compromise *within* the modern university's disciplining culture. In the new service learning programs that emerged, a commitment to engaged citizenship was tempered by a modern disciplining culture that set limits on modes of action of both students and institutions.

A common narrative trope in academic writing on student protest and the university is the "co-optation" narrative. The history of service learning fits neatly into patterns of co-optation. When asking what happened to mass student politics in the United States, one ought to turn to the ways the service learning programs and civic engagement centers have functioned to redirect and fragment student political energies. Yet, we have very little understanding of the process of co-optation itself within the university. Why do university leaders seem to respond to broader political challenges in predicted ways? It is easy—and tempting—to treat academic leaders themselves as at best reform oriented and at worst nefarious. As this book demonstrates, their ideas and political beliefs do matter, but institutional culture matters just as much. After all, student activists and academics were equally shaped by a disciplinary culture that—for better or worse—promotes a set of rules and boundaries reflective of the university's place as a mediating institution.

The intent of this book is not to be a history of student activism or campus administrative politics. Nor is this simply a history of a new teaching approach. Rather, the book's goal is to use a particular institutional development—new civic engagement programs—as a lens onto the political role of the university in modern American life. The history of service learning is the history of how the university mediates competing claims on what it means to be a "good" citizen in American political life. This book, then, is a biography of the modern American university's political tradition since the 1960s—its institutional formation, programmatic outcome, and impact on ideas of education and a student's political role in a democracy.

The backbone of this book is a series of institutional case studies from the 1960s to the 1980s. The first four case studies focus on the political roots of disciplining democracy in the 1960s and early 1970s, while the next three examine the political recycling of disciplining democracy in the 1970s and 1980s. Given the organizational structure of this book, most of the source material is drawn from case study institutional archives. This includes presidential and dean papers, student newspapers, and, where available, student affair offices and programs. But institutional archives also raised a set of dilemmas. Because of the cycles of funding and underfunding, the programs themselves only left traces of efforts, initiatives, and student perspectives. Presidential, board of trustee, and other administrative papers are also limited, sometimes due to institutional policy restricting access for a certain period of time. To address the constraints of institutional archives, I also examined source material outside the university. This included documents and materials of key organizations affiliated with the first campus programs, such as the Peace Corps and Student Nonviolent Coordinating Committee (SNCC), and the organizations and public forums associated with the anti-apartheid movement in the 1980s.[12] Additionally, I drew on memoirs and oral histories of key activists from the 1960s while also conducting oral history interviews with those willing to speak about their experiences and efforts in the 1980s. The process of "reflecting back" revealed salient features of the experience of activism and formal education. The combination of institutional archives, movement documentation, and oral history interviews enabled me to analyze both the formulation and effect of the university's political logic from multiple perspectives.

Political Roots

The logic of disciplining democracy was rooted in the ideological tensions of the post–World War II university. When a new generation of college students enrolled in American universities in the late 1950s and early 1960s, they entered institutions that were far different from what previous generations experienced on campus. On one level, American institutions of higher education were just bigger—more students, larger buildings, and campuses that stretched for miles. But on another level, the place of the American university in political life was also bigger. The political crises of the mid-twentieth century—from the Great Depression to World War II—expanded the academic-federal partnership. Policy makers turned toward the university for technical research to support new domestic and foreign policy initiatives designed to address the political crises. They also turned to the university for education and training purposes, especially in preparation for World War II. In exchange, academic institutions received federal financial support that not only stabilized the American higher education system but enabled universities to expand their intellectual and educational footprint in social and political life.

The scale of the post–World War II expansion of the federal-academic partnership presented a distinct institutional challenge. Academic leaders had to develop a new social mission that accommodated competing impulses—the university had to be directly engaged in contemporary political questions through public research and education while remaining institutionally neutral on those very questions. To address this challenge, policy makers, academic leaders, and intellectuals across the American higher education landscape developed a model of general education that promoted a particular idea of citizenship associated with the disciplinary characteristics of the modern university.[13] First, they emphasized the intellectual traits associated with a value-neutral science, believing that objectivity and disinterested judgment were the requisite attributes that would prepare modern citizens for the needs of the American nation. Second, they eschewed normative arguments for democracy—arguments explaining what it could or should be in America—and hewed instead to naturalizing assertions that the political structures and institutions of democracy represented the model of democracy itself.[14] The combination enabled academic leaders to describe the university as a neutral party that promoted independent inquiry among its students while maintaining its role as a mediating institution of state, federal, and market policy.

The institutional mission and pedagogical vision of modern citizenship that triumphed on American college campuses proved difficult to maintain in the context of the various social movements that arose in the 1960s, most prominently the classical phase of the civil rights movement, anti-colonial movements around the world, and the anti–Vietnam War movement. Shaped by the social urgency of these political struggles as well what they learned through their direct involvement, students confronted what they saw as a fundamental contradiction at the heart of their educational pursuits. Expanded federal funding to the university enabled increasing numbers of students of diverse backgrounds to attend higher education institutions, where they were exposed to new political, cultural, and social ideas. Yet, students often found their colleges and universities frustratingly aloof to the political concerns off campus. They were also troubled by claims of neutrality when the university was deeply engaged in the political world through federal grants and research. How could the university, many asked, be an engine of democracy if it remained neutral on the pressing issues of the time?

The most famous student analysis of this question was the Port Huron Statement. When student activists met in Port Huron, Michigan, to articulate a vision for the nascent progressive student movements of the 1960s, a primary focus of their discussion—indeed, a primary focus of what became the Port Huron Statement—was the university's approach to civic education. "The university," wrote Tom Hayden, the main author of the statement, "'prepares' students for 'citizenship' through perpetual rehearsals." As Hayden explained, "That which is studied, the social reality, is 'objectified' to sterility, dividing the student from life—just as he is restrained in active involvement by the deans controlling student government." The result was an apathetic student body, he argued, who did not value political activity as a citizen. Yet, even as Hayden critiqued the staid curriculum of the university, he also believed that the other attributes of the university—including "social relevance, the accessibility to knowledge, and internal openness"— when combined together with political action, would "make the university a potential base and agency in a movement of social change."[15]

Hayden's critique of the modern university resurrected a progressive tradition of education more closely associated with the core ideas of John Dewey. As the historian Robert B. Westbrook noted in his biography of Dewey, "Perhaps nowhere did Dewey's ideas echo more resoundingly than in the 'Port Huron Statement.'"[16] The differences between the student movements and university leaders in the 1960s reflected a tension at the heart of the American progressive tradition—one that had direct implications for the modern American university. The debate operated between technocratic and reconstructive progressivism. Academic leaders adopted one strain of American progressivism—what the historian Ethan Schrum identifies as technocratic progressivism—to define the university's role as an instrument of economic and state policy making. Student activists sought to resurrect reconstructive progressivism—a political and educational tradition that promoted broad active participation in the public sphere not only as discrete learning situations but as incubators of new knowledge.

What was the model for a reconstructive progressive educational philosophy? Hayden believed that the modes of study emerging from the student movements provided a new model of civic education. The student movements—from the civil rights movement to what Hayden defined as the "student peace corps movement"—shared a commitment to "action." He saw in both a shared set of values that contained the seeds of a new civic and educational outlook, including the simplicity of volunteer living, the commitment to serve marginalized populations, and the participatory nature of the community development process.[17] What thus united both movements was a belief that learning was a collective endeavor situated in community involvement and deliberation. Hayden emphasized that action was more than just a political commitment; it was an expression of a nascent educational worldview. Students understood action as a distinct form of civic education, one that took its cue from the broader political appeal of the 1960s. If the goal of the student movements in the 1960s was to realize a participatory democracy, what was needed was a *participatory* mode of civic education.

The differences between students' visions of university leaders and those of student leaders did not fall neatly along a dividing line between reconstructive and technocratic progressivism. In drawing inspiration from the Peace Corps, Hayden and others embraced elements of technocratic progressivism in their pedagogical visions of action education. Community development efforts within the Peace Corps were linked to national projects, both for the United States and the host country. This link constrained the type of politics volunteers could engage in as part of community development. Just as significantly, community development in the Peace Corps was also intertwined with modernization theory—a prominent postwar academic theory that shaped ideas of service in the federal-academic partnership. Key modernization theorists argued that what they defined as undeveloped or traditional societies were economically stagnated because they lacked the West's—in particular, America's—technical knowledge and modern political system. This academic theory was central to the modern American university's technocratic model of service, one that taught students that the problem of poverty was the lack of American technology and knowledge, not political and economic power.[18]

The theoretical framing in the Port Huron Statement thus simultaneously challenged and reinforced the university's role in educating citizens for a democracy. The modes of action education that emerged from the student movements accommodated competing impulses that, depending on the context of their activism, shifted between critiquing the university and desiring to belong in the university. Moreover, the student appeal to action also shifted between providing service and engaging in acts of civil disobedience. Hayden's analytical innovation—to relate the appeals of the civil rights struggle to the volunteer programs like the Peace Corps and thus to define the new left broadly—also made the demand for action education susceptible to more narrow interpretations within the university.[19] On campus, then, the broader appeal of action education was pedagogically flexible, and this flexibility is key to understanding the ways action education was translated into the modern American university.

In the first four chapters, I examine the pedagogical flexibility of the students' political critiques of the modern university at four different institutions: Howard University, Michigan State University, San Francisco State College and Harvard-Radcliffe. All the institutions established new volunteer centers that promoted iterations of service learning, a reflection of the emergence of disciplining democracy as a broad political development across the higher education system. In focusing on a diverse set of institutions, I also reveal the particular formulation of disciplining democracy as shaped by the particular culture of each institution and the character of students' political demands.

The book begins with Howard University. How should a historically Black, elite institution like Howard University support the Black Freedom Struggle? This question took on profound significance at Howard during the classical phase of the civil rights era in the 1960s. Many key faculty members and university leaders took an active role in supporting student activists in the civil rights struggle. But student activists and Howard officials took different stances on the appropriate role of the university. The differences provoked wide-ranging debates on ideas of service and justice at Howard—debates that culminated in the Toward a Black University Conference and subsequent campus strike in 1968 and 1969. What emerged from both the conference and strike was an extensive set of action programs in the professional fields that, on paper, linked the institution to civil rights and the pursuit of justice. However, in examining how the university responded to a student-run initiative, this chapter makes clear that even at a historically Black college like Howard, the prevailing institutional ideologies of national service set limits on the ideas of social action. The institution's links to—and dependency upon—federal funding meant that the types of university programs that received funds were those promoting national service. The limits were not just a reflection of the institution's federal dependency. Howard University's historical development and promotion as an elite Black institution also constrained programmatic efforts. The university was to cultivate elite Black leadership. Service learning programs better fit that mode than forms of activism that sought to transform this institutional culture.

Chapter 2 focuses on Michigan State University (MSU), with a particular emphasis on the ways that student activists challenged the prevailing institutional idea of service. Both MSU presidents in the 1960s and 1970s—John Hannah and Clifton Wharton—agreed with students that the university should be involved in the social world. They disagreed on the type of involvement—in particular, the type of service to the public. The campus civic movement at MSU led to the establishment of the Office of Service Learning. The creation of an institutional home for civic engagement demonstrated the university's commitment to students' demands for a more socially relevant education. However, the new home for service learning marginalized other efforts on campus, including programs that linked the university more closely to the civil rights struggle. It also had the effect of deflecting students' efforts that challenged the university's research ties to the Vietnam War. What emerged at MSU was a particular cultural logic associated with disciplining democracy. In establishing the Office of Service Learning, MSU leaders employed a rhetorical strategy that contrasted what they defined as the constructive activism of students associated with service learning programs with the destructive forms of activism associated with civil rights and the anti-war movement. Promoted across American higher education by the Nixon administration, the Office of Service Learning at MSU became the model for other universities when responding to campus activism.

Chapter 3 turns to another state university: San Francisco State College (SFSC). The campus movement at SFSC is best remembered for the Third World Strike in the 1960s. Led by a broad and diverse coalition of students, the Third World Strike helped establish the School of Ethnic Studies. The demand for ethnic studies included a demand for "action education." The appeal to action education, however, was not shared by all activists. Some worried that university-sponsored programs would limit the political possibilities of student activism. Just as importantly, action was much more narrowly defined by academic leaders and faculty members in the new School of Ethnic Studies. In the extracurriculum, academic leaders established a volunteer bureau that promoted action in the form of community service, while faculty members in the School of Ethnic Studies developed a model more akin to fieldwork in which action became primarily a mode of inquiry. With the volunteer bureau in student affairs, the process of disciplining democracy at SFSC thus took on characteristics of both Howard University and MSU. SFSC also had an added component; it represented an expansive example of a more traditional form of disciplining—the use of both the administrative and police apparatus of the state to punish student efforts.

Chapter 4 examines action education at another elite university, although one that was historically White. What is the place of service in the elite curriculum at Radcliffe and Harvard? For many faculty and academic leaders at these institutions, service to community was an expression of elite leadership and a key mechanism to enhance student learning. Thus, when student activists demanded new modes of education linked to the civil rights struggle at home and international volunteerism abroad, academic leaders provided institutional support. Harvard and Radcliffe rose to national prominence in the 1960s for their unique action program—Education for Action (E4A)—which was embedded in the general education. The program linked traditional coursework to Peace Corps international service and Volunteers in Service to America (VISTA). However, when students attempted to expand the definition of action beyond domestic and international service, academic leaders worried this would politicize the curriculum. In response, they moved E4A out of the regular curriculum into student affairs. What emerged was an activist clearinghouse disconnected from the central educational mission of the university. In contrast to other institutions, Harvard and Radcliffe's mode of disciplining was strictly administrative. The autonomy of the university as a private institution enabled academic leaders to provide a campus home for students' political efforts. But, in moving E4A to student affairs, they made clear that activism was separate from one's intellectual pursuits.

Political Recycling

The next set of case studies transitions to the mid-1970s and 1980s. I examine how academic leaders recycled the logic of disciplining democracy and its programmatic component in the context of anti-apartheid activism on American college campuses. The political era from the mid-1970s to the 1980s was characterized by a set of higher education policy shifts associated with the rise of a market ethos within the university. With the economic downturn of the 1970s, federal policy makers in both the Ford and Carter administrations justified continued support for higher education by promoting the university's distinct role in preparing young people with skills for professional success.[20] This policy emphasis persisted even as direct federal support to higher education was cut in half by the Reagan administration. The funding cuts were justified by the 1980 Bayh-Dole Act, which enabled universities to profit from institutional research funded by the federal government.

The technocratic tendency within the university remained, but with a stronger focus on market investment and return. Indeed, the policy shift and market emphasis transformed every part of the institution. University leaders increasingly turned to corporations and foundations to make up for the budget gaps and identify areas of profit on new research developments. The Bayh-Dole Act shifted the research mission from a broad commitment to knowledge production in service to the nation to one that focused on the most profitable research proposals. The emphasis on financial return also transformed the purpose of education, with many academic leaders promoting the university's role in preparing students for success in the marketplace.[21] Although university leaders continued to utilize the rhetoric of citizenship, with the older emphasis on objectivity and disinterested judgement, they increasingly prioritized the development of marketable skills as the primary goal of education.

The American university's focus on education as a financial investment was directly challenged by the campus anti-apartheid movement. Over the course of the 1970s and 1980s, the African National Congress and the American Committee on Africa helped develop a broad campus network in the United States that called on American policy makers to shift the country's economic relationship with South Africa. A key tool of the anti-apartheid movement was institutional divestment from corporations operating in South Africa. When calling on the university to also divest, student activists in the 1980s raised larger questions about the university as a moral actor. Recycling activists' claims from the 1960s, students argued that if the university's role is to educate students as moral and ethical citizens in the marketplace, it should also act in a morally and ethically consistent way. How students and academic leaders sought to address the role of the university pivoted on different historical interpretations of the mass student movements of the 1960s and their institutional legacies, both of which informed what they believed the university could do.

Indeed, what emerged on campus in the late 1970s and 1980s was a politics of institutional memory. Student leaders in the anti-apartheid movement understood the call for divestment as carrying on the legacy of the mass student politics from the 1960s. They also turned to existing institutional programs that emerged in the aftermath of the 1960s. In linking the call for divestment to existing institutional programs, student leaders sought to resurrect their lost visions—connecting the programs of action to the university's actions as an institution. In response to calls to divest, university leaders supported the Sullivan principles, which required companies working in South Africa to hire Black workers and pay a minimum wage. But, over the course of the 1970s and 1980s, university leaders increasingly acknowledged that the principles did little to challenge apartheid.[22] They thus agreed with students that the university needed to do more. Echoing academic leaders from the 1960s, they focused on expanding volunteer and public service programs—forms of action that fit within institutional culture—while deflecting the demands to redefine the university's role in American political life.

The resurgence of service learning programs in this era demonstrates the persistence of disciplining democracy, albeit in the ways the institutional logic was adapted to the political economy of the 1980s. Here, I examine Stanford University, Brown University, and Georgetown University. I focus on these institutions for three reasons. First, all three institutions had existing service learning programs, many of which were initially established in the late 1960s. Second, the academic leaders of these institutions played a key role in forming the Campus Compact, a top-down public service initiative that led to a proliferation of service learning programs now common across American higher education. Third, all three institutions emerged as "elite"—as defined by the newly established *U.S. News* college rankings in the early 1980s—due to their increased endowment from market investments. These institutional case studies provide different sets of analytical lenses on the political logic and reuse of disciplining democracy: the role of research in education at Stanford University, the application of ideas in the liberal arts tradition at Brown University, and the characteristics of moral commitment within the Jesuit tradition at Georgetown University. As such, these chapters are not an exhaustive history of the divestment movement. Rather, the primary focus is on the larger arguments that students and academic leaders made about the political role of students and the modern university itself.

Chapter 5 examines the anti-apartheid movement at Stanford University in conjunction with President Donald Kennedy's promotion of public and community service. Kennedy's efforts took two forms. The first was the more traditional model, one associated with volunteer and charity work. The other was an internship or research model. The latter reflected Kennedy's efforts to update service learning for the professional development of students. Both models came under fire by student activists at Stanford for the ways they seemed to redirect anti-apartheid efforts that challenged the university's investments in South Africa. Yet, many of the key student leaders at Stanford also drew upon the institutional programs to support their political efforts. Students saw their anti-apartheid activism—especially the research they conducted to provide an empirical basis for their critiques of university investments—as an expression of Stanford's research mission. However, university administrators largely ignored the knowledge developed within anti-apartheid activism for findings that supported Stanford's existing investments. Kennedy recycled disciplining democracy as an epistemological force by dismissing the experiential and research knowledge developed by student activists in the anti-apartheid movement.

Chapter 6 considers the modern philosophy of the liberal arts at Brown University. Howard Swearer, the university president, was a strong supporter of public service. In the 1980s, he turned to the ideas of the Peace Corps in the 1960s as a way to expand and update the liberal arts tradition at Brown. Student activists supported these efforts. In the context of anti-apartheid activism, students also demanded that Swearer and the university administration do more. In the same way Swearer turned to the Peace Corps in the 1960s as inspiration, he also turned to that time period to defend an orthodox conception of institutional neutrality. He believed that the university could not commit to divestment because doing so would run counter to its mission as a neutral institution for public debate. Drawing on this idea, Swearer believed that student activists failed to commit to civil responsibility. He thus maintained a commitment to institutional neutrality while also promoting action in the form of public service. The Brown University case study demonstrates the ways that university leaders in the 1980s recycled disciplining democracy as an ideological force that treated student efforts as counter to "good" citizenship on and off campus.

Chapter 7 examines the politics of religious morality at Georgetown University in the 1980s. A commitment to service was central to the mission of Georgetown. Since the 1960s, the university had established and supported a range of programs that enabled students to participate in community service. In the late 1970s and early 1980s, many student activists—a number of whom participated in these service programs—believed that Georgetown University failed in its commitment to Jesuit values because of its investments in companies that worked in South Africa. Albeit more slowly than students, university leaders agreed. In 1987, Georgetown University divested from its holdings in companies working in South Africa. But the political alignment obscured the ways that Georgetown leaders, including President Timothy S. Healy, utilized the logic of disciplining democracy to define what were appropriate actions of student activists within the Jesuit tradition of service. Indeed, Healy promoted the university's commitment to service by creating a service program for Georgetown students to teach in South Africa while arresting those who participated in campus activism. The logic of Georgetown's action rested upon a particular historical interpretation of the service programs on campus. Ignoring the ways they emerged from mass student politics, university leaders framed those programs as deeply rooted in the Jesuit tradition. In making this interpretive claim, they dismissed political activism as a component of Jesuit service and education. The Georgetown case study illuminates the ways that institutions that publicly promoted a strong value commitment were still shaped by the political logic of disciplining.

The series of institutional case studies from the 1960s to the 1980s reveals both the emergence and reuse of an institutional political logic that has mediated student politics throughout the modern era. The conclusion links the case studies by analyzing the federal and foundational higher education reports that reproduced and normalized disciplining democracy as the prevailing form of the university's civic mission. I focus on the "Atlanta Service-Learning Conference Report" in 1969; the Nixon administration's *Report of the President's Commission on Campus Unrest* in 1970; and the series of Newman reports in the 1970s that culminated in the 1985 Campus Compact. In the conclusion, I also explore the emergence of a subset of scholarship that has begun to respond to the institutional logic underlying prevailing service learning and civic engagement programs that now dominant American higher education. This scholarship provides a helpful framework for considering the tensions within and legacy of service learning for American higher education and political life. But I hope that in reading this book, you see that the tensions within—and ultimately the political limitations of—contemporary civic engagement programs in American higher education are not something new. Rather, they are rooted in the logic of disciplining democracy. Excavating the political roots and recycling of this logic is one of the central goals of this book, but it is not my only one. I also hope that the lost visions of the university as a civic actor that emerged from student movements can inspire new thinking on the form and nature of the modern university in the United States.

CHAPTER 1

Howard University

Making the Campus into a Base for Social Action

In 1903, W. E. B. Du Bois penned his essay "The Talented Tenth." At the time, he was witnessing firsthand the dawn of a select cohort of African Americans accessing higher education. One of those colleges producing educated African American leaders was Howard University. Founded in the middle of the nineteenth century, on the heels of the Civil War, Howard University was an early expression of Du Bois's idea. Howard's founding motto—*Veritas et Utilitas*, or "Truth and Service"—reflected the university's commitment to educating an elite stratum of African Americans who served the Black community writ large. In the first half of the twentieth century, the university produced notable alumni like Thurgood Marshall and Pauli Murray, two figures who personified a commitment to serving the legal cause of racial justice. The university also garnered national fame for other reputable scholars, including Alaine Locke and Ralph Bunche, both of whom helped define distinct formulations of American Black culture and politics. The prominence of Howard alumni led to global recognition of the university as an intellectual safe house for African and diasporan networking and intellectual exchange.[1]

Even as Howard University created a space for the development of Black leadership and culture to thrive, its mission and academic culture were defined by structures of class and race. Du Bois's idea of education rested upon a dichotomy between the "talented tenth" and the "masses" that promulgated an elite definition of education. Howard University functioned in the same way. Indeed, the first Black president of Howard, Mordecai Johnson, emphasized the vision of Howard as an elite institution. In his inauguration speech, he envisioned Howard as an institution that could "compete favorably with any liberal arts university in America."[2] The result of this vision was an institution that primarily served a small, elite population, especially the emergent Black middle class. While maintaining an elite conception of education and leadership, the university's service mission was also constrained by White philanthropy and economic and political structures in America. Howard University's initial funding was dependent upon White congregations. Even as the university received appropriations from the federal government, it continued to depend on White philanthropy.[3] Recognizing that the Black college and university were dependent upon the White economic power structures in both government and foundations, Black academic leaders struck a compromise. The curriculum of the institution would support the development of Black leadership and culture without directly challenging White power structures. This compromise depended upon a sharp division between education and political action. The mission of Howard University was to support the cause of racial justice and civil rights but in a way that was disciplined by a commitment to both developing an elite Black academic culture and protecting White political and economic interests.

This institutional compromise was challenged in the 1960s. Indeed, the explosion of sit-ins during the first part of the 1960s and the associated formation of a Black student-led organization—the Student Nonviolent Coordinating Committee (SNCC)—created new campus conditions for reconstructing Howard's education and service mission. Students associated with SNCC attempted to turn Du Bois's idea on its head. They hoped to create an institution that was for the Black "masses," not just a Black elite. But students believed that to realize that vision, the university had to directly support civil rights action. In the view of SNCC activists at Howard, this was not an argument for the university to engage in politics in a traditional sense. Rather, they understood their various actions—the sit-ins, freedom rides, and community organizing efforts—as distinct modes of study. They thus argued that civil rights action represented a way to expand and redefine Howard University's educational mission.

This chapter examines how academic leaders at Howard responded to the efforts of student activists to link the institution directly to civil rights activism in the 1960s. Academic leaders at Howard University argued that students should engage in civil rights action, but not in association with Howard. This is why Howard's chapter of SNCC—the Nonviolent Action

Group (NAG)—never received institutional recognition at Howard University. Efforts to separate Howard from direct action were politically savvy, especially in the short term of the university's relationship to the civil rights struggle and the navigation of its financial dependency on federal and foundational funding. Yet, the political logic used to justify this separation had long-term effects on the form and nature of Howard's updated civic mission by the end of the classical era of the civil rights movement. Indeed, the mode of disciplining democracy that triumphed at the end of the decade adopted the logics associated with Howard's founding institutional culture.

In the context of the civil rights struggle, academic leaders agreed that the university needed to provide some type of institutional support and programmatic initiatives. Over the course of the 1960s, Howard leaders and faculty members instituted new programs. But student efforts—ranging from NAG organizing efforts in the first part of the 1960s to a student-run initiative called the D.C. Project at the end of the decade—did not receive the same institutional support as other programs. The student-led D.C. Project maintained political action, while the new programs at Howard prioritized community service within the professional fields as the new and ongoing expression of the university's support of the civil rights struggle and the institution's civic mission. On one level, what type of efforts and programs Howard leaders supported reflected the political and economic constraints of the university. Academic leaders at Howard walked a fine line, balancing their commitments to the political demands of the movement with the financial constraints of the university. On another level, the decisions reflected the persistent influence of Howard's founding institutional culture. The university was designed to cultivate Black elite leadership. Service programs aligned more closely with this mission than did those that attempted to reconstruct Howard's culture in a more activist mold.

Pursuing Truth

In the first part of the 1960s, Howard students took on prominent leadership roles across the American South. Some of the most significant events associated with the student wing of the civil rights movement—from the sit-ins and the freedom rides to rent strikes and community boycotts—included Howard students.[4] While deeply committed to the civil rights struggle, the same student activists remained connected to Howard. Indeed, they saw that connection as strategic to their civil rights work. Howard student activists believed the university—located just south of the Mason–Dixon Line, between the struggle against de jure segregation in the South and de facto segregation in the North—could serve as a key hub of the student wing of the civil rights movement and its direct-action efforts. With this vision in mind, Howard student activists formed NAG, an affiliated campus group of SNCC. The primary reasons for seeking institutional recognition as a student organization were practical and political. First, institutional recognition would enable the students to access student government funds and utilize campus spaces for meetings. Such access would provide financial support for student efforts while also creating an intellectual respite space for planning between civil rights actions. Second, institutional recognition as a student organization would enable the group to use Howard to recruit students into political action, whether it be the Northern or Southern civil rights struggles.

When students formed NAG, they were optimistic about the leadership and vision of Howard President James Nabrit, believing Howard officials would support efforts to link the university to the civil rights struggle. As a respected civil rights attorney, Nabrit stood out among university presidents, especially those at Black institutions, for defending the civil liberties of students. In 1961, Nabrit's administration publicly supported NAG's efforts to organize Project Awareness.[5] The NAG project brought Malcolm X and Bayard Rustin to debate the civil rights struggle. The Nabrit administration allowed NAG students to promote the event on campus and use Howard's Cramton Auditorium to hold the debate. Nabrit's support for the project, Stokely Carmichael wrote, "enhanced the reputation of Howard as a source of leadership in the struggle for human rights," especially the Black struggle for freedom in the United States.[6] It seemed, at least early on, that NAG and Howard leaders agreed on the goal of Project Awareness, which was to "help liberate the minds of students."[7] Indeed, as Nabrit explained after attending the event, "this discussion has been a very thrilling experience because Howard is dedicated to the task of making young people think."[8] Nabrit's enthusiastic support was not all that surprising. The educational logic of Project Awareness—a debate between two prominent Black intellectuals—aligned closely with his vision of Howard University. Nabrit believed deeply that the university's primary role was to encourage debate and free inquiry. Central to Nabrit's ideal was a commitment to an orthodox conception of institutional neutrality. "The pursuit of learning," he argued, "must be free from the biases of race, religion, nationality, politics, and all else which would obstruct its functions as a center of intellectual activity."[9]

The administration's support of NAG's efforts, such as Project Awareness, proved to be the exception rather than the rule. When it came to institutional recognition of NAG, Nabrit and the dean of student activities, Carl Anderson, denied every request. The public reason for denying institutional recognition was based on an existing university policy that prevented student organizations from using the campus as a base for social action. The policy aligned with Nabrit's philosophy of the university. Interpreting students' civil rights actions as a form of engaging in politics Nabrit believed support for such actions would obstruct the functions of the university. The problem with Nabrit's argument—or at least what students saw as the tension within it—was that the policy itself was political. Johnson, the predecessor to Nabrit, had initially created the policy in response to the first sit-ins led by Pauli Murray and other Howard students in 1942. The reasoning was not for Johnson's personal politics, even if they tended to be conservative. Rather, Johnson developed the strategy as a method of deflecting further congressional oversight rather than as a deliberate attempt to mitigate student efforts on campus.[10]

Nabrit employed this same strategy. In his view, NAG's appeal ignored institutional realities, particularly the prevailing economic arrangements that made Howard University possible. In the 1960s, funding for the university was processed through the Health, Education, and Welfare agency, which also meant that Howard's budget, including for student organizations, was under supervisory review of congressional members. Johnson sought to protect the financial solvency of Howard, even if it meant a more constrained Black politics on campus. Nabrit's administration largely built on this strategy. In the first part of the 1960s, with the sit-ins and freedom rides capturing national attention, congressional leaders—especially those coming from Southern states or those near the Mason–Dixon Line—called on Nabrit to control student efforts in the civil rights struggle. Nabrit was especially concerned because Howard's federal appropriations increased significantly in the years that the sit-ins and freedom rides captured national attention. In 1959, Howard received $5,498,000 in federal appropriations. Two years later, in 1961, those appropriations jumped to $12,010,000.[11] By strategically denying institutional recognition of NAG based on the policy of social action, Nabrit was able to argue at congressional budgetary hearings that the organizations leading the sit-ins and other forms of direct action were not associated with Howard University.[12]

University leaders developed a secondary argument—one that also had an associated political strategy—for denying institutional recognition of NAG. Publicly, Anderson used the financial constraint framework for denying recognition of NAG. Dependency on and oversight by the federal government, Anderson argued, meant the university could not use the funds to support NAG and related student efforts in a movement that directly challenged federal and state laws. Privately, Anderson believed that recognition would also constrain the radical potential of NAG. Given the university's constraint, Anderson argued that NAG students should desire the opposite: to be unaffiliated with the university. He argued "that the strength [of the movement] remained in being outside of the institution, not inside the institution."[13] In Anderson's view, the "outside" work of NAG and "inside" intellectual work on campus was a beneficial arrangement to student efforts in the civil rights struggle. The university provided the means for intellectual exploration, while NAG, as an unaffiliated organization, could provide a separate space that enabled students to move ideas into action off campus.[14]

The political reasoning and strategy of Howard leaders divided members of NAG. Anderson's argument resonated with some NAG activists, especially when interpreted strictly in terms of the political goals of the movement. Geri Gustavo was skeptical of NAG's efforts to achieve official recognition. A Howard student and member of both NAG and SNCC, Gustavo believed the focus on the institution, especially as a hub for movement building, was misplaced. Gustavo ultimately saw the real work of the civil rights movement—and political consciousness building—to be off campus.[15] Echoing the views of Anderson, Gustavo argued that focusing on Howard would limit politics to student life. Fellow NAG and SNCC member Phil Hutchings disagreed. He believed focusing on the university would help build and sustain the civil rights struggle. Hutchings argued that having an official student social organization on campus would "gather new recruits and more students will become politically involved." Moreover, he believed that the campus offered a natural space to "experiment with new techniques" as part of the civil rights struggle. In connecting NAG to the university, "we do not sacrifice the work now being done in the Washington area," he further explained; "if anything, we will strengthen it."[16] The strategies of the Nabrit administration and the secondary reasoning of Anderson seemed politically sound, especially given the constraints of Howard University. In a parallel fashion, the differences between Gustavo and Hutchings also concerned political strategy, in particular how best to sustain the student wing of the civil rights movement and whether focusing on the university was politically sound. The division between students and administrators and between students themselves partly came down to disagreements about political strategy, especially as it related to the university's role in the civil rights struggle.

But there was also a deeper debate that concerned the role of the university as a political institution. The reasoning—whether articulated by academic leaders like Anderson or student activists like Gustavo—rested upon a division between political action and education that ran counter to a core epistemological belief of most NAG members who sought institutional

recognition. Howard students in NAG embraced the underlying epistemol-
ogy of nonviolent direct action, even if they disagreed on the philosophy
of nonviolence itself. *Satya*, or truth, was central to Mohandas Gandhi's
understanding of nonviolence. In Gandhi's view, knowledge was always partial.
Nonviolent actions such as civil disobedience represented a set of experiments
that could realize a common truth among its participants.[17] Like others of
the founding cohort, Howard students participated in nonviolent workshops
facilitated by James Lawson, the primary adviser to sit-in leaders and early
SNCC members on nonviolent direct action. In his workshops, Lawson translated Gandhi's conception of truth into the American pragmatic tradition.
As he explained, the experience of nonviolent direct action was similar to
"being engaged in an experiment where you have to keep figuring out what
happened and why, what didn't happen."[18] The experimental emphasis at the
core of nonviolence served as the basis of SNCC and NAG's conception of
knowledge and the pursuit of truth. "Truth," students declared in outlining
the philosophy of SNCC, "comes from being involved, not observation and
speculation."[19] Action for NAG students was more than a political appeal; it
was a commitment to the pursuit of truth.

When Howard University leaders refused to recognize NAG as a student
organization, students interpreted that refusal as a contradiction of not only
their political commitments but also the institution's commitment to education and the pursuit of truth. Indeed, the stated position—that NAG's actions
fell outside the realm of the university's educational mission—shaped not
only the contours of the debates about the role of Howard University in the
struggle for civil rights in the 1960s but also how Howard University defined
the boundaries of what it meant to pursue truth and higher education at
a Black elite institution. The institutional salience of this epistemological
belief arose at the Gandhi Memorial Lectures sponsored by Howard University. The theme of the conference was "Youth, Non-Violence, and Social
Change." However, students challenged university leaders for sponsoring a
conference on nonviolence while denying support for NAG, an organization
that was engaged in nonviolent direct action. Indeed, the conference symbol-
ically captured the tension that went to the heart of NAG's efforts for institutional recognition. For supporters of NAG's efforts, the conference rested
upon the "unrealistic notion that 'education' was limited to classrooms."[20]

Paralleling disagreements on political strategy and whether to even focus
efforts on the university, members of NAG who supported institutional recognition made different arguments for the place of action at Howard University. Carmichael believed the university's policy contradicted a student's
academic freedom to pursue knowledge. A key flash point was in 1962,

when Carmichael and other NAG members organized a solidarity rally for Southern University students expelled by President Felton Clark for their involvement in the sit-in movement. Howard students like Carmichael had a deep connection to Southern University. Dion Diamond, a Howard student and NAG member, visited Southern to speak to the student body, only to be arrested. The purpose of the Howard rally was to bring attention to the violation of students' academic freedom at Southern University. When students gathered for the solidarity demonstration, the Howard administration responded by ordering the students to disperse. The problem, argued Carmichael, was "not merely one of legality." Rather, the problem was "the policy of the administration, which has decreed that the university shall not be 'used as a base for social action.'"[21] Carmichael found the policy, in the ways that Nabrit and others used it, confusing. The stated concern by Nabrit was that NAG students, through their political actions, would be speaking on behalf of Howard University. As a prominent student leader within NAG and SNCC, Carmichael found such claims to run counter to his experiences within both organizations. "Howard students who have participated in protest activity have never claimed to speak for the University, only for themselves," Carmichael wrote, "so there can be no question of the University's having been 'used.'"[22] Carmichael argued the issue seemed to come down to the perception of association rather than official use of Howard for direct action.

Carmichael also argued that the policy contradicted the position of the student as a political actor. In Carmichael's view, the university was the logical place at which a student should organize for social action. "The intellectually aware student," he continued, "quickly perceives the injustices of the system in which he lives and moves to act against them." As a result, the student "has no other base from which to act than his own campus." Moreover, Carmichael argued that political activity was vital to a student's intellectual growth. Turning to the examples of student movements in Hungary, South Korea, Poland, and Spain, Carmichael argued that the movements demonstrated the "inseparability of intellectual ferment and social ferment, of thought and action."[23] The bourgeoning civil rights struggle—in which students like Carmichael took a prominent role—also demonstrated the inseparability of thought and action. In his critique of the university's response to the 1962 solidarity rally, Carmichael ultimately defended NAG's actions by taking an orthodox position on academic freedom: the university had no right to impose any regulation on student activities. But he did not advocate for institutional sponsorship of civil rights activism, either. Rather, Carmichael's views, at least early in his activist career, hedge closely to a traditional conception of the university and that of Nabrit's—as a space for free inquiry. The only difference was that Carmichael saw civil rights action as an intellectual activity in ways that Nabrit did not.

Carmichael's defense of NAG—and how he translated the core episte-mological belief of civil rights action—was but one argument. The decision by Howard University leaders to limit the activities of NAG—especially its solidarity rally for Southern students—was personal for Ed Brown. The pre-vious year, he had been expelled from Southern University for his role in the sit-in movement in Louisiana. Brown transferred to Howard University in the hopes of finding a more intellectually and politically aware student life. However, he was dismayed by what he interpreted as Howard's tepid intellectual and political life. He argued that intellectual apathy at Howard was a by-product of Nabrit's defense of a traditional idea of the university. Despite Nabrit's public presentation as an advocate for the cause of civil rights, Brown noted that Nabrit regularly avoided "any reference to politi-cal activity" on college campuses. Brown argued that this absence was not a surprise. Rather, it reflected the ways Nabrit and other academic lead-ers imbibed the cultural norms associated with the American university's development as a liberal institution. "This absence," Brown explained, "is in perfect agreement with the liberal-democratic assumption that such activity should not be influenced or directed by University policy." Brown argued fur-ther that the lack of such activity was also a reflection of Howard's particular institutional culture. The tendency of Howard students to show intellectual apathy was an expression of the institution's prevailing culture that "served as the capstone of the Black Bourgeoise" and as a "factory for the produc-tion of job fillers."[24] Brown believed the way to combat the intellectual apa-thy in the university—and to transform Howard from a university for the Black bourgeoise to an activist institution that serves the Black public—was to make political action a central activity of the university. Doing so would bring about "a revolution in ideas and values" at Howard University.[25]

If Carmichael's reasoning hedged closely to a defense of an older idea of the university and Brown sought a radical reimaging of the university, Michael Thelwell charted a middle-ground argument. He wrote that the refusal to recognize NAG touched "upon broader areas of educational philosophy."[26] Although the university exposed students to new ideas, he argued that it also set limits on the application or realization of those ideas. As Thelwell explained, "When the rare flame of deep commitment is kindled, and the student seeks to put into practice, or to proselytize on behalf of, an idea learned in the classroom, the university terrain suddenly appears too confin-ing and conflict with tradition and authority erupts."[27] However, Thelwell argued that activism and formal educational pursuits at the university were not mutually exclusive. Echoing core tenets of SNCC and NAG, Thelwell argued that action was "itself a generative intellectual flame."[28] In providing institutional support for NAG, Thelwell argued, Howard University leaders would be supporting similar education activities common to other political organizations on campus.

Thelwell's argument stood out for its broader claim and vision about the relationship between action and education. "It is possible for the University," Thelwell asserted, "to evolve a policy which will enable it to accommodate the new currents stirring in this generation and at the same time to preserve its intuitional goals and integrity."[29] In Thelwell's argument for institutional recognition of NAG, he noted that students would abide by the rules and regulations of the university, just as members of other organizations on campus did. The purpose of NAG, Thelwell wrote, "shall be to deepen the commitment of Howard University students to the ideals of human equality and to encourage the expression of that commitment by such means as shall be consistent with University policy."[30] Thelwell, in other words, believed that NAG's commitment to action could be made compatible with university policy and tradition. So too did Howard University leaders. Indeed, while Howard leaders never granted institutional recognition to NAG, they did agree with the broader point made by Thelwell: the university should evolve its educational policy to support the civil rights struggle. They promoted the Community Service Project, in contrast to the political action models that grew out of SNCC, thus setting the tenor for a new disciplining culture at Howard University.

Providing Service

In 1960, when Howard students gathered with other sit-in leaders across the country, they listened in as Ella Baker encouraged students to think of their movement as "bigger than a hamburger." She wanted the young activists to see the goal of the movement was to end racial segregation and discrimination "not only at lunch counters, but in every aspect of life." This goal, she underscored, required full-time dedication.[31] Howard students Carmichael, Courtland Cox, Charles Cobb, and Cleveland Sellers took this appeal to heart. During the winter and summer months, they became full-time "field secretaries" and began organizing community meetings and voter drives in the rural Deep South. At the core of community organizing was a deep commitment to relationship building and listening. Cobb personified this commitment. Organizing in Ruleville, Mississippi, a rural Delta town that contrasted with Cobb's upbringing in Massachusetts and Washington, DC, Cobb had to learn to navigate a different social world. "What I had to do in Ruleville," Cobb explained, "was learn how to listen to people and learn how to speak to people. There was nothing in my experience that taught me how to function in Sunflower County."[32] Cobb's key word—*learn*—was also important. Indeed, the relationship building and commitment to listening that were central to the organizing process also contained the seeds of a distinct political philosophy of experiential learning.

Experiential learning functioned on two levels within SNCC's organizing efforts. The first was a commitment to learning from those in rural Southern communities—the communities most affected and marginalized by the system of Jim Crow. Baker explained to students like Cobb that the process of community was about tapping into the wisdom and knowledge of experience. This focus had deep political salience for Baker. The overemphasis on formal education as a qualification for leadership, she argued, led people who were "not educated" to defer to people who had book learning. The goal of organizing was to empower the politically marginalized to see that they had the knowledge, from experience, for political leadership. The second commitment was to learn from the process of experience. Baker defined the community organizing process as experimental, much like the nonviolent models of education. The organizing projects and the distinct character of certain localities required different approaches. With the help of Septima Clark and Myles Horton from the Highlander Folk School, Baker and SNCC field-workers held regular workshops where students analyzed their experiences to develop new political knowledge about a particular locality or organizing effort.[33] Howard students in SNCC came to understand that the community organizing was a learning process that was oriented just as much toward them as young people as it was toward community residents.

Indeed, the experiential learning of community organizing directly challenged the academic culture at Howard. Baker believed that her own political education was rooted in what she learned on the streets and in meeting places and union halls, rather than in her formal training at Shaw. Such experiences informed her skepticism of Black colleges and universities. Baker critiqued Black universities, seeing them as largely conservative institutions because they did not "provide adequate experience for young Negroes to assume initiative and think and act independently."[34] Baker believed that the lack of opportunities to engage with and experience democracy in practice produced a narrow conception of education. She believed the prevailing idea of education across Black higher education primarily served to advance individual professional careers that were accommodated to the system of Jim Crow. In the view of Sellers, the academic culture of Howard University was a direct reflection of this model of education. Transferring from Voorhees, where students were on the front lines of the sit-ins, he assumed that Howard—because of its status as an elite academic institution—would be a hotbed of activism. But he found the university's student culture to be more class-based and focused on the development of the "professional, white-collar." It was "a kind of bourgeois campus," he explained, that taught students "to become part of the status quo."[35] Baker's philosophy of organizing that became inculcated in SNCC and associated organizations like NAG came to represent a counterpoint to prevailing notions of what it meant to be "educated" in the early 1960s, especially at institutions like Howard University.

But the knowledge, perspective, and relationships gained through organizing work had both epistemological and political limitations. While the process of organizing enabled field-workers to identify particular local conditions to exploit as part of their efforts and taught students value-laden skills and perspectives missing from the regular curriculum of the university, the experiential knowledge itself was limited in helping students understand the larger structural conditions of their work. As part of the organizing efforts, SNCC field-workers set up economic programs to address high unemployment and the lack of economic power among Black residents across the South.[36] Yet, SNCC field-workers recognized that many of their self-help projects had very little impact on the economic conditions of Blacks in the South. Many of these same field-workers also lacked a broader knowledge of existing federal programs and other resources that might aid their community projects across the South. The limitations of their community organizing and projects across the South raised larger questions within SNCC concerning the relationship between formal education, expert knowledge, and the experiential knowledge of community organizing.[37]

Howard Zinn, an adult adviser to SNCC, argued that the issue that SNCC confronted was the gap between its experiential knowledge and the university's expert knowledge. He believed that SNCC was "unique in that we are in touch with the grass roots of society in a way in which most of these minds in academic pursuits are not."[38] But, Zinn argued, many students within SNCC "feel a loss because there is information we need which is available in the academic world." In order to develop more effective economic programs, Zinn argued, "We need to enlist some of the best minds around in thought on reorganisation [sic] of society." Zinn suggested a new model of education that allowed for temporary shifts of study and community organizing. The combination, Zinn believed, constituted a "union of moral commitment, social action, and intellectual inquiry, which education should give."[39]

Indeed, in Zinn's view, SNCC needed to develop a sustained and intentional mechanism that connected knowledge gained through the experience of organizing to knowledge developed in the context of academia. Zinn's idea became a central goal of SNCC more broadly. "In recruiting potential student leaders from college campuses and sending them to work in rural communities," students explained in SNCC's recruitment pamphlet, the organization provided a means "to bridge the gap between the centers of learning and the work-a-day communities."[40]

Privy to these discussions and shaped by Zinn's ideas in SNCC, Howard students Brown, Thelwell, and Bill Mahoney went to work on organizing programs that linked academic research to organizing efforts in the South. They focused their energies on Howard, believing the university, with its existing graduate programs in medicine, social work, and law, represented a vital resource for developing new education programs. Mahoney emphasized the value of having the conference at Howard. "It is imperative at this time that all sections of the community close ranks in this struggle," and to accomplish this task, he wrote, "we prefer that the conference be held at Howard rather than at one of the white universities in the District."[41] In Brown's view, the conference was an expression of an existing tradition at Howard. "Howard University," he wrote, "has a tradition of making its facilities available to programs primarily concerned with the Negro in America."[42] Like Zinn, Howard students in NAG also believed that a formal SNCC-university conference not only reinforced existing traditions but also could model alternative forms of education at Howard. Indeed, the model NAG activists developed sought to flatten the hierarchy typical of academic cultures like Howard. The workshop model treated SNCC field-workers, community representatives, and Howard faculty as equal experts, despite the wide variance in their degrees and backgrounds. Howard faculty and other outside academic researchers were to provide relevant information, while SNCC field-workers and community representatives—those with experiential knowledge of community organizing—would "relate the information to the real situation in the communities they come from."[43]

Howard officials supported the conference, albeit in a way that employed the same political strategy and logic associated with the policy on social action. Because neither NAG nor SNCC were recognized student groups, the event was sponsored by a chapter of the National Association for the Advancement of Colored People (NAACP). Like Project Awareness, a SNCC-sponsored conference at Howard was also an expression of the university's role in providing a space for free speech and deliberation. But Nabrit and other academic leaders also believed the conference connected to the educational mission of Howard. Indeed, the role of Howard was to provide expert knowledge and training in the areas of job training and economic relief and relate the information to SNCC's community work in Mississippi and other parts of the South. In Nabrit's view, the conference was a natural extension of its existing disciplinary and expert culture. This is the point that Mahoney made after the completion of the conference. To Dean Evan Crawford, Mahoney wrote, "This event was testimony to Howard University's continued rededication to its founding principles of training for all youth regardless of race."[44]

Even as NAG activists and Howard leaders agreed that the conference aligned with the mission of the university, the conference itself revealed key differences in the cultures of learning in SNCC and at Howard. Mahoney raised two key issues. First, many of the academic experts presented findings that did not match the experiential knowledge of the community. As Mahoney wrote in the conference report, "The speakers who were asked to address themselves to policy questions made some statements contrary to SNCC's experiences." Second, the approach to conveying information did not enable SNCC field-workers to connect the research knowledge to the community. While the technical experts "were successful in giving pertinent information," Mahoney wrote, they were "not successful in directing conversations toward the area of Southern rural problems."[45] On paper, these differences read as largely logistical, but they revealed deeper philosophical differences around the Howard-SNCC partnership. The conference model largely prioritized a technical and expert-led model of service, one in which involvement for the student meant extending university research into the community via data collection and social service. While recognizing the need for expert research, student activists associated with SNCC and NAG critiqued the university's approach to serving the community for the ways that it marginalized the perspective and knowledge of local residents.

The differences mattered, especially in how Howard developed new institutional programs—and civic culture—in response to the appeals of NAG and SNCC in the first part of the 1960s. Howard leaders and faculty agreed that the conference represented a model for expanding education. The same year that Howard sponsored the SNCC conference, Howard leaders expanded the Community Service Project. Partnering with local churches, the stated mission of the project echoed a core idea of SNCC's organizing ethos. The purpose, explained Gilbert Lowe, the project director, "was to learn from the residents themselves the problems they considered most important, the services lacking and the residents' attitudes towards working on these problems." Moreover, Lowe's framing drew on the nascent critique of Howard by

NAG activists—what he described as the "lack of concern for the communities in which [universities] are located." But the process of learning from the community took the form of survey research. Lowe translated the ethos of the movement into the value-neutralist logic of the university. Indeed, Lowe argued that the Community Service Project offered a two-tier educational model for other urban universities—what he defined as an "action-research program." Lowe's report on the project articulated a particular model of disciplining that served the academic development of the student while also providing direct service to the community. As Lowe explained, the project served as "a training facility for Howard University students" by providing "field work experiences for students in methodology or for subject matter for papers and theses."[46]

While Lowe focused on the academic and professional benefits of the project, seeing the work largely as an extension of social science fieldwork, university administrators and outside supporters believed the project represented a way to connect the pursuit of knowledge to value commitments. William Stuart Nelson, the vice president for special projects and a professor of religion at Howard, played a prominent role in the civil rights movement. He served as a mentor to Martin Luther King Jr. in his development of nonviolent direct action and facilitated nonviolent workshops with student activists in Atlanta, Georgia, in 1960. At Howard, he helped plan the Youth, Non-Violence, and Social Change conference in 1963. Nelson understood that Gandhi's idea of nonviolence had two sides: civil disobedience and constructive service.[47] In his view, the university's appropriate role within the civil rights struggle was to provide constructive service. He was a staunch supporter of the Community Service Project, seeing it as an expression of his interpretation of nonviolence within the American political context. In 1964, Nelson invited King to meet with students at Howard. Only on campus for a brief afternoon, King focused mainly on the Community Service Project. As reported in the campus newspaper, *The Hilltop*, King believed the project "united the knowledge of the school with the betterment of the community."[48] University administrators like Lowe and Nelson believed the project fit into the disciplinary culture of the university with its emphasis on research while also providing an outlet for students to participate in the civil rights struggle as an integrated part of their education.

The institutionally supported project seemed to be an expression of Howard's efforts to reimagine its mode of education to better support the civil rights struggle, especially in the DC area. Indeed, many of the churches affiliated with the project also worked with NAG and SNCC in DC. The survey data was utilized by NAG and SNCC as part of their organizing efforts.

Just as importantly, the project was moving students into the community. By 1964, 150 students participated in the project, many of them coming from the Sociology and Anthropology Club, campus sororities and fraternities, and those in social work. Working with Howard faculty, students went door-to-door canvassing, meeting with church members, and observing patterns of the neighborhood. They also provided needed services, volunteering with Big Brother, Big Sister, the Urban Corps, and related organizations that offered educational programming. But direct institutional support for the project came at the same time that NAG students were advocating for recognition on campus. The promotion of the project had the effect of redirecting socially conscious students away from NAG's efforts to community service and fieldwork that aligned with Howard's traditional research mission. Indeed, the logic of the Community Service Project approach—with its emphasis on data collection and volunteerism—not only served as the basis of the new disciplining culture at Howard but also marginalized the political philosophy of experiential learning associated with the community organizing work of NAG and SNCC in the first part of the 1960s.

Reimagining a Black University

A new generational cohort of students at Howard in the mid-1960s focused efforts on reforming the university by calling for new service programs in the community. But the change in focus was not simply due to the influence of the institution; it also reflected shifts in the civil rights struggle. The intellectual project of Black Power on campus was both a demand for Black studies and a demand for programs that served the Black community. The most prominent organizational iteration of Black Power in the mid-1960s was the Black Panther Party, an organization that was deeply committed to "service to the people" programs.[49] At Howard, the community service ethos of Black Power shaped a generation of activists who sought to carry on the legacy of NAG and SNCC in redefining the political role of the Black university in the civil rights struggle. Starting in 1967, the student assembly at Howard made community service a key element of reforming the university. With the end of the Community Service Project in 1966, the assembly called on the university to open the campus resources to the surrounding community by creating a "training program" in human relations, Black arts and culture, and community action. They emphasized that these efforts must be determined by local community members. "Periodic meetings," the students explained, must "be held between students and community people being worked with in the programs so that people in the community can determine with which problems they wish Howard University to deal."[50] Even as Howard students focused their appeals on community service, the commitment to service among Black Power advocates still involved an associated commitment to political activism. The emphasis on community action and knowledge was a central component of the nascent vision of a new Black university articulated at Howard's conference "Toward the Black University."

Despite students' appeals and the guiding ethos of the conference, Howard leaders did not provide any new programs that served the Black community. Frustrated by the lack of opportunities, students in social work, law, and medicine boycotted classes in the winter of 1969. They pressed university administrators on the curriculum. Arthur J. Cox, a student in social work and participant in the boycott, argued that many students had come to Howard looking for that "extra something that would help us be more effective in the black community," but he had never found such opportunities in his coursework or on campus. By the spring, Howard undergraduates joined in the protests, making similar demands for educational relevance and programs for community involvement. What emerged from the spring conference—and its more famous campus strike that fall—was a shared call for new programs that connected university resources to the community. In the open letter and list of demands to Nabrit, key student leaders of the campus protest—Anthony Gittens, Ewart Brown, and Barbara Penn—demanded that "Howard must be made relevant to the black community. The university campus must be made more available to all black people and programs must be instituted to aid the black community in the struggle against oppression."[51]

But that shared vision hid different conceptions of community involvement. In Carmichael's vision of a Black university, one that he articulated at the Toward a Black University Conference, the Howard graduate and former NAG student maintained an emphasis on institutional autonomy while further framing his vision in the context of Black liberation and Third World political struggles. Black Power advocates like Carmichael saw their political task as revealing the ways that the stated claims of universalism in institutions like the university were in fact color-blind claims that masked the prevailing culture of Whiteness. Carmichael argued that the goal of a Black revolution on campus was not to create a "black Harvard." "The white education system has placed technical development over human development," Carmichael argued; "we must reverse the system—to put human development over technical development." He worried that the calls for Black studies and a "Black university" continued to be shaped by prevailing conceptions of White higher education. "We cannot just have Swahili or Afro-American studies taught by the same methodology and ideology as the white system," Carmichael argued. Like other Black Power advocates within SNCC, he envisioned the Black university as a community-based university, or what fellow activist Ivanhoe Donaldson defined as "an activist oriented institution."[52]

Other SNCC and civil rights activists agreed that Howard must redirect its intellectual resources to the Black community. However, their visions largely aligned with the technical and academic character that Carmichael associated with the White university system. Indeed, for some, the concern was less about institutional revolution and more about institutional reform. E. W. Steptoe and Jesse Morris had deep roots in Mississippi and knew the concerns of its Black residents. Steptoe was a farmer who intimately experienced the struggles of Black sharecroppers in the South, and Morris helped form the Poor People's Corporation, a self-help organization that provided loans and technical assistance to Black residents seeking to start cooperative businesses. Steptoe and Morris advocated technical aid and research that would help advance the economy of rural agricultural communities in the South.[53] Their vision was largely a land grant extension service model that would connect expert and academic research to economic and agricultural programs.

This conception of the Black university's role in the community resonated with a group of Howard students who formed Students for an Educational Institution (SEI). SEI members disagreed with the focus on Black identity at the institutional level. Vernanders Black, the cochairman of the organization, worried that an emphasis on race and Black identity would not fully equip students to live and appropriately engage in a diverse society. Group members also did not see their academic education as Whitewashed. Rather, the purpose of the organization was to improve academic education at Howard and focus on academic research opportunities. Like others at Howard, SEI members sought ways to develop more "academic-community projects." In contrast to Carmichael and others who believed that a community-based education would challenge and transform notions of knowledge and education, SEI students argued that the task of community projects was to extend university education and knowledge to the community.[54]

In the aftermath of the strike, Michael Harris, the Howard University Student Association (HUSA) president, started the D.C. Project. Fully funded by HUSA, the D.C. Project was a student-run effort that sought to realize the various calls for a community-based education at Howard. The project served as an institutional compromise, at least among the students. Similarly shaped by appeals to Black Power, Harris echoed a key tenet of Carmichael's vision. "Howard University," he explained "should serve another purpose other than preparing people to fill slots in white society." That purpose, in his view, was to serve as an intellectual resource to the Black community. Indeed, he wrote, Howard should "belong to the black people in Washington, D.C., the black people surrounding the university."[55]

What Harris proposed in the D.C. Project synthesized the SNCC elements of experiential learning and the cultural appeal of Black Power with the academic models associated with SEI and the research culture of Howard University. The first goal was to develop community-based research mechanisms that enabled students to determine whether Howard University's curriculum and research could support community organizations adjacent to campus. Second, based on this research, they envisioned developing programs designed to eliminate "social ills which have plagued the community for so long." A key component of these two goals was the creation of "community information centers" that made "available information sought by the community and that will serve as a resource of information for Howard University to design new programs and provide needed services." It also involved a reshaping of university governance that included not only increased student input on institutional decisions but also the input of "community representatives" who engaged with university affairs. The D.C. Project was an attempt by students to create a research and educational model that maintained SNCC's commitment to community knowledge and Black culture while also developing a service arm that provided research to Black communities in the DC area. In both ways, Harris explained, the project sought to combat the prevailing existence of Howard—what he saw as an "ebony tower of social detachment and philosophical neutrality."[56] The D.C. Project went into full operation in 1969.

One component of the D.C. Project—called the Southeast Community Summer Project—was designed to involve students and faculty in youth and adult education in DC. The project employed a particular model of teaching that took on key characteristics of the experiential learning models of SNCC. Called Operation Zygote, the model started with the particular conditions and situations of the student. The goal, explained Harris, was to "use the environment to teach and give knowledge about the environment." This commitment allowed for learning to be multidirectional. Area students on the "receiving" end of tutoring services took on key leadership roles in the programing. Tony Stewart, a Howard student and project coordinator, explained that the "majority of the students participating in the program are from the inner city schools, they are, therefore, equipped to attack the problem." By using the environment and the community experience as a source of knowledge and promoting the leadership of the high school students, the program positioned the professional college student as a learner in the tutoring relationship. At the same time, the college student also brought to the relationship academic and expert knowledge to help contextualize the experiential knowledge of the student. Indeed, at the core of the project was a political critique of the schooling system. Stewart argued that the fact that inner city schools required a tutoring program indicated that "the present approach to inner city education is inadequate."[57]

As part of the D.C. Project, students also established community health care and legal aid centers to redirect the research and education in those schools to address community issues. The Center for Clinical Legal Studies combined community organizing with coursework. The combination, students believed, would develop both a student who would be a "legal advocate for the poor" and an "integrated program of legal study in the law of the poor."[58] The center served as a legal arm of civil rights efforts in Augusta, Georgia, and Jackson, Mississippi, in the late 1960s. Ike Madison, a law student who oversaw the legal clinic, explained the philosophy of the center as an approach that recognized community members' need not only for legal advisers but also for legal advocates who understood community problems and "the need for the effective combination of all community resources to solve these problems."[59] Other law students went so far as to connect the efforts of the D.C. Project to a complete reframing of what it means to study law and become a lawyer. Les Gaines, a Howard student and president of the Student Bar Association, argued that those enrolled at the law school would be known as "liberators" rather than law students. Gaines explained that, like those participating in the efforts in Alabama and Mississippi, "we're going where the people are, where ever they're being oppressed, shot down, and killed."[60] For students like Gaines, community-based work via the Center for Legal Studies was part of the broader movement to remake Howard into a base for preparing students to challenge social and political systems.

The D.C. Project accommodated the varied efforts of Howard students over the course of the 1960s. The project reflected the early appeals for action made by NAG students, albeit in ways that were reflective of the evolving political strategies of the movement. Members of the D.C. Project continued the work of SNCC field-workers in the South, where they led political mobilization efforts in Alabama. The D.C. Project also funded student work with the National Welfare Rights Organization. In 1972, five students helped plan the conference in Miami, based on the theme "People before Politics." As part of the conference, the students also organized a protest of the Democratic National Convention.[61] While the D.C. Project enabled participants to use Howard as a base for organizing students and moving them into political activism. The student-led initiative also accommodated legacies of the Community Service Project. The tutoring program focused on providing tutoring services as well as charity donations to families in the neighborhood. Indeed, for some students, the project's experiences in the school provided an outlet to connect community service to coursework. As Leonard Harvey explained, the D.C. Project enabled students to "get a chance to apply what they have learned in the classroom to a real working situation."[62] Students thus attempted to create a model of community education that balanced student learning, community service, and political activism. This balance carried on the legacy of SNCC—one in which service was always tied to structural analysis and political struggle.

The rhetoric of the new administration at Howard suggested that the D.C. Project would garner additional institutional support, especially with the emphasis on community service. James E. Cheek, the new president at Howard in 1969, supported the creation of new community programs. "The total resources of this university," he explained in his inaugural address to students, "will be mobilized to engage the entire spectrum of social problems which have emerged as crises in our national life." In particular, he hoped to create "new public service activities" and "community programs" to address the issues of social justice. He believed that a university like Howard, with its unique history, required a different position as an institution, one that "cannot stand aloof, morally and neutral and socially passive."[63] Andrew Billingsley, the new vice president of academic affairs at Howard, shared similar views. He believed that the institution was "strategically located to transform American education." As such, he argued, the institution offered a natural setting to develop what he defined as "liberation techniques," and the faculty, students, and administration had to work together to "use all available resources of the society to help liberate Black people from oppression outside and dissent within our own community."[64]

Even as student activists and university officials aligned on the need for new education programs that both supported Black community needs and extended learning beyond the campus, Cheek and Billingsley tended to support those efforts that prioritized community service over political activism. Indeed, the D.C. Project never received institutional and financial support because it focused on community organizing and political activism in the DC area. Both Cheek and Billingsley used the same logic as Johnson and Nabrit, seeing such direct political activities as both outside the scope of Howard's mission and a risky activity given the institution's financial dependency on federal funds. Cheek and Billingsley were also informed by the logic of the new federalism of the Nixon administration. Cheek signed onto the University Year for Action (UYA), an initiative by the Nixon administration that promoted volunteerism among college students. Howard's participation in the UYA attracted more federal appropriations. Those appropriations also came with further limitations on the type and form of community involvement. Lawrence E. Gary, a social work professor, oversaw the initiative and interpreted volunteer work as a key experience for preprofessional development. Although the UYA shared elements of the D.C. Project, students involved in the UYA were prohibited from participating in political activism. The type of activities allowed to address the UYA's goal of the "alleviation of poverty" was limited to community service. One of the successful projects, as Gary interpreted, was when student volunteers working in a DC nursery found the school in disrepair and organized a group of students to paint it. Students enriched their education and developed a sense of community concern through their work, but broader questions related to the cause of the disrepair or structural inequalities were marginalized in UYA programming.

The logic of UYA and associated funds also shaped the other community programs started by the Cheek administration. Cheek also provided funding for a Volunteer Assistance Bureau at Howard. Operating under student affairs, Darrah F. Hall, the associate director, used the language of educational relevance and activism to describe the Volunteer Assistance Bureau. "Days of universities as 'ivory towers' are almost over. We can no longer isolate ourselves," she explained. The bureau, she argued, provided students an opportunity "to work towards alleviation of social ills affecting society."[65] The forms of community involvement that the bureau promoted were short-term volunteer opportunities such as the Day in the Community, an effort that recruited student volunteers to clean up trash and litter in the surrounding Cardoza area. Hall connected the volunteer experiences to learning. "A student must be actively involved in his own educational process," she explained. "The student can greatly enhance his theoretical classroom experience through the theoretical experience gained as a volunteer." Hall worked with faculty to create alternatives that allowed "volunteer work to take the place of another course requirement."[66] The Volunteer Assistance Bureau encouraged student involvement but in ways that were focused more on charity work, service, and professional development.

With the establishment of the bureau and institutional involvement in UYA, student interest in the D.C. Project waned. In some ways, its demise was the result of student mismanagement. By the spring semester of 1971, HUSA called for a complete reorganization of the D.C. Project. Sam Wallace, the treasurer of HUSA, had found that many of the student coordinators were delinquent and failing to do their work in the community. Other advocates of the project challenged Wallace's interpretation. They believed its issues resulted from the lack of support from the administration and the development of alternative community programs. D.C. Project staff believed that the university never supported their efforts, either through granting credit or funding. Some staff members noted that when the university began to develop its own programming, such as the Volunteer Assistance Bureau and the UYA, it redirected students away from the D.C. Project and its goals. Students who participated in institution-sponsored programs received five times more in funding and academic credit. As some D.C. Project staff also worried, these "community projects tend to get lost or become institution-alized that they reflect the university's need rather than that of the Black community."[67]

From 1973 to 1975, students held multiple referendums that attempted to revive the D.C. Project. Supported by the HUSA student body in a 1974 vote, the new D.C. Project laid out a set of principles that called on students and university officials to make the resources of Howard more readily available to the Black community. Despite wide-ranging student support, the university administrators attempted to undermine the new program. In 1974, after a summer in which students ran the program, the office of the vice president for student affairs impounded the funds of the D.C. Project. Carl Anderson, who was then the coordinator of the UYA, refused to release the funds to the project, even after a referendum by students that demanded their release. Publicly, he argued that the issue came down to competing interpretations of the referendum in HUSA. Privately, he was skeptical of the project. He noted that the project did not have support from the board of trustees and himself. He also had reservations about the efficacy of the endeavor, believing the project was "too broad in focus and scope." Moreover, he believed that "the project cannot stand as an independent unit, outside the University."[68] Anderson had changed course. In the mid-1960s, he believed the university should neither support nor be involved in the activities of NAG. By the mid-1970s, the political environment and context had changed. With community involvement now accommodated within the university, any efforts off campus now fell under the rules and regulations of the university, constraining students' efforts associated with the D.C. Project.

Legacy

Anthony "Mawu" Straker led the effort to revive the D.C. Project, critiquing prevailing university-sponsored community projects in the process. In an editorial for *The Hilltop*, Mawu captured the fundamental difference between the programs adopted by the university and those that were defunded. He believed most efforts at Howard, especially in response to the activism from 1966 to 1969, tended to only give "lip service" to the needs of the community. But, Mawu emphasized, this was not a result of a broader effort to deflect student efforts. He argued that universities like Howard, dependent upon federal money, faced a dilemma when trying to connect students, education, and activism to community problems. In order for a university like Howard to exist, Mawu argued, it had to "adhere to the systems of this racist nation or be destroyed by political and economical forces of the system." At the same time, the stated purpose of Howard was to provide requisite skills and education that students could use for Black liberation. This tension put pressure on university officials and the board of trustees to make a choice in terms of what programs they could and could not support. Using Howard as an example, Mawu concluded that "most 'Black' institutions of higher learning pretend to be the middle of the road, thus giving lip service and tokenism to the needs and aspirations of the Black communities, while actively campaigning for the systems that oppress them, exploit them, and degrade them." Mawu's analysis of Howard's financial dependency on federal and foundational money reflected the constraints of using the university as a means for political liberation. At its best, at least in Mawu's view, Howard's financial dependency meant that the institution could only support elements of social reform.[69]

Mawu's analysis of the institution's financial dependency identified one factor that constrained efforts to reimagine the Black university in the 1960s and 1970s. The other factor was an academic culture, promoted by Howard leaders and reinforced by the student body, that defined Howard as an elite institution for the privileged few of the Black middle class. Ruth Robinson, a longtime Shaw neighborhood resident, negatively viewed Howard University, especially in the 1950s. "Howard University students saw the Negro community in Washington as a poverty-stricken ghetto. They saw our citizens as block boys and mammies," Robinson explained. As a result of this view, she emphasized that "we saw the students as snobs."[70] Even with the expansion of new volunteer programs, the relationship between Howard and its surrounding community rested upon the same class divide. "Many of our fellow students claim to have the ultimate goal of using their education to help the Black community but after being a part of the 'Howard mentality,'" Bilal Sunji Ahmaddiyya, a student at Howard, explained, "they refer to their brothers and sisters of the very community they claim to want to provide leadership for as Blockgirls & Blockboys," a derogatory reference. Ahmaddiyya believed that the academic culture of Howard—even those programs that supported community involvement—reinforced class barriers between privileged Black students and their counterparts in Shaw and the broader DC area.[71] The programs supported by academic leaders at Howard University were made to fit the academic culture that defined the university as a space that cultivated a "talented tenth."

The analytical reflections of Mawu, Robinson, and Ahmaddiyya identified the twin institutional factors that set limits on student efforts at Howard. Over the course of the 1960s and 1970s, students pushed Howard leaders to rethink both prevailing ideas of education and the role of the Black university in the struggle for civil rights. Academic leaders were supportive of the larger appeals. But, at different stages in this era of mass Black student politics, university leaders at Howard set boundaries as to what were appropriate modes of action both on and off campus. Initially, the focus was on whether the university could directly support the actions of NAG, which included sit-ins, freedom rides, business boycotts, and rent strikes. University leaders denied every request for institutional recognition and support of NAG, reasoning that maintaining an institutional distance from direct action would protect the financial solvency of Howard while ensuring students' political freedom. The underlying logic was politically realistic, but it also shaped a broader disciplining culture that set limits on other efforts to support students' engagement in the community and redefine the idea of the Black university.

At the same time, Howard leaders recognized the value of supporting student efforts in the community. In response to the community organizing efforts of SNCC in the mid-1960s and the broader appeals for community action that emerged out of the 1968 campus strike, Howard leaders provided institutional support for a range of new education projects and institutional hubs for community service and involvement among students. The type of programs that academic leaders supported rested upon the same logic used to deny the recognition of NAG, although with different emphases. In the first part of the 1960s, the dean and civil rights activist Nelson interpreted community service as an element of cultivating students' sense of moral concern and an expression of one component of Gandhian nonviolence. Faculty members like Lowe and Gary interpreted programs like the Community Service Project and UYA as an extension of academic coursework and social science field research. By the 1970s, Cheek's views largely synthesized both views: the goal of volunteer service was to enhance students' academic and professional learning while developing students' sense of moral and social commitment. The efforts of the Cheek administration in the late 1960s and early 1970s—at once promoting alternative community programs while refusing to support the D.C. Project—solidified the new culture of disciplining democracy at Howard University.

Indeed, the financial dependency on federal appropriations and maintenance of Howard as an elite institution disciplined the more expansive vision for a Black democratic university. But the culture of disciplining democracy at Howard was not solely a product of Howard academic leaders seeking to deflect or mitigate student activism, even if the programs primarily resulted in students moving toward community service over political action. A majority of Howard students also adopted the political reality of the university. "All right," acknowledged one Howard student amid the campus protests, Howard is "'bourgeoisie' and not 'revolutionary,'" but if Howard were to become "revolutionary" and cut ties from the federal government and other White philanthropic outlets, where would students and academic leaders get "$500 million to even replace this school?"[72] The political and institutional reality, in other words, shaped students just as much as academic leaders. It also shaped its legacy. Q. T. Jackson was a leading figure in the Howard movement in the late 1960s. As an advocate for the D.C. Project, he maintained a vision of Howard that combined the emphasis on Black thought with Black community action.[73] In the late 1970s, as he looked back on the legacy of the Howard campus movement, he noted that "the relationship between Howard and the community has improved tremendously over the years." But, he emphasized, "we still have a long way to go."[74]

CHAPTER 2

Michigan State University

Evolving the Land Grant Philosophy of Service

The idea of service to the public was deeply embedded in the founding of Michigan State University (MSU). Like other land grant colleges established in the middle of the nineteenth century, MSU's founding mission was to make education and research accessible to the working class population of the state. Although the university maintained an emphasis on the classical liberal arts in its early years, its primary focus was on training and the development of practical knowledge in agriculture and engineering. A key institutional mechanism of MSU's teaching and research mission was its community extension programs, which connected university research to communities across the state of Michigan. Over the course of the nineteenth and twentieth centuries, MSU's service mission expanded from its regional focus on Michigan to a national and international focus. While MSU's mission exemplified a broad commitment to serving the public, the type of service was shaped by the economic needs of the state of Michigan and the geopolitical interests of the nation. Indeed, John Hannah, the longest serving president of MSU, underscored the national character of MSU's service mission in the mid-1950s. "Our colleges and universities," Hannah proclaimed, "must be regarded as bastions of our defense, as essential to the preservation of our country and our way of life."[1] MSU had a clear institutional mission: to serve the public through research and teaching in a way that was explicitly disciplined by national policy needs and interests.

In the 1960s, a coalition of student activists and faculty members sought to reconstruct MSU's service mission and expand the philosophy of community extension. They made a set of overlapping arguments that extended the logic of MSU's service mission. Since the university supported community extension programs, students and faculty supporters argued, such initiatives should also include opportunities for students to participate in the community as citizens, which included actions such as civil disobedience and other forms of activism. Moreover, since the mission of the university was to serve the community, they also argued, the service mission should include efforts to challenge local, national, and international policies that affected certain members of the community. At MSU, it proved institutionally easier—and more politically convenient—to expand the community extension philosophy to include student volunteerism while delegitimizing other forms of political action and deflecting critiques of the service mission of the university more broadly. In a variety of situations in the 1960s—from civil rights and anti-war activism to domestic and international service—the university's response was clear: field research and volunteer service fell within the realm of community extension and were appropriate forms of civic action for students. Acts of civil disobedience or political dissent were neither appropriate activities in community extension nor allowable positions for the university.

While MSU maintained similar distinctions between political action and formal education to those embraced by other universities, the collective institutional response over the course of the 1960s—and its legacy at MSU—came to represent a particular model of disciplining democracy reflective of the land grant extension mission and the national character of the American public university. The first form of disciplining was institutional categorization between different types of community extension activities for students. By the end of the decade, MSU administrators established two programs that expanded students' education in the community: the Center for Urban Affairs, which later became the College of Urban Development, and the nation's first Office of Volunteer Programs, which was housed in student affairs. In forming distinct institutional homes in response to student appeals, MSU also codified and distinguished between the volunteer service opportunities in the extracurricular and what came to be defined as "academic field placement" experiences that emerged in the College of Urban Development. By institutionally categorizing different forms of community action, the university was regulating not only the type of action that was appropriate for MSU students but also how such action related to other modes of inquiry there. Indeed, the institutional homes reflected the logic of the large university—one that tacked on added opportunities rather than fully considering the core questions raised by activists about MSU's service mission.

The effect was more than academic categorization and regulation. The establishment of the new programs also enabled MSU administrators to develop a rhetorical and institutional strategy to respond to campus activism. In the late 1960s and early 1970s, university leaders contrasted what they deemed was the constructive activism associated with the Office of Volunteer Programs (what became the Office of Service Learning) with what they deemed as the deconstructive efforts of those associated with the ongoing anti-war and civil rights movements. The new programs, in other words, enabled MSU administrators to deflect critiques of the university's broader service mission while pointing to the ways the university was involved in preparing engaged citizens. What emerged at MSU was a disciplining process that allowed academic leaders to highlight the institution's role in supporting students' civic engagement, but in a way that continued to support national policy. MSU disciplined student activism by redefining it as a form of volunteer service and as a model of academic research that aligned with the new national policies of the Nixon administration.

Limiting Field Research Demonstrations

The new disciplining culture at MSU that emerged at the end of the decade was rooted in the institution's initial response to civil rights activism in the East Lansing area. Located in the middle of Michigan and with a predominantly White student population, MSU seemed like an unlikely place for students to engage in civil rights action, let alone develop an interest in the civil rights struggle. Except for occasional solidarity protests, MSU's campus was quiescent in the first part of the 1960s. But the geographic location of MSU and its quiet atmosphere were misleading. MSU students in the campus NAACP Youth Council chapter were focusing their attention on a pervasive problem in the East Lansing area: housing discrimination. MSU was located in East Lansing, an area where Black citizens could not live, even if they attended the university. This contradiction was palpable for Black students like Ernie Green. Green found the MSU context to reflect the conditions of his upbringing. Green had graduated from Central High School in Arkansas, which was located in the same school district where the Little Rock Nine had captured national attention. The contradictory position of the university—at once opening up access to Black students while abiding by local segregation practices—also took on international tones. In 1960, MSU had partnered with Nigeria. This partnership brought a small contingent of Nigerians to MSU who, like Green, could not access housing near campus. In this context, Green and others in the campus NAACP chapter sought to challenge MSU for its failure to address and take a stance on the pervasive problem of housing discrimination in the East Lansing area.[2]

In the first part of the 1960s, the primary approach by the NAACP Youth Council campus chapter was to research housing discrimination in the East Lansing Area. MSU chapter members—Green and Joe Syfax—implemented a case-study approach that was common to the national chapter of the NAACP. The MSU NAACP chapter would send Black students to look for off-campus housing. If they were refused housing based on their race, the group filed formal complaints with the East Lansing housing director. The group also developed a database of instances to substantiate their claims of the problem of housing discrimination for Black students. The goal of the research effort, explained members of the MSU campus chapter, was to make "democracy a matter of political action."[3] Even if framed as a mode of democratic action, the efforts of the MSU chapter reflected the influence of the disciplinary culture of the university on student thinking. After all, their model of political action was fieldwork research, a common methodological approach in sociology. In this light, faculty members at MSU, especially in the sociology department, saw the work of the NAACP as an extension of students' academic training. Wilbert Brookhover, a sociologist, linked his course to NAACP research efforts. Brookhover was interested for both political and academic reasons. A trained social psychologist with a focus on the minority experience in schools, Brookhover had testified in *Brown v. Board of Education* as an expert witness. In the context of his course, Brookhover had integrated teams—one White and one Black student—meet with realtors to record their reactions to their efforts to receive housing. What emerged in the context of Brookhover's class and the efforts of the NAACP was a model of research that connected the tools of fieldwork methods to the political project of civil rights.[4]

Unlike NAG at Howard University, the MSU NAACP campus chapter gained institutional recognition. This is not too surprising. The work of students in the NAACP aligned with Hannah's own politics on civil rights. Hannah was on the Civil Rights Commission, created by the 1957 Civil Rights Act. The commission's mission was to investigate and make recommendations concerning civil rights issues in the United States—an approach that was largely replicated by the NAACP Youth Council. Moreover, NAACP's field research largely fell within the realm of the land grant philosophy of higher education. Indeed, like other land grant presidents, Hannah believed deeply that research should serve a practical purpose that could inform public policy making. As such, a student and faculty team conducting field research on housing discrimination was a reasonable service activity on campus because it fit prevailing disciplinary research cultures and the extension philosophy of MSU. But even if NAACP actions fell within the realm of Hannah's philosophy, it did not mean that Hannah or the university administration provided active support for their efforts. The MSU administration's stance on the NAACP was largely laissez-faire.

Hannah took a different position when NAACP students translated research into political action. Despite being faced with multiple years of research that demonstrated racist real estate practices in the area, the East Lansing city government neither addressed individual cases nor developed policies that banned racial discrimination in housing. Students' frustration with the slow response from the East Lansing City Council led them to organize a sit-in at the East Lansing City Hall in 1965. "The leaders of the community have failed to grasp the moral urgency of this problem," explained NAACP members who engaged in the sit-in. Thus, they concluded, "stronger action was necessary."[5] In contrast to how they responded to NAACP's field research, Hannah and MSU administrators intervened directly in the sit-in, coordinating with the East Lansing Police by sending university vans to transport the students to the county jail.[6] The coordination with the police department—and the visual effect of sending vans with the MSU logo to help arrest students—sent a clear message: MSU not only discouraged student political action; it actively disciplined students for engaging in such actions.

Hannah's response to the sit-in went to the heart of MSU's service mission. On one level, the sit-in and the response by the Hannah administration represented divergent interpretations of the land grant teaching mission. Students believed the sit-in was in line with the community extension philosophy of education at MSU. In MSU's extension programs, once problems were identified, a research demonstration program was designed to address them. Similarly, NAACP students believed the sit-in served as a research demonstration that highlighted the problem of housing discrimination in East Lansing. Indeed, Sheldon Imber, a student at MSU, interpreted the sit-in as educational similar to the research demonstrations in community extension programs. As such, she called for more civil rights activity in the next year. Those activities, she believed, could serve as an "enlightening experience for students."[7] Students who engaged in the sit-ins also argued the activity was itself a form of education. Responding to East Lansing community members who called on students to return to their education, sit-in participants retorted that "a 'real' education is not contained in books alone."[8]

While students interpreted the sit-ins as an educational opportunity in line with the land grant mission, Hannah interpreted acts of disobedience as not being a legitimate activity for the university and as being counter to his idea of good citizenship. Nationally, Hannah was an outspoken critic of the freedom rides and other acts of civil disobedience as an effective political strategy for achieving civil rights. He believed deeply in change through the process of law. Indeed, in his speech to the graduating class that same spring, Hannah underscored his support for the cause of civil rights and encouraged students to be on the forefront. But he believed that "they must work for change under the rule of order." Hannah explained that students engaging in forms of civil disobedience "creates a climate of unrest" that disrupted the normal function of the university.[9] If students interpreted the sit-in as a form of education, MSU leaders like Hannah largely interpreted the action as disruptive.

On a broader level, the sit-in and the response by the Hannah administration represented divergent interpretations of MSU's service mission as an institution. Indeed, students believed that the sit-ins also concerned the role of the university within the community. Peter Cannon, an MSU student from South Carolina, argued that the position of Hannah and of MSU was a "double standard."[10] Hannah promoted and called for civil rights around the country while remaining neutral on discriminatory practices within East Lansing. Similarly, the university recruited students of color, even as the institution turned a blind eye to the experiences of the problem of housing faced by those students. He argued that MSU as a public institution had an obligation to take a clear political position on the problem of housing discrimination in East Lansing. Hannah, however, believed his position—and that of the university—was ultimately limited. He distinguished between his private position as a citizen and professional role as a president, believing that he did not have the authority to speak on behalf of MSU. "I am dedicated to open housing," he explained to students, "but I cannot tell East Lansing how to run its affairs."[11] Hannah explained further that off campus, he was only one citizen of the city and had only one vote.

Whether encouraging students to work through existing systems or defining his institutional position in a narrow fashion, Hannah defended the idea of institutional neutrality. The problem was that Hannah was far from neutral. In addition to sending university vans to support East Lansing Police, Hannah also directed its Public Safety Department to work with the East

Lansing Police to establish a political surveillance unit of faculty and student activists who helped organize the sit-in.[12] Hannah's response to NAACP's protests and forms of civil disobedience shaped a particular institutional logic of disciplining democracy at MSU. In a range of different ways, MSU supported field research or student engagement in the community, seeing such experiences as part of the community extension philosophy. But the research "demonstration" aspect of the land grant philosophy had limits. Students could only demonstrate what they learned if it was deemed non-political by the university.

Tutoring in the Community

The distinction made by Hannah between appropriate and inappropriate forms of field research "demonstrations" also shaped the boundaries of the provision of academic service to the civil rights struggle in the South. In the first part of the 1960s, a cohort of student activists and faculty members also sought a more public position from MSU that made clear to students and community members that it supported the movement for civil rights within its institutional mission. Two individuals played a key role in pushing MSU in this direction: Mary Ann Shupenko, a White student at MSU and member of the campus NAACP, and Robert Green, a Black faculty member in MSU's sociology department and faculty adviser to the NAACP. Green was a soci-ologist of education who, like Brookhover, committed himself to the civil rights struggle both as an academic and as an activist. While Shupenko and Green initially connected through Green's course on "Race in the Schools," the model that inspired them was the 1964 Mississippi Summer Project.[13] In recruiting students and faculty across the country, SNCC field-workers argued that the Mississippi Project, with its connection to the political proj-ect of organizing the Mississippi Freedom Democratic Party, represented "pedagogical revolutions," especially for the college students who came from the "much-maligned liberal arts undergraduate education."[14] Shupenko and Green agreed, believing the summer project contained the seeds for a peda-gogical revolution at MSU.

The Mississippi Summer Project connected formal education to politi-cal organizing. Students like Shupenko were to serve as tutors in traditional academic subjects, while faculty members like Green were there to provide academic expertise to both staff and local community residents. But their roles as "teachers" and "experts" were misleading. Liz Fusco, the Freedom School coordinator, believed the experience in the South would encourage volunteers like Shupenko to and Green reconsider "what education is, since the people we presume to be 'teaching' know and understand so much more than any of us from the middle-class white North do."[15] The emphasis on experiential learning was also embedded in the political organizing of the summer project. The political structure of the project linked the Freedom School to the formation of community centers, where Mississippi residents and Northern volunteers could meet, discuss relevant social and political issues, and develop organizing strategies. In connecting the Freedom School and community centers to the formation of the Mississippi Freedom Democratic Party, the summer project aimed to develop a grassroots model of democracy that sought to not only transform the political system in Mississippi but also to create a mode of "participatory citizen-ship" education.[16]

Shaped by their experiences in Mississippi and utilizing their MSU campus connections, Green and Shupenko started the Student Tutorial Education Project (STEP). STEP was a cross-institutional model between MSU and Rust College in Mississippi. They focused on partnering with Rust College because it was facing accreditation and financial issues due to the role of its students in the Mississippi movement. Green and Shupenko believed a partnership could help provide direct financial support to Rust College as it navigated state-level politics of funding while also engaging MSU students with a college that took a prominent role in the civil rights struggle in the South. At the core of the partnership was the Freedom School model. The goal was to bring MSU faculty and advanced undergraduate and graduate students to Rust College to provide academic support for Rust College and local high school students. MSU volunteers were tasked with tutoring students, while MSU faculty members provided support to Rust College staff. Like the Freedom Summer, the STEP program also included "a 'community' project with maximum participation of local adults." Indeed, Shupenko and Green understood STEP as another institutional hub in the political organizing for the Mississippi Freedom Democratic Party.[17]

Green, in particular, saw the STEP project as an effort to reorient the service mission of MSU. He saw the political goals and aspirations of the civil rights movement not as outside the university but as a central part of the institutional service mission. "Most people in the university don't see social change as the role of MSU," but Green believed that "anything that causes pain and injustice is in our domain. The university has to be an instrument of change."[18] To build support for the program and its vision, Green invited Martin Luther King Jr., who likewise linked formal education at MSU to civil rights activism. King interpreted the program as a means to infuse a sense of moral concern and commitment into the formal curriculum of the university. King challenged the four thousand students in the audience to get involved and encouraged them to transform "conviction into action." He linked such involvement to their education. He defined the STEP program as a "broadening" experience for students, one that would help individual students identify their own individual prejudices and lead to further political commitment. For both Green and King, the STEP program represented a model for other universities to engage students in the struggle for civil rights.[19]

While both Green and King interpreted STEP as a political project, the program was interpreted differently in the context of MSU. Indeed, the political vision of the STEP program was constrained by two factors. The first was leadership. Inspired by his experiences in the South, Green took a leave of absence from MSU. He joined the Southern Christian Leadership Council (SCLC), where he served a director of the Citizenship Education Program. Shupenko, who also helped organize the connection between MSU and Rust College, took a gap year and worked directly with SNCC. With these changes, the STEP program fell under the leadership of John Duley, who had worked with Green in forming the partnership. Duley prioritized King's spiritual interpretation of the STEP project but did not share the same political interpretation articulated by Green. A campus minister with the United Christian Ministry, Duley was concerned with what he defined as the spiritual gaps in modern higher education. Duley interpreted student demands for educational "relevance" as the "new morality for higher education." In contrast to Green, Duley was less interested in social transformations led by students and more in their individual and moral development, primarily through community service.[20]

The second factor was the logic of the institution that distinguished between formal education and political action. In turning to MSU to support the STEP program, students and faculty participants confronted institutional regulations of student groups. Since it was an affiliated project of MSU's student government, students had to sign what was called a "non-agitation" agreement that prevented students from engaging in political activities as part of the STEP program. This requirement influenced how students defined the mission of the STEP project within MSU. In material for the promotion of the program, the student coordinator, Laura Leichitler, refrained from including language that supported SNCC's efforts or that of the Mississippi Freedom Democratic Party. Instead, she promoted the STEP program as a "non-political tutorial program" and a "community education tutorial."[21] Of course, these rhetorical moves were also politically strategic. After all, the program was navigating not only the institutional politics of MSU but also those of Mississippi. Even if the rhetorical shift was politically strategic, the new mission had the effect of influencing how MSU student volunteers understood their roles in the civil rights struggle. Wayne Albertson, a STEP participant, acknowledged the intentional, nonpolitical nature of the program. "We acted on the premise that our activity was educational and not explicitly political," Albertson explained.[22]

Green attempted to maintain the STEP program's political commitment. Indeed, SCLC's citizenship program provided Green with a model that connected tutorial education in political and constitutional rights to community organizing at the local level. In 1966, he met with MSU volunteers at Rust College and encouraged them to join the Meredith March Against Fear. For Green, participation in the march was an extension of the STEP mission to be engaged with the community as well as of his work with SCLC. Green's efforts confronted a programmatic context shaped by the program's emphasis on tutoring as its primary activity. In a community meeting to discuss whether to join the march, MSU volunteers debated a range of issues. Some students assumed the distinction between the educational nature of the program and the political nature of the march, while others adopted the view that such political engagement might endanger the program itself. While the student community overwhelmingly supported involvement, it set strict limits: interested volunteers had to receive parental permission and could only participate in the march on Sunday, outside of program time.[23] Activism in the form of political protest and community organizing—the other "learning situations" from the Freedom Summer—was no longer interpreted as a core educational activity of STEP; rather, it was treated as outside the program mission.

With these programmatic constraints, only a small cohort of students, including Albertson and Kathy Wolterink, participated in the march. Albertson concluded that his involvement was vital to his work as a tutor, noting how the protest enlivened the meaning of education between him and the students at Rust College. Wolterink also noted that the Meredith March "gave me an opportunity to experience what it means to stand up for what you know is right, in the face of hostility, hatred, and the threat of violence."[24] But Albertson and Wolterink were the exceptions, not the norm. The STEP program discouraged and limited student involvement in political activism. Many student volunteers maintained the view that the program's purpose was to serve an academic need in Mississippi—a view that was infused into the student culture at MSU. Indeed, when STEP volunteers returned to campus, Char Jolles's headline presented a juxtaposition between the STEP volunteers and sit-in leaders: "STEP Sent Educators, Not Agitators."[25]

What triumphed was a tutorial model of education disconnected from civil rights activism. This tutorial model shaped the institutional conditions of a new culture of disciplining democracy that promoted MSU's service to civil rights without a political commitment. When Jim Krathwohl reflected on whether the STEP project was successful, he focused on the educational experience of the MSU college student. "The volunteers," he wrote, "learned as much as the students."[26] A nascent culture of service learning emerged in the context of student life—one that was increasingly supported by university administrators. Indeed, this interpretation—of learning through non-political community service—took on even greater institutional salience in MSU's partnership with the Peace Corps.

Defining Service Learning

The civil rights struggle captured the political imagination of students at MSU. But it was not the only experience reshaping ideas of education and community extension at MSU. In the first part of the 1960s, the first director of the Peace Corps, Sargent Shriver, turned to American universities to provide training for international volunteer work overseas. In a letter to Hannah, Shriver asked: "How can institutions best participate in the Peace Corps program to enhance their educational functions and to increase their capacity in world affairs in the U.S. interest?"[27] The question connected deeply with Hannah's philosophy of the land grant university and his focus on connecting academic research and education to a national policy goal. Hannah believed the Peace Corps training exemplified the university's public service. Indeed, MSU's training partnership with the Peace Corps in the 1960s provided MSU administrators with another model for updating MSU's public service mission and expanding the undergraduate curriculum.

Within the context of the Peace Corps–university partnership, Peace Corps officials emphasized the educational potential of the volunteer service. Shriver believed the Peace Corps–university partnership would serve two purposes. First, the volunteer experience would serve as an educational experience for young Americans, thus contributing "to the education of America and to more intelligent American participation in the world." Second, the partnership would also influence American universities like MSU. As Shriver envisioned, the partnership would help "American education expand its horizon—its research and curriculum—to the whole world."[28] Using Shriver's focus as a guide, MSU administrators also prioritized the potential of the volunteer experience as a form of education. In MSU's proposal for Peace Corps training, Donald Grummon, a professor of counseling who oversaw the Peace Corps training, emphasized the need for volunteers to embrace a learner's mindset, even if they were there to provide educational support to Nigerian students. The whole program must be "broadly educational," Grummon explained in the proposal; he emphasized that "an attitude of 'we have much to learn from the host country' should be assumed."[29]

The primary focus at MSU was thus pedagogical—how to train volunteers as both experts who provided technical aid and learners who worked in collaboration with host country communities. The dual learning goal was best captured by the volunteer role. The role of MSU in Nigeria was to help develop the University of Nigeria, Nsukka, as well as the elementary school system. In both capacities, Peace Corps volunteers served as teaching assistants who also worked on community development projects. They were thus positioned to be both academic experts and experts-in-training. The main emphasis of MSU's Peace Corps training was on balancing American expertise with respect for local culture and traditions. "While scholarship . . . must be the first consideration in sending our people abroad (else why send them?)," a MSU training guide explained, "merely the possession of these skills is far from enough to act as a specialized representative of our American society." The training guide also emphasized that the volunteer should be "thoroughly educated in cultural relativistic views and in the implications of the cultural concept" so that the volunteer can be both "tolerant and understanding" in their overseas work. This position was deemed necessary for the Peace Corps mission. The volunteer must learn from the community so that they "furnish our citizens with accurate information about peoples and customs in other lands."[30]

David Schickele captured the educational vision of the MSU–Peace Corps partnership. Schickele participated in Peace Corps training at MSU, prior to serving for two years. He interpreted the volunteer experience itself as a distinct form of learning, one that endowed his intellectual understanding of the world with social and cultural meaning. "No real intellectual understanding," he concluded about his experience, "can exist without a sense of identification at some deeper level."[31] This was more than a fleeting reflection on his experience. He also believed it offered a new model of updating the American liberal arts. He challenged what was often treated as two warring camps: liberal arts defenders and progressive educators. Schickele described the Peace Corps as a "total education, a bonding of the active and contemplative in which experience is made meaningful and books become experience." The volunteer experience, he further argued, closed "the gap between thought and action, academic education and experiential education, education and work."[32]

The perspectives of volunteers like Schickele provided MSU administrators with an example of the educational possibilities of the Peace Corps experience, both in terms of educating young Americans and in supporting MSU's service mission. Eugene Jacobson, the assistant dean for international studies, believed MSU's partnership with the Peace Corps enhanced both the overseas work of the agency and the academic research and teaching at MSU. He underscored this point in a letter to Shriver. "We are convinced that the integration of Peace Corps training with the regular University program," he wrote, "enhances both the Peace Corps training effort and the capability of the University for making meaningful international contributions."[33] George Axin agreed. A seasoned expert in professional development in land grant personnel and the coordinator of the MSU-Nigeria training program, Axin interpreted the training program and volunteer experience as being akin to the land grant tradition of extension programs. He understood the experience in terms of advanced fieldwork research. "Because of the nature of the work they are doing," which included gathering data for future study projects and uses in theses, Axin explained, the Peace Corps experience represented "significant academic achievement." As such, he worked with faculty in the program to codify the experience within the traditional disciplining culture of the university through the granting of academic credit for not only the training programing but also the overseas experience.[34]

MSU administrators' excitement for the Peace Corps partnership, especially as a model for education, masked two critical issues. The first was how the MSU–Peace Corps partnership promoted a political goal in the guise of volunteer service. From its inception, there were concerns about the Peace Corps raised by students, especially regarding the national character of volunteer service. Indeed, Nigerian students at MSU raised a fundamental issue at the core of the partnership: MSU's support of American political goals in Nigeria. In the *State News*, Daniel Archibong argued that the Peace Corps was "another tactical move to win the cold war." As such, he continued, the imposition of the Peace Corps onto host countries represented "the image of the disliked or the just ousted representatives of colonial governments" and thus "will aid in prolonging ill feeling against colonial thinking and values."[35] In Archibong's view, the Peace Corps was an extension of both Cold War politics and colonial legacies that demonstrated the very political nature of volunteer work overseas. The partnership with MSU—as a research and teaching university—concealed the political goals of international volunteerism in the form of education.

The second issue concerned the training itself. The training model that MSU administrators celebrated was largely a replication of academic and disciplinary models at the university. The program took on characteristic patterns of academic instruction. At the end of the training program, prospective volunteers wrote two papers; one explored the functions of education in American society as compared to other cultural contexts, and another focused on the opportunities and problems of teaching in a cross-cultural context. In other training contexts, students were given exams. This "excessively academic approach," wrote the Peace Corps training evaluator Meridan Bennett, "caused much of the material to remain dead." Most materials presented, she further noted, "were simply a re-run of one of the regular undergraduate courses." Bennett's conclusion became a common refrain among Peace Corps evaluators. "Places like Michigan State," Bennett wrote, produce "a simulacrum of training" that is "largely irrelevant to the field experience." The limitations of the training program, Bennett argued, led the Peace Corps to fail in its stated mission, both in expanding the university and in providing aid to host countries. She wrote, "In trying to educate the universities to the realities of the world (if, indeed, that is one of our purposes), we are prejudicing the service of thousands of rural development and CD [community development] workers. The losses to the countries we are trying to help is staggering."[36]

Roger Landrum—a volunteer who also trained and served with Schickele—raised both of these issues in his reflection on his experiences at MSU and in Nigeria. Landrum returned home critical of the ways the MSU–Peace Corps training promoted the role of the volunteer overseas. He reinterpreted his training on volunteer and development aid—in particular, the view that institution and nation building in Nigeria required American knowledge—as perpetuating a colonial logic. As he told Peace Corps staff and university officials when he returned home, "volunteers object[ed] to the image the Peace Corps has created because it is essentially Americans moving into darkness with light."[37] In challenging the political nature of his volunteer work, he also prioritized what he learned from the experience itself. "Most of us feel differently," Landrum explained—"that we learned more than we gave. That needs to be defined."[38] Landrum inverted the idea of development in the Peace Corps, but in a way that limited the very mission of the organization. He prioritized the ways he learned and "developed" through experiences over the ways American knowledge and expertise—the mission of the Peace Corps–higher education partnership—professedly helped develop the host countries.

At MSU, advocates who saw Peace Corps volunteerism as a new model of education responded to the criticisms of the pedagogical problem of the Peace Corps training model raised by evaluators while ignoring the political and social limitations of volunteer service. Indeed, MSU advocates interpreted reflections like Landrum's in terms of cross-cultural learning rather than as a critique of the colonial logic of the Peace Corps–MSU partnership. A key figure at MSU who prioritized the experiential and cross-cultural learning of the Peace Corps experience was Duley. He believed the Peace Corps provided a theoretical framework for his thinking on the new models of civic education emerging at MSU. In outlining his theory of experiential learning at MSU, Duley drew on the work of the psychologists Richard Hopkins and Roger Harrison. In their analysis of the Peace Corps, they focused their attention on the cross-cultural elements of the volunteer experiences. A key theme in their report was the place of emotions and values in the Peace Corps experience versus the academic focus on higher education. At the university, Harrison and Hopkins wrote, "feelings and values may be discussed but rarely acted upon." In contrast, they argued, in the Peace Corps, "values and feelings have action consequences, and action must be taken." Like Peace Corps staff and volunteers, Hopkins and Harrison concluded that the methods of higher education were successful in preparing students' intellectual capacity, but Peace Corps training prepared students for situations that required them "to adapt to or to act in unfamiliar or ambiguous social situations."[39]

Duley thus adopted one component of the Peace Corps–MSU partnership. Using the frameworks proposed by Harrison and Hopkins in their study on cross-cultural training, Duley developed a pedagogy of experiential learning that combined seminars with community experience. The objectives of the community experience were to "relate intuitive response and the intellectual understanding of experience" and to "use experiences as a source of knowledge about oneself and other cultures."[40] Duley believed that the volunteer service, whether in East Lansing or overseas, functioned as a form of "field" experiential learning where "meanings and values can be explored and experimented with; not just examined abstractly, but tried out in living situations." Discarding the underlying politics of international volunteerism and its limitations, Duley focused on the need for field experience learning situations to better prepare students for adaptable thinking.[41]

While Duley used the Peace Corps to inform his theory of experiential learning, MSU students connected the Peace Corps model of service learning to the work in the East Lansing community. The Peace Corps, argued MSU student Frank Bianco, brough to light "the potential of American youth to aid undeveloped nations." He applied the appeal of the Peace Corps to the American context. "It has lately become apparent," he wrote, "that our own nation is in need of contributions that can be made by volunteer youth in combating the poverty problem in the United States."[42] When the Peace Corps captured Bianco's attention, he was taking a sociology class on education taught by the sociologist David Gottlieb. The class focused on school funding and racial inequality in the East Lansing area. Reflecting on the idea of the Peace Corps, Bianco and other students asked Gottlieb what students at MSU could do to address these issues at the local level. They linked the question to their own education at MSU. "While part of the function of the University is to prepare young adults for responsible citizenship," the students argued, "no outlet is provided where these responsibilities can be assumed."[43] With the Peace Corps serving as a model and with the support of Gottlieb, Bianco started the Student Education Corps (SEC), a program in which MSU students served as volunteer tutors in math, English, and science in Lansing schools.

Bianco interpreted the SEC as a carbon copy of the Peace Corps and its domestic counterpart, Volunteers in Service to America (VISTA). "The kind of concern and service shown by the originators of the SEC," Bianco wrote, "is the same type of concern and service shown by new volunteer organizations in the United States today." In this way, the SEC program adopted the same logic of development and education that informed the Peace Corps. The project ignored the political and economic conditions that produced educational inequalities in the Lansing area. Instead, its mission was "to help alleviate the social and educational inequalities of culturally disadvantaged groups" through mentorship and "providing needed inspiration and motivation to continue with their schooling."[44]

Bianco also believed that the SEC represented more than just an opportunity for students to volunteer. He argued that the SEC addressed the critiques of the university's curriculum while also serving as an expression of the university's service mission—one that aligned with Hannah's vision of good citizenship. "Citizenship should not be an indefinable abstraction," Bianco explained, "but rather, a concrete state of social consciousness which embodies both privilege and duty."[45] In Bianco's view, volunteer service made citizenship "concrete" and encouraged students like himself to recognize their privilege and duty. How a student volunteer learned from community service—whether at home or overseas—thus became the model of the new civics as MSU. As MSU administrators expanded and codified such opportunities in both the curriculum and extracurriculum, those opportunities were also used to delegitimize other forms of political education and dissent that emerged on campus in the late 1960s.

Promoting "Constructive" Activism

In 1965, the MSU Committee for Peace in Vietnam organized a teach-in on the Vietnam War. The event attracted over two thousand students. The teach-in was one part of the organization's political education. Students on the committee also linked the teach-in to protest and organizing. Two weeks later, the committee organized 150 students to join the anti–Vietnam War protest in Washington, DC. The MSU Committee for Peace in Vietnam also organized the Lansing Chapter of the Vietnam Summer Project. The Vietnam Summer Project sought to engage students and community residents in a political education campaign. At the core of the effort was a model that combined formal education with community organizing. Training for the Vietnam Summer Project included the development of a study group program that focused on the historical and political backdrop of US involvement in Vietnam; role-playing exercises that focused on engaging with difficult conversations on American foreign policy and community members' belief systems; and what was defined as "neighborhood work." In "neighborhood work," MSU students were encouraged to choose precincts where they lived, because "the most effective volunteers are those who live in the neighborhood being canvassed." The role of the student was also to take the position of a learner. The volunteer should "listen closely and discern how various types of people think about the war" and "discover what other issues arouse most concern in the community." The effort, in other words, took on other modes of community engagement that were increasingly common at MSU in the 1960s. But there was one distinguishing characteristic, and it reflected both the political reasoning of MSU's NAACP chapter and the original vision of STEP; if the other university-sponsored programs linked their engagement to either academic or national service, the Vietnam Summer Project linked community engagement to political dissent.[46]

The anti-war movement at MSU again revealed ideological preferences within the service mission of the university. In response to the teach-in and anti-war organizing around the East Lansing area by MSU students, Hannah largely expressed rhetorical support. Hannah interpreted the teach-in model as being akin to the ethos of academic education and research. "No conscientious university president would refuse to give consideration to recommendations from responsible students," he explained, especially if "arrived at through careful study and serious reflection."[47] However, Hannah's support for MSU students' right to dissent changed with the publication of the 1966 *Ramparts* article that highlighted MSU's link to the CIA in Vietnam and its role in developing the security apparatus of the Diem regime.

The controversy centered around MSU's public service mission. Hannah defended MSU's role in Vietnam, seeing security training as an extension of the university's mission and philosophy of instruction, research, and service. "To say that a university should never undertake to serve the national policy," Hannah argued, "is to deny the right of the public university to exist." Indeed, in Hannah's view, the sole purpose of the university was to support national policy efforts. He continued, "In everything it does, the public university carries out the national policy."[48] For anti-war activists at MSU, research and education activities tied to the war reflected the university's misconstrued understanding of service. As Stu Dowty, an activist for SDS, explained, "universities are 'service stations' par excellence to those institutions we seek to alter—they are part of the institutional structure preserving the status quo."[49] Like some student activists at MSU and in SDS, Dowty wanted university officials to not only create opportunities for students to engage in "service" for the movement and related political struggles for social change but also separate the institution from those "service" activities they deemed immoral.[50]

The efforts that grew out of earlier activism at MSU, such as the STEP and SEC programs, were recast as counterexamples to the anti-war movement and the critiques of the university. Indeed, it was in the context of increased anti-war efforts that focused on the university that Hannah established the Office of Volunteer Programs, a campus clearinghouse that consolidated the SEC, STEP, and other student-run volunteer programs. The first administrator of the Office of Volunteer Programs was James Tanck, an MSU graduate who was deeply involved in student government and coordinating the SEC. Tanck aligned the office with Peace Corps volunteerism in a way that differed from Duley's philosophy of experiential learning. In outlining the mission of the office, Tanck took a position similar to that of Hannah on "social action" at MSU in the 1960s. Highlighting both civil rights activism and the Peace Corps, he prioritized what he deemed as the more constructive and nonpolitical elements, in particular student tutoring and volunteering with local charities. Involvement in the freedom rides, sit-ins, and voter registration allowed "students to look and serve beyond the 'ivory tower,'" Tanck wrote, but he concluded that the volunteer development work of the Peace Corps "refocused student involvement from picketing to constructive social action."[51]

In making this interpretive argument about action at MSU, Tanck at once associated student "action" with the land grant tradition of providing service to the community and discounted the value of other forms of activism and civic participation. While such action was typically taken by faculty and administrators at MSU in the form of scholarly research and lectures, Tanck believed students could offer similar types of service through volunteerism. "The concept of student volunteer action," he wrote, "is simply an extension of this tradition to include the service of the University's students as well." The office also became the interpreter of what appropriate student service looked like. The new office, Tanck explained, represented the main contact point for residents and ensured that no promises were made to a community "without the University's knowledge or consent." As the liaison to community residents, the office was thus set up as a way to interpret where and how students got involved, creating a filter that shaped students' conception of community engagement. It also served to mollify residents of East Lansing, where the university was expanding.[52] On both levels, the new office created disciplining boundaries of what could and could not constitute community and civic engagement at MSU.

Tanck also believed that the new office served a secondary purpose: good public relations. As Tanck noted, student volunteerism would promote a positive public image of the university. Informational news releases "on positive student action," he explained, held "tremendous public relations value" for "the public at large and particularly to alumni." In the context of anti-war activism on campus and broader critiques of the service mission of MSU, university administrators employed a rhetorical strategy that delegitimized anti-war activism. They juxtaposed what they defined as the constructive activism of those doing volunteer work with the perceived deconstructive efforts of anti-war protesters. Clifton R. Wharton, the new president of MSU in the 1970s and the first Black president of the institution, was a strong supporter of the various volunteer programs on campus, providing institutional funding for the growth and expansion of the Office of Volunteer Programs. During the student strikes and protests regarding the Vietnam War, Wharton used the programs and student participants as a way to deflect from the broader questions concerning appropriate service on campus. In public interviews and reports on anti-war activism at MSU, Wharton explained that the protests on campus distracted from the students who were "committed to positive activism as student leaders, tutors for the blind, ghetto workers and the like."[53]

Indeed, this institutional move that juxtaposed what Tanck deemed as the positive activism of student volunteerism with the perceived destructive activism of students associated with the anti-war movement became a rhetorical tool of the Nixon administration. In the early 1970s, the Nixon administration provided federal support and funding to university-based volunteer programs tied into regular coursework and used the MSU office as the model for the University

Year for Action. Tanck became the head of Nixon's National Student Volunteer Program, which oversaw the University Year for Action. A couple of months after the student strike at MSU in 1970, the Office of Volunteer Programs invited representatives from the Nixon administration to MSU's campus as a way to promote an alternative type of student social action. Tanck helped facilitate the visit of Pat Nixon, the wife of President Nixon. On her visit to campus, Nixon encouraged students to get involved in volunteer projects because, as she explained, "volunteering is protesting in a beneficial way."[54] Like Wharton, Nixon emphasized what many in the administration defined as more constructive forms of activism.

Nixon's visit was also part of a broader promotion of a particular kind of volunteerism in the university promoted by the administration, one that served state manpower needs. On a visit to MSU two years after Pat Nixon's visit, Elliot Richardson, the director of Health, Education, and Welfare under Nixon, defined community action as the "new volunteerism" that tapped into the compassion and concern of students to address "problems of manpower and financial shortages."[55] Shaped by institutional responses to anti-war activism and broader political shifts at both the state and federal level, volunteer service shifted from being a key element of students' various forms of social activism and education to being one of state manpower needs.[56] Indeed, the mission of the office took on the priorities of the "new volunteerism" as outlined by the Nixon administration. Under both John Cauley and Jane Smith, the two directors of the office from 1969 to 1979, most programs focused on volunteer management and the most effective ways to allocate student volunteers in community service opportunities. Office reports over the course of the 1970s counted the hours of students working in a variety of social service agencies to demonstrate the "manpower" impact of student volunteerism. Volunteerism was quantified and commodified for the university's public relations.

University officials also distinguished the efforts of the Office of Volunteer Programs from the other forms of community engagement that emerged at MSU in the late 1960s. As Cauley explained, the goal of the office was to distinguish "between legitimate voluntary activity and what is realistically academic field placement."[57] This institutional categorization had the effect of not only disconnecting student volunteer commitments from field research experiences but also fragmenting the student movements' broader critique of MSU's service mission.

One of those programs that Cauley distinguished from the Office of Volunteer Programs was the Center for Urban Affairs. Like the Office of

Volunteer Programs, the Center for Urban Affairs was also started in the context of and in response to campus protest activism focused on civil rights. In the mid-1960s, a new student group was formed on campus—the Black Student Alliance—that carried on the legacy of the MSU chapter of the NAACP, demanding the university to fight housing discrimination. In addition, the Black Student Alliance called for the university to create more programs that better supported the Black community. "The university should develop a project," said Barry Amis, one of the founding members of the alliance, "for the black students of Lansing and take a greater interest in the Lansing community."[58] In response to the advocacy of the Black Student Alliance—in particular, the occupation of the administration building in 1968—the Hannah administration established a new office designed to support projects that connected Black students to the Lansing area. Operating under the Office of the President, the center was made to fit prevailing institutional logic. Indeed, the new office reflected other organized research units established in the postwar university and focused on ways to apply social science research to policy and social problems.[59]

In the late 1960s and early 1970s, students and faculty attempted to expand the center's mission. Indeed, the center was overseen by Robert Green. Drawing on his experiences in the movement, Green became a leading advocate for reorienting research models from the perspective of the university to that of the community. "Community residents and a growing number of concerned researchers," he argued, "have asserted that community-based research rarely benefits the residents of the communities researched." Too often, he argued, researchers believed their role was to "define and describe the problems" rather than begin from the perspective and knowledge of the community. For Green, the issue came down to the lack of community input and power. Local residents—often those who were the subject of research—"feel their voices have been overruled by the 'experts,'" even though many of those residents "see no relationship between the proposed study and the problems as they see them." In Green's view, the issues were compounded by the fact that most researchers who came into the community were White, middle-class individuals who brought a set of assumptions about the "ghetto." As such, Green argued, scholars needed to redesign research and education models to create cooperation that prioritized the knowledge and experiences of residents on the one hand and the political implications of research at the community level on the other. Too often, he explained, "neutrality" had been "concealed by a cloak of 'academia.'" He argued that the university needed to develop a different approach that taught students and scholars to "perceive [his or her] role not necessarily as neutral but as one that will directly benefit the community."[60]

Green believed the center would serve as a model for redesigning education and research in the university, especially in relation to minority students. "Past efforts to educate in our society have basically dealt with the 'transmission of culture,' with a common core of white middle class values," he argued. The transmission tended to "justify and perpetuate the oppression of Black people, American Indians, Mexican Americans, and other minority groups."[61] Under Wharton, the center was expanded and became the College of Urban Development. As the university's first African American president, Wharton shared Green's concern about Black residents in Detroit and the broader role of the university in addressing urban issues. Wharton believed that the purpose of the college was to provide researchers and students with a means to bridge the theory-application gap.[62] In contrast, Green saw the role of the college and in particular its work in the community differently. He was more concerned with community empowerment than the application of a particular theory or research problem. Green attempted to develop a model of "service learning" more sensitive to community knowledge and concern. "The Intent of the S-L [service learning] program being the provision of a service to the community, all efforts will be made to avoid the misuse of the community," he explained, and "in this regard, faculty advisors/consultants should make certain that an outcome of the S-L project will be of direct benefit to the community."[63]

Green's efforts at the center were constrained by administrators and faculty who interpreted such activities as being outside the service mission of the university. During the transition from the Center of Urban Affairs to the College of Urban Development, many faculty members were skeptical of the education and research models articulated by Green, arguing that universities should not be compromised by involvement with outside communities. In particular, some faculty explained to Green that the program lacked intellectual standards because of its activist leanings.[64] Members of MSU's board of trustees expressed similar concern about the perceived politics of the center. In 1970, Clair White, a trustee member, called for a probe into the operation of the center. "If this [institution] is being used as the basis of a political operation," he explained, "I want to know."[65] Although the board did not cut funding, the institutional culture and skepticism, especially as the center transitioned into a full college, set limits on Green's broader goals for the college. Concerned with the perception of the new college, Green increasingly focused on the academic and learning elements of community involvement over broader goals of community empowerment and social activism. "With the advent of college status," Green concluded in 1972, "the academic function must take on the overriding and unifying emphasis of our efforts; it is no longer one among equals." As such, he explained further, "all non-campus work must be carefully coordinated so that it is a contributory part of the academic function."[66]

With the prioritization of the academic components of community outreach in the college through such education projects as the Urban Service Program and Field Experience Program, student learning took precedence over community impact and input. In the academic year 1973–1974, students were involved in a range of community projects, including a consumer education program, urban planning for a community center, and an outreach effort for ex-offenders returning to the Greater Lansing area. While the experience provided a needed service to the community, the broader purpose, especially for students, was defined in terms of academic goals. Maxie Jackson, a graduate student and assistant in the college, oversaw the field experience program. He explained that its value was that it took the "student out of the traditional classroom setting and into a practical, applied experience." Jackson underscored that the experience was "no less demanding than the classroom" and was designed to "supplement and complement the student's academic program" in terms of skill development and career exploration.[67] The evolution of the center to the College of Urban Development reflected the disciplining boundaries of rethinking education, research, and student involvement in the community. Inspired both by his former students and his own activist experiences, Green and other faculty members challenged and extended the meaning of research and education. Institutional concerns over whether the kind of community research Green did was "political" or appropriately intellectual set limits on the meaning of student action as part of research and education at MSU.

Legacy

Writing in 1965, Trudie S. Barreras, a master's student at MSU, was supportive of recent demonstrations at MSU. But his support came with an important question. He worried that the increasing emphasis on demonstrations and other forms of political action at MSU had the potential of becoming the "cheapest form of involvement." "Good citizens, your desire to 'stand up and be counted' is admirable," Barreras wrote. "But here is the critical question: Is this all that you can do?" He encouraged his peers to link their political actions to service work in the community. Doing so, he believed, would demonstrate a deeper commitment to the community and to the political cause. If students did not make this connection, he argued, "we should not be surprised if our efforts generate little but disgust among the unconvinced members of our community and, perhaps, do more harm than good to the cause which we are trying to support."[68] Indeed, Barreras's point was vitally important to discussions of good citizenship; a sole commitment to political action without other forms of involvement was a limited form of being a "good" citizen. The problem, however, was the inverse: MSU discouraged students from—and actively disciplined them for—connecting their various forms of community service to political activism in the form of civil disobedience and dissent.

Over the courses of the 1960s and into the 1970s, student activists and faculty supporters at MSU attempted to reconstruct the meaning of service and education by developing new community programs. With faculty support, students organized a range of community involvement projects, from STEP in the South and SEC in Lansing to the Vietnam Summer Project. MSU administrators offered support as well, interpreting student efforts as a means to expand the definition of community extension programs. There were also new partnerships—such as that between MSU and the Peace Corps—that directly connected a student's education to volunteer service in the world. The new projects inspired MSU administrators to establish the Office of Volunteer Programs and expand the offerings in the Center of Urban Affairs or what became the College of Urban Development. However, university support always came with an important caveat: the university could not support efforts that were deemed political, such as civil disobedience or political dissent, or actions that challenged the institution's commitment to national service. Indeed, in the middle part of the 1960s, MSU established offices that supported new community engagement programs as it actively disciplined students who participated in the civil rights sit-ins and anti-war protests both on and off campus. The emphasis on community service also served a strategic purpose. In response to campus activism that criticized the role of MSU, university administrators promoted the what they deemed as the constructive activism of volunteer service associated with its new offices and programs.

The institutional reasoning for supporting some types of action in the community over others was multipronged. The emphasis on volunteer service and academic field placement aligned with Hannah's politics: he ultimately saw forms of civil disobedience as counter to his understanding of good citizenship. But his political views only partly explain the evolution of new community engagement programs at MSU. Hannah also interpreted

activism as incompatible with formal education and research and thus outside his philosophy of community extension. In contrast, the emphasis on
volunteer service fit with the existing mission of MSU as an institution that
served national policy goals. Indeed, the promotion of volunteer service
aligned with the Nixon administration's efforts to utilize student volunteers
to support the "manpower" of Nixon's New Federalism. A coalition of students and MSU supporters, especially those who helped form STEP and
SEC, also adopted the institutional logic of community extension. Barreras's
op-ed reflected the more general view of students at MSU. The broader political visions of community engagement and the role of the public university
articulated by students like Ernie Green and Dowty and faculty members
like Robert Green proved to be the exception rather than the norm.

By the mid-1970s, MSU administrators could point to a range of opportunities, from volunteer service through the Office of Volunteer Programs
to academic field placement in the College of Urban Development. MSU
administrators saw those opportunities as an expression of the university's
updated service mission. So too did the new students who participated in
those programs. "Students still care," argued MSU student Peggy Gossett in
an editorial for the *State News*, "but in a realistic way." Challenging the idea
that students in the 1970s had become apathetic, Gossett argued that "this
generation of students has not abandoned the social and political concerns";
rather, "those concerns have merely been rerouted and reconstituted into
more workable attitudes to fit in the world in 1974." With the end of the
war and the broader civil rights movement, she explained, "no longer are students advocating for peace and love for all," but "instead they are becoming
Big Brothers and Big Sisters and volunteering their time to Family Planning,
the Listening Ear, or the Women's Resource Center." Over one thousand
students, she proudly claimed, were doing volunteer work.[69]

CHAPTER 3

San Francisco State College

Striking for Community

When Herbert Wilner, an English faculty member, described the key physical arrangements of San Francisco State College (SFSC) in the early 1960s, he wrote that a prominent feature of SFSC "doesn't belong to the college." Rather, he explained, it "is the municipal streetcar marked 'M' which passes one of the college's corners on a main artery." SFSC, Wilner concluded, "is essentially a streetcar college."[1] "The streetcar college" is a helpful metaphor for understanding the character of SFSC and the politics that emerged on campus in the 1960s. The metaphor reflects the ways that California's 1960 Master Plan for Higher Education enabled a diverse, working-class student population to attend SFSC even as they remained deeply connected to their cultural identities and the political concerns of their communities. While the streetcar helps us visualize the movement of students from campus to community, it also symbolized the superficial relationship of SFSC as an institution to the surrounding communities in the 1960s. Outside of the streetcar that took students to and from home, there was very little connection between SFSC and the surrounding communities.

Indeed, students challenged the institution's identity as a *community* college. "San Francisco State, a community college," explained SFSC student Fred Wong, "exists in a moral vacuum, oblivious to the community it purports to serve."[2] Over the course of the 1960s, students developed a range of initiatives that sought to reimagine SFSC's identity as a community college.

These included the Community Education Tutorial, the Community Action Curriculum, the Community Involvement Program, and what became the Community Service Institute. The goal of these efforts was to endow the community aspect of SFSC's mission with political and social meaning. "The Community Involvement Program," students explained, "was established as a vehicle for students committed to learning skills of community organizing, and as a vehicle for students committed to exploring new ways of creating alternatives to current power structures in the community."[3]

The political vision of students' various community involvement programs was limited by the very policy framework that enabled them to access college: the financial and administrative structure of California's 1960 Master Plan for Higher Education. The plan created a tripartite system, broken down into three segments: junior colleges, state colleges, and universities. SFSC sat in the middle as a state college. The goal of the plan was to provide administrative order and a financial logic to what was a diverse landscape of institutions in the state of California. However, the plan's institutional hierarchy and centralized administration placed SFSC in a precarious position. Without the superior external funding and endowment associated with the university in the master plan, SFSC was less financially flexible than its institutional counterpart in Berkeley. Moreover, the centralization of higher education at the state level limited the power of SFSC's president and administration to institutionally experiment with programming, such as the new student-led community involvement programs.

The tension between a diverse student body who developed a range of community involvement programs and a centralized state system that determined the allocation and use of state funds in higher education created volatile campus conditions that produced not only the longest student strike in US history but also a draconian model of disciplining democracy. In the first part of the 1960s, SFSC President John Summerskill provided rhetorical support and administrative accommodation to students' various community involvement programs but, constrained by the logic of the master plan, very little financial support. Indeed, a core issue of the strike was the limited financial support for community involvement programs. The issue was further exacerbated by the Reagan administration's policy efforts to curtail the autonomy of student programs in the community, many of which they deemed too political. Summerskill's limited institutional accommodation also troubled California policy makers, especially those associated with the new Reagan administration who looked negatively at what they saw as the liberal leniency of California universities. When both Summerskill and his temporary replacement, Robert Smith, resigned, the new SFSC president, S. I. Hayakawa, became the intuitional face of the Reagan policy on higher education in California—a policy that defined disciplining with physical and financial force.

The institutional legacy took on similar characteristics at MSU in the form of a volunteer bureau for student affairs and distinct field programs in the newly established School of Ethnic Studies. However, the process of disciplining democracy at SFSC was much more politically explicit than it was at other institutions. First, there was the explicit use of city police as a violent force to discipline the Third World Liberation Front, the campus coalition that developed the various community involvement programs at SFSC. Second, there was the explicit use of the regulatory instruments of the state. California state policy makers granted the chancellor's office with the power to determine if funds used by students were allocated in ways that aligned with state or institutional policy, even if the funds came from external resources. The new plan developed by the Reagan administration—what became known as the Dumke plan—severely limited the type and form of community involvement at SFSC. The symbol of the institution's response—Hayakawa—not only instituted the policy but used it to limit the student body's use of funds by setting up an approval system. The approach enabled university leaders to advertise the institution's commitment to community involvement and address student critiques, but in a way that supported rather than challenged existing power structures.

Defining Community Involvement at SFSC

In the first part of the 1960s, student activists at SFSC agreed: the institution should be more involved in the community. But what was the goal of community involvement, both for the students and the institution? Jimmy Garrett, the Black Student Union student president, understood community involvement as a form of political education. This belief was rooted in an education that occurred more in the streets and rural backroads of Black communities than in the classroom. Growing up in Dallas, Texas, Garrett witnessed the mass demonstrations by the NAACP Youth Council at the Texas State Fair. The experience led him to become actively involved in the NAACP Youth Council and participate in the sit-ins and freedom rides in Houston. He also joined SNCC, serving as a Freedom Summer volunteer for the Mississippi Summer Project. Like others of his generational cohort, he was inspired by the Freedom School model, with its emphasis on readings in Black culture and history and its connection to community organizing in the Black community. He believed the Freedom School represented a new model of community-based Black studies at the university.[4] At SFSC, Garrett argued that the goal of community involvement was part of the broader process of political consciousness raising that connected the Black cultural resources to the experience of organizing in the community.

In his first year as president of the Black Student Union, Garrett transformed the community-based tutorial program—an institutionally supported effort run by the Associated Students—into a hub for political recruitment and organizing. He connected the tutorial to the institution's Educational Opportunity Program, a modest affirmative action program that waived admissions criteria for 2 percent of incoming students. The combination enabled Garrett to develop a tutorial project relevant to the community and political concerns of young Black residents in the Bay Area while also providing a channel for those students to attend higher education after high school. The recruitment of Clarence Thomas demonstrated the effectiveness of Garrett's efforts.[5] Garrett helped Thomas get into SFSC through the Educational Opportunity Program and the community tutorial. As part of his admission, Thomas participated in a Black Student Union–organized seminar that included readings by Che Guevara, Frantz Fanon, Nathan Hare, and W. E. B. Du Bois. He also engaged in community organizing in the Black community. The whole experience, Thomas believed, exemplified "Black Power in action."[6]

In contrast to Garrett's efforts with the Black Student Union, Karen Duncan's ideas of community involvement were defined in terms of making academic education more personally and socially relevant to a student's education. Duncan interpreted the Freedom Summer in much the same way many other White volunteers did: as a commitment to public service. She also believed it was a commitment that was missing in the regular curriculum. While enrolled at SFSC, Duncan was a member of the National Student Association, where she helped develop the "community action curriculum." The goal of her efforts was to encourage university faculty and administrators to develop programs that provided students with "direct experience" in existing community organizations while also offering "valued assistance to a desiring community."[7] Duncan cited the University of Chicago Public Affairs Program as the ideal model. The program allowed students to work temporarily in organizations involved in problems of public concern while still receiving academic credit.

The differences between Garett and Duncan paralleled those among activists associated with SFSC's community involvement programs. Jo Ann Ooiman, a fellow Freedom Summer volunteer, supported Duncan's framing of the "community action curriculum." Ooiman believed that the Freedom Summer was a valuable form of political experiential education. Yet, she was critical of a common refrain during the summer, what she described as an effort to make everything "unacademic." As a result, she worried, the treatment of academic as a dirty word had led her to teach "lies half the summer" and "propaganda the other half."[8] Working within the Bay Area Friends of SNCC, Ooiman believed that what was missing from the movement's education was a deeper commitment to academic forms of inquiry that would serve as an aid to community organizing while also endowing a student's education with political meaning.

Others associated with SNCC had reservations about efforts to connect the university to community organizing in the Bay Area. Jim Nixon and Tom Ramsay, two Bay Area SNCC activists, were skeptical of efforts that defined community involvement as a way to enhance academic education. As both Nixon and Ramsay argued, many "SNCC people will say to the student, 'who are you; what are you doing; what are you in this for? You don't have the same stake in this as most of us do; you can pull out of being born in a ghetto.'" Ramsay wanted "students who will come into the community as people who are able to go to work," rather than "kids who are 'learning'" as part of a university-sponsored program.[9] Ramsay's concern was that students who did not have a racial or cultural connection to the community or could not empathize with the conditions in the community would just use the experience of working with the poor as a means for their academic education and that the experience would reinforce rather than challenge economic and racial inequities.

Some students deeply engaged in the planning and funding of community involvement programs at SFSC did not see the positions of Garrett and Duncan or those that emerged between students and community organizers as inherently at odds. Rather, they believed there was a middle-ground interpretation of community involvement for students, one that balanced the needs of the student, political organizer, and resident. Michael Vozick was a student activist who participated in the Route 40 freedom rides in Maryland. At SFSC, he was the Associated Students president and played a prominent role in developing SFSC's portfolio of student-supported community involvement projects. He believed that students and community organizers needed to see beyond a simple dichotomy between the college and the community. "The real difficulty is in trying to work inside and outside at the same time," he argued, "the really radical experiment is trying to be both places."[10] Vozick's view included the other goal of community involvement programs. Such programs were created not just to engage students in the process of community organizing or service but also to transform SFSC as an educational institution.

Indeed, even as students defined the goal of community involvement differently, they agreed that building connections to the area would transform the college. Both Garrett's and Duncan's critiques of the university shared a common theme: the university's curriculum and approach to education were irrelevant to community issues. At the university, Garrett argued, "intellectual curiosity" was too often "'channeled' into academics and abstractions so that real questions aren't related to the lives of students."[11] Likewise, Duncan argued that the modern university had two interrelated issues: the irrelevancy of education to community life and the lack of involvement in community issues by students and faculty. Duncan explained that education at the university rested upon a theory that assumed "that experts create knowledge and teachers transmit it and that students are the passive objects of that transmission—i.e. the receivers of 'the Truth.'" She argued that this dichotomy tended to serve an institution "that wants to reflect rather than evaluate the norms of society" and acted as a filter that allowed "certain 'qualified' people to receive certain 'important' information."[12] Even Ramsay, who expressed reservations about linking SFSC to SNCC, shared the critique of the institution. Prior to joining SNCC full-time as an organizer, he was a student at SFSC, where he helped develop the Experimental College that offered an alternative approach to education.

The critique of the university served as a common thread across the different ideas of community involvement and also garnered support from faculty members at SFSC. Fred Thalheimer, a professor of sociology, and Eric Solomon, a professor of English, believed that student efforts in the community offered a means to reimagine the curriculum at SFSC. "Students working in the community," Thalheimer noted, "were returning to campus with serious questions about the relevancy of their education." In Thalheimer's view, the problem was that the structure of the university—both the organization of intellectual life into disciplines and the administrative process—limited experimentation in the curriculum. Indeed, Thalheimer redefined student efforts in the community, seeing the experiences not as being confined to student affairs but as central to the core curriculum of the college. "Student activity off the campus had been regarded as extra-curricular," but, Thalheimer argued, "many students found that the bulk of their educational experiences were happening outside the confines of the institution." Thalheimer continued, "If students were in learning situations off the campus, then the institution should recognize that activity as a valid, co-curricular activity and provide assistance and support."[13]

Thalheimer's discussion of the educational value of community involvement was part of a broader proposal cowritten with Garrett for developing an institute for community involvement. The core idea of the proposal was to expand and organize the various campus-community programs run by the students into a single institute. In doing so, students envisioned reorienting the university to make it more "responsive to individual human needs" and provide outlets that "enable individuals to effectively confront and engage the critical problems of American culture and society."[14] SFSC president Summerskill supported the new community involvement program. "They wanted a different society and they were prepared to work for it," Summerskill believed, and "they should have all the constructive opportunity they could handle."[15] Like the faculty members, he understood community involvement as being in line with the liberal spirit of the American college and intellectual life. As Summerskill noted, students wanted to understand the world "not only through analysis but through experience."[16]

This was more than a fleeting proposal. Summerskill provided university support for a two-day conference on experimental studies and community involvement programs with a focus on the relationship of the college to local and national issues. What emerged from the initial proposal and conference was the Community Service Institute (CSI), which served as a link between the different community efforts. The CSI was a joint operation between the Associated Students, the governing body of students, and the School of Education. Through campus seminars and planning sessions that involved local residents as instructors, students would create a "basis of cooperation" of different student organizations and community efforts.

In its first two years of operation, the CSI was led by Sharon Gold, a graduate student in the humanities at SFSC. Prior to attending SFSC, Gold worked as an SNCC volunteer in 1965, teaching in a Freedom School in Selma, Alabama. Gold made two important theoretical and practical interventions that addressed the internal tensions within student efforts. The first intervention was reconciling the educational goals of the students with the political goals of the organizers or residents in the community. In explaining the purpose of the CSI, Gold emphasized the educational value of community participation but underscored that such involvement must be directed at broader political struggles. "It would assume that participants in the process of the Institute would accept the responsibility to use their intellectual resources not only to analyze and describe contemporary problems," Gold argued, "but also to attempt to solve them" through student involvement and community organizing.[17]

By combining formal education with political activism, it would, Gold believed, reconstruct the relationship between the college and the community. Residents had "a great deal of hostility to college students and other members of the academic community," and many had told them that they "resent having outsiders tell them what their problems are and how to solve them. They do not want 'experts' to take over leadership of their organizations because then the organizations no longer belong to them." Moreover, Gold continued, community members "do not like to be studied particularly when they do not know who wants the information and for what purpose it will be used. Often, in fact, this information is used by agencies for purposes which are viewed by the residents as inimical to their interests." Gold thus envisioned the CSI as a way to "alter this distorted relationship" by involving community residents in the operation of the center, which would include facilitating seminars and determining how the resources of the university would be used to address issues in the community.[18]

The second intervention centered identity as a means to enhance rather than inhibit the educational process. In the context of broader debates concerning the role of White activists in the civil rights movement and the transcendence of Black Nationalist and Third World politics, Gold was sensitive to the relationship between racial identity and student involvement in different communities. Indeed, the emphasis on community was not a universalist claim; rather, it was about the particular. The key student groups who organized community involvement projects within the CSI—the Black Student Union, La Raza, the Philippine American Collegiate Endeavor, and Inter-Collegiate Chinese for Social Action—prioritized their cultural and racial identity. At the same time, the CSI was run through the Associated Students, SFSC's student government whose leadership was predominantly White.

Informed by the particular context of the diverse student groups at SFSC, Gold concluded that students had to work in communities that aligned with their racial backgrounds, believing it would enable students of color to "acquire the skills, information and perceptions necessary to work effectively" and "to assist residents in their efforts to gain more control over the quality of their daily lives." She also argued that the emphasis on working in communities that aligned with a student's cultural and racial background served a similar purpose for White students. Community involvement would "provide a process of reeducation for white students so that they may experientially understand the culture and society for which they are responsible." In particular, she believed the experiences would provide White students with "skills and abilities necessary to confront the inhumanity, racism and oppression" perpetuated by members in their own communities.[19] The underlying assumption was that students would be better equipped with insider knowledge and cultural empathy, enabling them to understand the concerns of the community more intimately.

Gold developed a flexible philosophy of community involvement that was attuned to the racial and cultural identity of the student while still committed both to the political project of community organizing and transforming the SFSC as a community college. The philosophical flexibility in the CSI attracted wide-ranging support among students at SFSC. In 1967, when the CSI went into full operation, over four hundred students worked in twenty-two different communities across San Francisco. One of those students who participated in the summer session was Wendy Alfsen. A White student from rural Southern California, Alfsen attended SFSC because of its urban setting and diverse student population. Conversations with La Raza president Roger Alverado during her first year inspired her to get involved in the CSI, where she worked in the South Market Community Center. Self-identifying as a "third generation activist" of the 1960s, Alfsen developed a political awareness through her conversations with the residents of South Market, especially around issues concerning housing discrimination and poverty. The CSI encouraged students like Alfsen to see the work beyond community service and learning as part of a broader social movement attempting to transform American society. "It was all about social change," Alfsen explained, both at the community and institutional level.[20]

A Financial "Strike" against Community Involvement

The program mission of students' community involvement program—especially the explicit focus on challenging power structures—concerned state-level policy makers in California. This was not a perceived concern, either. Indeed, the new politics of higher education in California further constrained what was already a financially limited set of community involvement programs. At the same time that students began to expand community involvement programs, new policies in the California system of higher education began to curtail those very efforts. In 1966, California elected Ronald Reagan as governor. Part of Reagan's campaign focused on what he saw as the political leniency of university presidents and administrators, especially in response to the 1964 sit-in at the University of California, Berkeley.[21] Reagan's 1968 state higher education budget sought to constrain student efforts in the community. Chancellor Glenn Dumke outlined a new funding proposal that aligned with Reagan's budget. Two key elements of that budget concerned student activists at SFSC. The first involved funding cuts to the Educational Opportunity Program. In 1968, Reagan struck $250,000 from the program, and his next budget did not include the $2.5 million recommended for it to operate.[22] The second expanded the authority of the chancellor, who had final say in how certain funds for student programming could be used by students, even if the funds were raised by students themselves.

Students active in the community involvement programs expressed concern about the potential impact of what became known as the Dumke plan. Russell Bass, the president of Associated Students in the fall of 1968, argued that Dumke's funding proposal "effectively eliminates or curtails student . . . autonomy." Alverado expressed concern about its impact on students' various efforts in the community. He explained that "the proposal takes away from the college whatever autonomy it may have had in its own activities—not just fiscal authority but authority over the kinds of activities it may sponsor as well."[23]

Alverado and Bass were not alone. Other students were worried that the new policy was intentionally designed to limit student activities in the community. The policy, SFSC students argued, directly challenged the needs of student organizations and their autonomy. "The sustained growth of student participation in their education and communities over the past few years," they wrote, required "increasing necessity for greater decentralization and sharing of institutional controls by those individuals directly involved in the college." However, the new regulation was "an extremely sophisticated and well-organized plan to thwart this present trend of student activism by instituting a system of hierarchical decision making and centralized policy."[24]

University leaders likewise expressed concerns about the new policy. Even though Summerskill provided institutional support, it mostly came in the form of access to campus spaces. Despite his advocacy with other college presidents in California, Summerskill was never granted more money or institutional flexibility with how the money was spent. The grant proposal to the Carnegie Foundation was not awarded either. When Reagan was elected governor, Summerskill interpreted his higher education policy efforts as a deliberate scheme to expand financial control over the institution. "The trustees and the chancellor," he concluded, "wanted to keep tight control of expenditures." In particular, he noted, the trustees and chancellor were concerned that "state money would be spent for programs that might be politically unacceptable."[25] Given these limitations, Summerskill resigned in early 1968, blaming the increasing volatile campus situation on state interference. In his resignation, he underscored the lack of support—and funding flexibility—for community involvement programs. "In the midst of a city with a human rights revolution," he explained, "it is impossible when you do not have the discretion to spend $1000 here or $20,000 there to solve a problem."[26]

Robert Smith, a professor of education at SFSC, was appointed as Summerskill's temporary replacement. Like Summerskill, Smith engaged the students, seeking ways to constructively expand the programs. Smith met with Bass and Alverado, both of whom highlighted the language in the proposed Dumke plan. The budget, Bass and Alverado argued in their meeting with Smith, set limits on what students could do on campus and in the community. "The proposal specifies that no student funds can be allocated to a student program or an activity if that program deviates from Trustee policy," Bass noted, because the report sets up "the Chancellor's Office as interpreter in this matter and requires his specific approval to any program or activity using student organization funds." Bass called the phrase "in accordance with college policy" the "catch-22" of the document.[27] Believing these changes were the results of political pressures in Sacramento, Bass argued that the proposal was intended to provoke students. "The trustees are inciting the students to riot," Bass argued. "The pattern of events since July bears that out, and this proposal is consistent with that direction."[28]

Student concerns proved prescient. After learning about the budget cuts and the limits on student funds, the Black Student Union and the Third World Liberation Front, a coalition of student organizations who helped run the CSI, went on strike on November 6, 1968. The tipping point for the strike was the firing of George Murray, the graduate assistant who helped oversee the Educational Opportunity Program. In addition to the rehiring of Murray, the Black Student Union and the Third World Liberation Front and its supporters demanded an increase in both the admissions of "Third World students" and funding for students' various community involvement efforts. The students' broader appeal—what became the demand for a School of Ethnic Studies—emphasized a program of study within the context of community and political organizing. Thousands of students refused to attend classes and occupied campus spaces and buildings. The strike garnered wide-ranging support because of student activists' earlier efforts of coalition building around the CSI and among select faculty. With support from the Longshoremen Union and the American Federation of Teachers, the Third World Liberation Front and Black Student Union sustained the strike until March 20, 1969.

The strike knitted together student concerns about policy efforts with their belief in the educational value of activism. Indeed, students argued that the strike was a response to the administrative strike in the form of the Dumke plan against their education, both in the community and on campus. The students argued that "the real disruption of the educational process (what little there is) came from Chancellor Dumke and the Trustees, bent on crushing the black and white student programs like Tutorial, CIP, Experimental college, special admissions."[29] In their press release, student strike leaders further argued that the various measures passed to limit student autonomy and community involvement programming revealed the priorities of educational institutions. "The educational system is less concerned with freeing people," the students wrote, "than with perpetuating a given social system, of which institutionalized racism is a functioning part."[30] Even as students refused to attend classes, they maintained throughout the strike that their education continued. Indeed, the motivating belief was that the strike itself was a form of education. SFSC students understood their organizing on campus—the sit-downs and protests as part of the strike—as expressions of their philosophy of community involvement.

The extent and scale of the strike confronted Smith with a profound institutional dilemma: What was the right response? Having met with student activists and supporting their various programs through the school of education, he saw their demands as in line with the broader experimental efforts at the college. Smith organized a convocation early in the strike, one that brought together faculty, administrators, and students to discuss the core issues on campus. The campus-wide event proved educational for the faculty. Arlene Kaplan Daniels, a professor in sociology, learned that "the student strike was not just an educational experience for young radicals; it was a serious protest over long-standing grievances."[31] One of those grievances that stood out to Thomas Kroeber, a professor of psychology, was the lack of ongoing institutional support for students' various community involvement programs. "The student strikers made very clear," Kroeber noted, "that the source of their energy and the focus of their work were outside the college. Their connection and interest were in the community or communities from which they had come or where they were spending most of their energies."[32] In Kroeber's view, this conception ran counter to a traditional view of the college as an ivory tower and would make it difficult to "keep political issues from damaging the openness of their inquiry."[33] Even so, Kroeber also acknowledged that the isolation of the college did not prepare students to engage critically with the problems in the area. The problem, Kroeber concluded, was competing understandings of the public mission of the college.

What became clear from the SFSC faculty and administrator perspective was that the dilemma was more about the institution's educational philosophy than the political actions of the students. David West, who oversaw the Educational Opportunity Program, believed the conflict came down to a question of values and the purpose of education. Although he disagreed with the tactics of some students, particularly those who turned violent as a result of the increased police presence on campus, he argued that the issue that arose came down to "'tradition' vs. 'what's right.'" Many of the students, influenced both by civil rights activism and their experiences growing up in marginalized communities, sought ways to evolve the "traditions" of education to address social or moral concerns and realize "what's right." Yet, West argued, "the majority of college administrators dwelled more on tradition rather accept the challenge of making the colleges and universities address themselves to the needs of the students."[34] In West's view, university officials tended to prioritize the perceived tradition of the institution over students' critiques of the university's education and the institution's relationship to the community.

Even as Smith encouraged honest deliberation about the core issues of the strike, his position was limited by the chancellor's office. Dumke did not allow Smith to affirmatively negotiate with the students. The message from Dumke and the board of trustees was to reopen the campus. The convocation thus had a countervailing effect on the students. Without the power to negotiate and address the demands for student program autonomy, financial independence for community involvement, and programs in Black and Ethnic studies, students interpreted the convocation as a farce, leading to further frustration. This also frustrated Smith. Like Summerskill, Smith resigned due to the constraints placed on him. "I quit as president mainly," he later reflected, "because we failed in six months of strenuous effort on the part of the administrative staff and me to get from the chancellor and the trustees the resources and kinds of decisions I felt we needed."[35]

Upon the resignation of Smith, Hayakawa was selected as the new president of SFSC without the faculty selection committee. Arlene Daniels, the sociologist who participated in Smith's convocation, interpreted the hiring of Hayakawa without faculty consent as a "clear sign that the trustees meant to run our college without campus consent."[36] Indeed, Hayakawa was responsive to the board of trustees in ways that both Summerskill and Smith were not—specifically around the use of police to force the college open. Both Summerskill and Smith utilized city police in response to student protests, but action was minimal. Summerskill believed that students had a right to political action, even if directed at the institution. "I believe," he underscored, "that students have the right to assemble, rally, protest, teach-in, sit-in, and otherwise fight for their convictions."[37] Smith similarly believed that the use of police was for extreme situations on campus. "Our plan: use police only minimally to maintain safety and arrest lawbreakers," he later explained, "continue to seek ways of mediating the demands, and so keep communications and decision making open through department-student meetings, convocations, and other means."[38]

The differences between Summerskill and Smith and Hayakawa ultimately came down to degree of use. Both Summerskill and Smith were troubled by some actions of students—especially the minority of students who utilized violence as a form of intimidation as part of their political demands. In those situations, they called in the police. But what Summerskill and Smith interpreted as a small and rare form of political action state policy makers and Hayakawa interpreted as the dominant problem, and they used it to justify the need for an increased presence and response by the city police. In contrast to Summerskill and Smith, Hayakawa utilized city police as a primary tactic. He saw it as a means to end what he defined as student disruption and ensure that the institution returned to what he believed to be its normal function.

Under Hayakawa, the narrative of the strike changed. Foremost, Hayakawa framed student actions as counterproductive and outside the normal function of the university. Hayakawa attracted the attention of the Reagan administration for his outspoken views on the sit-in at Berkley in 1964. "The FSM [Free Speech Movement] is clearly not interested in orderly debate and rational argument," he wrote; "sitdowns, picketing and mass demonstrations are not forms of argument" and "are entirely out of place in the university."[39] He employed the same institutional logic in response to students at SFSC. "For the past two weeks faculty and students have engaged in a number of activities—convocations, rallies, bull sessions, etc. to confront 'the real issues,'" he noted, claiming that these are "'educationally more relevant' than scheduled classes." But, he argued, "such rationalizations for evading one's educational responsibilities will not be accepted."[40] If students understood their political actions as integral to their education, Hayakawa drew a sharp distinction between political action and education. He argued that the problem was the students' efforts to politicize the university rather than the administrative overreach by state-level higher education officials.

Faculty supporters who took on leadership roles in the academic senate's ad hoc committee during the strike—Jordan Churchill, Jules Grossman, Ann Paterson, and Ray Simpson—sought to maintain the focus on the educational basis of the strike and the critique of the state's administrative control. In their state of the college address, they argued that "the crisis is founded in a series of unresolved and fundamental issues which dramatize the general failure of education to serve adequately the needs of all of the people." The problem, however, was that the college "has yet to engage the basic issues in any profound way." Outside of the small Educational Opportunity Program (EOP) and the CSI, they wrote, "our responses have been limited to administrative accommodation."[41]

The faculty worried that the critique of the college was increasingly drowned out by the reporting on campus violence provoked by the presence of police. "Police force," the faculty committee also wrote, "is a wholly inappropriate and ineffective response to the needs of ethnic minorities." When police are used "to protect and continue a situation seen by students as a determined and continuing denial of rights," they argued, "police force serves to influence feeling, harden attitudes and to encourage vandalism and violence according to opportunity." A small cohort of students did take advantage of the situation by using the presence of the police to highlight the repressive response of the institution. However, their actions—including raiding classes, setting off bombs, and slashing tires—proved counterproductive to the goals of the strike. As a result, the faculty worried, "the basic problems are obscured by violence and the reactions to violence." They asserted that an "immediate resolution of conflict demands acknowledgement that violence is not the fundamental issue, but rather that profound educational issues have yet to be confronted by the college."[42]

The faculty members' appeal fell on deaf ears. Outside the college, the educational issues were lost to the narrative in the press, which largely adopted Hayakawa's logic that the students were the cause of violence and a disruption to the college. Most reporting on the strike put the blame on students from the Black Student Union and the Third World Liberation Front, creating an artificial distinction between students involved in the Third World Liberation Front and students in the Associated Students. A report by Ron Moskowitz for the *San Francisco Chronicle* presented students involved in the CSI and Experimental College as the "good guys" who worked constructively through the institution, as opposed to the "bad guys" of SDS and the Black Student Union. In a letter to the *Chronicle*, students from the CSI and Experimental College wrote that Moskowitz's framing was a "vicious distortion," arguing that such interpretations misconstrued students' shared critique of the modern university.[43] Other reports interviewed students from a small organization called the Silent Majority Against Revolutionary Tactics, or SMART. Connected to other campus organizations in the Bay Area, the group called for the arrest of student radicals, the reopening of the university, and the maintenance of "qualification standards" for admission to SFSC. Reagan's support, the narrative in prominent media outlets, and the presence of SMART substantiated the views of Hayakawa, who largely saw the various efforts of student activists as outside the university. Alex Forman, an SFSC student striker, believed the more important question that grew out of the student movement and strike at SFSC had been lost. "The question," he explained, "was what was the campus being used for? What were the resources used for?"

Administering Community Involvement

In the aftermath of the strike, Hayakawa recast student commitments to the community. Shaped by a Cold War logic, he interpreted students' efforts as akin to those of earlier Russian revolutionaries. It was a "sentimental identification with the downtrodden," he believed, "just like the idealization of the peasant among Russian student revolutionaries in the early years of this century." In framing their efforts as similar to those of Russian student revolutionaries, Hayakawa argued that student efforts in the community were a cover for what he deemed to be their revolutionary aspirations. "This sympathy with the underdog," he explained, "gives a factitious moral base to justify their outrageous behavior." He contrasted what he defined as the revolutionary minority with the "mass" of students who he believed genuinely were committed to serving the community. "The majority of students also identify with the underdog," Hayakawa wrote, emphasizing that "the seriousness of their concern with social problems is one of the wonderful characteristics." But he believed that seriousness was easily manipulated. "It is this seriousness," he argued, "that makes them susceptible to revolutionary propaganda, with the result that many young people who genuinely believe in democracy are often led around by those who do not." Hayakawa thus focused his efforts on promoting forms of community involvement that he believed genuinely identified with the underdog to help combat the "revolutionary" fervor of other student groups.[44]

Blaming the problem on a small cohort of "revolutionaries" influencing those truly committed to serving the community, Hayakawa believed that the role of SFSC was to develop new programs in community involvement that provided a genuine civic education for students. Indeed, like other presidents, Hayakawa argued that students misunderstood the legal mechanics and civic processes of political institutions in the United States. Despite the fact that leading activists at SFSC had been deeply involved in a variety of efforts, most expansively the Mississippi Freedom Democratic Party, Hayakawa believed the students did not understand "democratic processes." He argued that student unrest "lies in the fact that too small a segment of our population has availed itself of similar opportunities—at school board meetings, in city council deliberations, before regulatory commissions with state and federal legislative committees." The task ahead, he believed, was for SFSC to develop programs that allowed students to understand those processes and "build a faith among the young in those processes as vehicles for solving social and human problems."[45]

Under the Reagan administration and the Dumke plan, Hayakawa also had new administrative power to determine appropriate forms of student involvement in the community. In the aftermath of the strike, William W. Harkness, the new dean of student activities, sent out a packet of materials to the incoming students for the fall of 1969 that made clear that certain activities were off-limits in the context of the university. "Any organization with a national, state, or local group shall not be recognized if the parent (or otherwise related) organization requires the local group to support a specific position in political, economic, or social issues which contravenes College polices," Harkness emphasized in the letter. The administration framed this policy in the language of action and the pursuit of truth at the university, but with a caveat that maintained administrative power over student funds. "This college will encourage all forms of action," except those that interfere "with the essential functions of the academic community."[46]

One of the major changes was how student efforts were funded. After the strike, the university created a community service fund. The purpose of the fund was to develop "a positive approach to dealing with campus (unrest) problems."[47] The funding for student-sponsored programs had to align with Title 5 of the California Administrative Code, in particular Section 42659, which specified what "programs of cultural enrichment and community service" were appropriate and inappropriate on campus as determined by the chancellor's office. When students attempted to fund new efforts at SFSC, they were restricted by the administration's interpretations of the Education Code.[48]

In the context of expanded administrative power, SFSC continued to promote community involvement, but in a way that aligned with Hayakawa's vision of good civics. In addition to requesting input on governance and the mission of the student activities department, Harkness also asked for input on efforts to "work out ways to involve more students in relevant volunteer service both on campus and in the community." The emphasis on volunteer service was reflective of Hayakawa's civic worldview. He promoted national service as a solution to campus unrest. In the context of SFSC, this took the form of Operation Outreach, which focused on engaging students in efforts to "extend our educational services into parts of the central city not now served by our College." Hayakawa saw the program as a means to also benefit the community by providing skills training. "I believe that it should include many kinds of courses enabling working people to upgrade their skills and earning power," he explained.[49] In both ways, Hayakawa promoted community involvement and campus-community connections without the political organizing goals of students' earlier efforts.

Hayakawa's Operation Outreach created an institutional wedge in the collective efforts of the student groups. The student-led CSI balanced formal education, community service, and political organizing as part of the institute's philosophy of community involvement. Hayakawa's efforts split education and service from politics. Hayakawa sought to address the critiques of some students by promoting volunteer service as a way to update the curriculum of the college. The students, he rightly noted, were "tired of preparing for life" and demanded programs that enabled them to "tackle real problems, not classroom exercises."[50] By providing the opportunity to tutor or volunteer in the community, Hayakawa sought to address one of the major critiques by students. At the same time, the focus on volunteer service, especially tutoring services, also drew in students who were supportive of the strike. The students in the Philippine-American Collegiate Endeavor, La Raza, and InterCollegiate Chinese for Social Action all had developed distinct tutoring programs in their communities as part of their political organizing efforts. Participants in these groups continued to engage in community tutoring. But, in the context of Hayakawa's Operation Outreach, students had to abide by the new institutional policy against political organizing and activism. What was a broad coalition was thus fragmented by SFSC's new institutionally sponsored program in the community.

The institutional responses and new programs constrained student activists' more ambitious vision of SFSC as a community college. In the 1970s, students recognized that the key components of their earlier efforts—including the emphases on community knowledge, political action, and other elements—had largely been expunged from the institutionally supported activities. Tom Williams, who helped lead the Black Student Union with Garrett, attempted to resurrect the tutorial project along the lines of earlier practices associated with the CSI. The board of directors voted to deny Williams's request to use the tutorial program, arguing that the Associated Students had already reactivated the community tutorial in line with the new protocols of the university. In his explanation of the board's decision, Harkness argued that the Associated Students, under Henry Lehman, oversaw the tutorial program and had "proprietary right to such a name and program." Run by Gilbert Robinson, an English faculty member hired after the strike, the new tutorial model was based on VISTA and related federal volunteer programs. It focused more on professional development of the students and charity goals than political empowerment.[51] As outlined in the new handbook, the Associated Students tutorial program provided "the student considering a career in education with an introduction to the field while also providing him or her with the practical extramural experience essential to acquiring a teaching position in a tight job market."[52] Harkness encouraged Williams to fold his project into the institutionally supported one. But, as Williams argued, the program was drastically different than what he and other students had envisioned in initially developing the tutorial project and attempting to revive it in the 1970s. Williams was not alone. Solomon, a professor of English who supported the efforts of CSI and the Black Student Union, took a position at SFSC because the college had many "exciting educational ventures" that sparked student interest. But institutional responses "put out the flame," and as a result, "the spark went too."[53]

The university also created the volunteer bureau, a clearinghouse for referrals and information on student volunteer placements. In 1976, close to eight hundred students worked in the volunteer bureau, a reflection of continued student interest in connecting education to community work. Like the tutoring program, the bureau contrasted with earlier student efforts like the CSI. It was run by Bob Westwood, who viewed the bureau as a form of charity work that supplemented students' education. Westwood believed volunteerism provided students with opportunities to build their professional profile. "It's not only rewarding but students gain experience from it and it's fun," Woodward explained. "It's set up to serve the individual student."[54] David Turner, a student who volunteered at Shriners Hospital, personified how the mission shaped students' interpretation of their experience. "Money is not that important," Turner explained. "I'd gladly give my time without being paid if it means something."[55]

While professional goals replaced the political goals in the new community involvement programs, academic priorities constrained the new ethnic studies program. Along with developing the Operation Outreach initiative, the community service fund, and the volunteer bureau, Hayakawa also oversaw the formation of the School of Ethnic Studies, where community involvement was redefined. Nathan Hare, like Garrett, believed that Black studies required an experiential component of direct involvement within the Black community. In his view, the goal of Black studies was the development of a political movement, or what he described as "a mass movement and a mass struggle" that aimed "to rid the world of racism and achieve black self-determination." In the context of SFSC, he attempted to redefine field research as community organizing. Involvement in "the community," Hare explained, was akin to being in a "laboratory" in which one could learn the process of community organizing while also working "to transform the Black community."[56]

Hare was not part of the development of the School of Ethnic Studies. Indeed, during its formation, Hayakawa prevented faculty who participated in the early community involvement programs or in the strike, such as Hare, from participating in creating the new ethnic studies programs. This did not mean that the community involvement component was lost. The dean of the program, James Harabayashi, believed the community-based component was central to the broader goal of ethnic studies. He explained, "one of the educational concerns of all the ethnic studies programs has been to relate much, much closer to the peoples of the community." In contrast to what he saw as the way "traditional education separates itself from what is going on in the community," the School of Ethnic Studies created programs "where education becomes much more relevant to present-day life," especially in terms of "getting students out in the community, getting them more in touch with what's going on."[57]

Even as Harabayashi maintained a focus on community, community involvement was defined and practiced differently in the School of Ethnic Studies. One of the core demands was for the creation of community boards, similar to what Gold had developed within the CSI. The community board would connect students with residents and they would work with them on shared projects that addressed economic and racial inequality or challenged the abuse of power by local officials. However, Hayakawa prevented students and faculty from having the power to decide who was represented on the community board, largely making the board a defunct idea.[58] The failure to realize a board was just one component of the limited idea of community involvement that emerged in ethnic studies.

Hare's choice word—laboratory—also proved institutionally flexible. Indeed, the new faculty adopted Hayakawa's idea of community involvement as either volunteer service or field research. In the context of Black studies, Mary Lewis, the head of the Black studies department, prioritized volunteer service in existing social service agencies. In other programs, the focus was on field research, with a coursework focus on teaching students research methodologies for data gathering in state and related social service agencies. Don Patterson, the chairman of the Native American Studies program, explained that the classroom was used to effectively prepare students for the community work. Rightly concerned with a "do-gooder" and "paternalism" tendency among researchers and students alike, Patterson focused on teaching students the "difficulties and ethics involved in research" in the community. For Patterson, the purpose of community involvement was fieldwork and ethnographic observation and teaching students to gather data and conduct research at the community level.[59] Community involvement was redefined to primarily entail the academic development of the student while also collecting relevant data for social service agencies to better serve the area.

In the 1970s, when reflecting upon efforts at SFSC, Hare argued that Black studies—like the School of Ethnic Studies—was drastically different than what he and others envisioned in the first part of the 1960s. Over the course of the 1970s, most courses in Black studies focused on content over efforts in the community. But Black studies, Hare argued, was never meant to be restricted to an academic and conceptual inquiry removed from the social and experiential context of the Black struggle. Ray Tomkins, a Black student who was the chairman of the Black Students Union during the strike, believed the new Black studies department—a success of their efforts—had largely been adapted to institutional norms of knowledge production and formal education. "The faculty don't want to put their theories to practice, just want to theorize and intellectualize," he lamented. "It ain't helpin' me or my community to sit there in a class for 30 minutes and trip on what you may think or how you may perceive the problems of the black community."[60]

Urban Whitaker disagreed with Hare and Tomkin, believing they both ignored the institutional reality and political situation in California. Whitaker also taught in Black studies and served as the interim dean of the School of Ethnic Studies before Harabayashi. In his view, the vision of ethnic studies programs like Black studies was to develop a clear program of study that was a respected discipline within the college and aligned with the protocols of the new administration. Indeed, the new faculty focused on efforts to ensure the legitimacy of ethnic studies in the college. Whitaker acknowledged that "there are some students and some faculty who believe that the purpose of the program are to promote revolution and politization." But, Whitaker argued, "the law requires and the Administration believes that the Black Studies department should conduct an educational program giving instruction in approved courses."[61] Whitaker's key phrases—*the law requires* and *politization*—demonstrated the ways the new state-level policy and rhetoric set administrative boundaries on the vision of ethnic studies.

Legacy

When Del Stenson participated in the meeting among SFSC students and community organizers in the mid-1960s, he expressed skepticism about efforts to link community and political organizing to the college. Stenson worried that the connections to the university would inevitably limit the actions of organizers and students. "Organizers resent putting much hard work into a 'safe' program that's designed to be acceptable to college big wigs," he explained. "They're not interested in safe things; they want to do radical, risky things."[62] From an organizer's perspective, Stenson worried that integrating community political efforts into the operation of the college would mitigate those very efforts while also redirecting student political energies.

The meeting that Stenson participated in was part of the early discussions of instituting SFSC students' various ad hoc efforts in the community. Over the course of the 1960s, a broad coalition of students sought to endow SFSC's identity as a community college with political meaning. The community involvement projects culminated in the formation of the CSI, a campus hub designed to facilitate political organizing efforts both within and across different communities. Informed by their own political experiences in the civil rights struggle as well as their connections in the area, students developed a nuanced philosophy of community involvement that was attuned to racial and cultural context while still maintaining an emphasis on political activism. It was the latter emphasis—what Stenson described as the "risky things" of the collaboration—that concerned state-level policy makers associated with the Reagan administration. Stenson was right, but the concern was not necessarily about the college presidents. Indeed, both Summerskill and Smith did try to do "risky" things but were often constrained by the administrative apparatus and its employment by the new Reagan administration in California.

When student efforts in the CSI reached a critical consensus in the late 1960s, state-level policy makers empowered university leaders to limit both the nature and form of community involvement. Indeed, Reagan officials interpreted the institutional autonomy of the program in the same way they interpreted the Free Speech Movement: as a reflection of the liberal leniency of the college. In an effort to rein in student autonomy, the Reagan administration developed what became the Dumke plan, which empowered the chancellor's office and university presidents to limit student funds and programs. It was these conditions—the financial independence of the students and the proposed administrative response—that served as the basis of the student strike that put SFSC on the political map in the 1960s. The student strike was in response to the administrative strike by state-level policy makers.

The administrative strike served as a basis for the broader process of disciplining democracy that developed at SFSC and in the California system. During and after the strike, the California system and SFSC developed a disciplining process with political teeth. During the strike, Hayakawa employed city police to restrain and, at times, violently arrest students. After the strike, Hayakawa utilized the administrative power granted by the chancellor's office to limit how students utilized funds for their various efforts in the community. Even as the process of disciplining took on more explicit political forms at the state level, Hayakawa's reasoning was rooted in a particular interpretation of the movement and the role of the college. Hayakawa believed the campus movement represented "antidemocratic" tendencies. In framing it this way, he justified his actions as a defense of the college's role in a democracy. This also provided a justification for how he defined community involvement after the strike. In the 1970s, Hayakawa established new institutional programs that promoted community involvement through volunteer service and the extension of academic services into the community. These efforts both limited and replaced earlier community involvement programs. A similar process occurred in the School of Ethnic Studies, where community involvement was recast as a form of fieldwork research that taught students about the ethics of research in the community and helped collect data for existing social service agencies. To borrow from Stenson, the new institutional programs were much more "acceptable."

CHAPTER 4

Harvard University–Radcliffe College

Educating for Action

After World War II, Harvard took a leading role in articulating a new educational mission that remained closely linked to the national project. When Harvard made its new general education curriculum—what became popularly known as the Red Book—available to broader public audiences, it contained the university's century-old heraldic seal: the word Veritas, or "truth," over the image of three open books. But the pursuit of truth involved two key ideas reflective of postwar intellectual transformations. The first idea, which related to the content of the curriculum, promoted a conception of civics that defined democracy as a set of institutions and principles synonymous with the United States. The second idea, about the attributes that a student needed for modern citizenship, prioritized the particular outlooks associated with postwar science, in particular a commitment to "value-neutrality." Harvard President James Bryant Conant believed the "objective, disinterested judgments" of modern science would develop the requisite values and habits "in the formation of citizens for a free society."[1] The new curriculum sequence at both Harvard and Radcliffe garnered wide public praise among academics and policy makers in framing a postwar vision of general education. Within its first year, the book received first honors as the 1946 best seller of the Harvard University Press.

Despite the public popularity of the new general education curriculum, Harvard and Radcliffe students were unimpressed. Writing in the *i.e., The*

Cambridge Review, a student journal started in the 1950s "to assume the critical position which dissatisfaction with the University necessitated," students argued that general education courses assumed that "the problems of the world have been solved or at least mouthed out of existence, and the ideal turns into one of specialization." However, they argued that "thought can only become an idea if it has a relation to action, because in action it will become meaningful to the thinker and will produce more ideas."[2] What was a nascent critique of general education in the 1950s became a common refrain among a cohort of Harvard and Radcliffe student activists by the 1960s. The civil rights struggle in the American South inspired a group of Harvard-Radcliffe students to embrace new ideas about education and the role of elite institutions in American political life. The experience of activism within the civil rights struggle exposed Harvard-Radcliffe students to perspectives that both revealed the experiential and moral gap in their elite formal education and challenged notions of institutional neutrality.

This chapter examines how academic leaders at Harvard-Radcliffe translated student experiences in the civil rights struggle into the institution's modern conception of truth. Academic leaders at Harvard-Radcliffe understood the activist experiences as a modern expression of moral commitment and good citizenship and thus as an opportunity to update the institution's educational mission. Indeed, these leaders embraced the appeal to action as a way to infuse moral commitment back into the general education curriculum. That was the view, at least, of Radcliffe College President Mary Bunting, who helped start the Education for Action (E4A) program, which was offered to both Harvard and Radcliffe students. While acknowledging the influence of civil rights activism, Bunting promoted domestic and international volunteerism. Like other colleges in the 1960s, when student activists attempted to expand the definition of action beyond volunteerism, academic leaders at both Radcliffe and Harvard disconnected the program from the regular curriculum and the institution.

The effort by academic leaders to delink E4A from the regular curriculum was not a deliberate attempt to mitigate student activism. Rather, the process of disciplining at Harvard-Radcliffe encompassed a set of institutional value judgments and priorities reflective of the institution's pedagogical ideology. When deciding the new budget for the 1970s, academic leaders deemed E4A an experience that did not fit within the curriculum or the extracurriculum. In making this interpretive claim, academic deans at both Harvard and Radcliffe asserted that the traditional activities associated with the extracurricular—such as debate, sports, and arts—took financial precedence over E4A while the program itself had no institutional home. Academic leaders hid this interpretive argument—of what was and was not an appropriate activity on campus—behind a financial decision. Even if the process was less draconian than it was at other institutions, the effect was the same. As a program outside the regular curriculum, E4A redirected student energies away from critiques of the curriculum and the institution. By the mid-1970s, E4A became an activist clearinghouse that allowed students to get involved and take political stances in the world, but those activities had no relation to either the general patterns of formal education or the role of the university.

Learning Politics

When Bob Moses traveled South to become a full-time organizer with SNCC, his work in the back roads of Mississippi seemed to be a far cry from his graduate study in philosophy at Harvard. But Moses did not see his field of study as separate from his political work. He understood his political commitment as but an extension of his intellectual pursuits. Reflecting on his study of existentialism, Moses explained, "[Camus] comes out with something which I think is relevant to this struggle [for racial equality]. It's not a question that you just subjugate yourself to the conditions that are and don't try to change them." The problem and the challenge, he continued, "is to go on from there, into something which is active."[3] The formation of SNCC provided Moses with the chance to become active and translate his study of philosophy to a political commitment in the world.

In the context of SNCC, Moses also drew on his graduate study of Ludwig Wittgenstein, whose analytical philosophy focused on the nature of representation through language. Moses interpreted Wittgenstein's philosophy through the lens of community organizing. One of the central goals was working through different perspectives and experiences or multiple representations of reality. As Moses explained to SNCC staff when describing the work of an organizer, his view of the world was only one part of the truth. The conclusions that he came to were "no more or less valid than yours," and he told his peers to "consider what I see and what you see and from it all we can ultimately find Truth."[4] Moses believed that one of the key tasks of an organizer—like the analytic philosopher—was to clarify and develop a shared language that all parties agreed represented a political or social reality.

Moses thus did not see his academic field of study and his activism as competing positions. Rather, he synthesized his study of existentialism and analytic philosophy with the political work of an organizer. This intellectual synthesis was at the core of Moses's educational worldview. He deeply believed that the experience of activism enabled the development of new political knowledge, especially for young people who engaged in conversations with adults and elders in the Black community of Mississippi. As he explained, students who engaged in the work of SNCC, even older students like himself, "found that we are learning and becoming 'qualified' by acting out these things in which we deeply believe." By serving the community, he continued, students discovered "in the process that they are serving themselves in a more complete way than they could have were they to spend four straight years in school."[5] However, he maintained that academic knowledge and formal education, like his graduate study in philosophy, were also vital to the pursuit of truth and justice. Over the course of the 1960s, Moses worried about a central problem within SNCC, which he described as the "conflicts between the college and the movement, the problems of a continuing student leadership and student leaders continuing their education."[6] When debates emerged in SNCC about the need for further education—the same debates that shaped some of the efforts of students at Howard University—Moses also advocated for increasing opportunities for students to take time out of action to engage with formal study.

Moses maintained a connection with the Harvard-Radcliffe campus even as he committed to the civil rights struggle in Mississippi. Early in his efforts in the South, he wrote letters to the *Harvard Crimson* describing the draconian nature of Mississippi's response to SNCC's efforts in the state. He also made several visits to campus.[7] The letters and campus visits served three important purposes. First, Moses hoped that sharing his political experiences in the South would inspire the Harvard-Radcliffe student body to also engage in the movement. Second, he maintained a connection with Harvard because he believed that the institution could provide vital intellectual and academic resources for SNCC's educational programming. Third, Moses recognized that the Harvard-Radcliffe campus could be used as a political resource that put pressure on states in the South. With a predominantly White, elite student body with families who came from positions of power in both finance and government, Harvard was a bastion of power. Likewise, with prominent scholars like Arthur Schlesinger, who had the ear of the Kennedy administration, the Harvard faculty could provide political support for the civil rights struggle in the American South.

Moses helped shape a new political culture on campus that linked education to the civil rights struggle. Inspired by the firsthand experiences of Moses and other young Black students in the South, students at Harvard-Radcliffe organized the Boston Friends of SNCC. Started and expanded by Dorothy Zellner, a White student who worked full-time in SNCC's Cambridge office, the Boston chapter developed the philosophy and fundraising model for other Friends of SNCC chapters across the country. A central approach to fundraising was bringing SNCC field-workers on campus to build awareness about the civil rights struggle in the South. In promoting those campus visits to Harvard-Radcliffe, students underscored that the key leaders of SNCC were also students. "A social revolution is being led by students," the Boston group explained in its program outline for Friends chapters, "and we hope that you, as students, will join us in trying to make democracy a realit[y] in the South."[8]

Like Moses, the Boston Friends chapter also synthesized the political and educational. The organization used fundraising for SNCC as a means for developing a model of political education that would bring about the "formation of a concerned, informed, and active student public, willing to commit itself to continued support of the struggle."[9] The chapters linked fundraising and food drives to the community organizing tradition that emphasized political education and civic participation. "We in the Student Nonviolent Coordinating Committee look on Northern Support as more than fundraising: we want to find a way for concerned individuals and groups outside the South to play a role in creating racial justice in the South," SNCC staff explained to Northern supporters. Zellner underscored that "each fund raising drive should be seen as an educational effort also, for change in the South depends on a climate of opinion all over the country which will cause people to support the movement in the South and demand action from the Federal government."[10]

As Moses envisioned, the Boston chapter also proved essential to providing academic resources to the movement. In 1964, when SNCC expanded its voter registration drives, they turned to the Boston chapter to provide books and other academic resources for "crash education programs" that helped local Black residents pass the literacy test to vote.[11] The book drive was part of SNCC's national recruitment effort for the 1964 Freedom Summer. As SNCC began recruiting volunteers, Moses also sent a letter to the academic community that captured the broader educational vision for the summer. "This letter is being sent to hundreds of faculty members across the country," he explained, "in an effort to involve the intellectual community in America's most serious social problem—racial discrimination." Moses envisioned faculty members providing staff seminars in American history, economics, sociology, and political science for project volunteers while also assisting research volunteers in understanding the ways the tax structure, education system, and welfare programs perpetuated racial inequality. In this way, the Freedom Summer project attempted to redirect the intellectual resources of elite institutions like Harvard-Radcliffe in service to the civil rights struggle while also encouraging faculty to learn directly through the experience. As Moses explained, the project hoped to involve university faculty members, "for we think it is important for the best minds in the country to know first hand what is happening in Mississippi."[12]

Faculty members at Harvard responded to Moses's call by developing an SNCC faculty fund. Prominent members of Harvard's faculty, including Schlesinger, Thomas Pettigrew, and James D. Watson, supported students' engagement in the civil rights struggle, seeing their commitments as part of their intellectual pursuits at Harvard and Radcliffe. Indeed, the goal of the SNCC faculty fund was to not only raise funds for student efforts in the South but also to build collections of resources that they believed would help supplement students' political experiences there. The faculty interpreted their efforts as part of their civic obligations as members of an intellectual community and the core learning goals of the general education curriculum. "As members of the academic community," they wrote, "we have a special concern with realizing in practice, in our country, the philosophical ideals of liberty and democracy that are embodied in the Constitution of the United States."[13]

The Boston Friends of SNCC chapter, the SNCC faculty fund, and the 1964 Freedom Summer encapsulated Moses's vision of utilizing Harvard-Radcliffe to build political awareness among liberal Whites in the North while also drawing upon the educational and intellectual resources of the elite institution. During the 1964 Freedom Summer, fifty-two students from Harvard and Radcliffe volunteered in Mississippi, representing one of the largest collegiate cohorts during the summer. Over the course of the summer, students wrote to their families and published reflections on their experiences in local newspapers and the campus circular. But the impact of SNCC's connection to Harvard-Radcliffe went beyond utilizing local and campus newspapers to build political support in liberal circles in the Northeast. The combination also influenced some students at Harvard-Radcliffe to reconsider the what and how of their education there through their experiences in the South.

Some students who volunteered for the Freedom Summer expressed a similar sentiment to that of Moses about the relationship between formal education and activism. Radcliffe junior Gail Falk volunteered as a Freedom School teacher in Mississippi. Although she served as a teacher, the experience made her skeptical of formal education. Working with Black community leaders and local students, Falk concluded, "I am far from believing that education is a universal panacea, and I have tried to show the kids in my classes that formal education isn't everything. They can do a lot that I can't do." In coming to this conclusion, Falk still maintained the value of formal educational pursuits. Indeed, what she came to realize was that political participation in the civil rights movement and intellectual pursuits at Radcliffe were reciprocal commitments in her development as a citizen. In a letter home, Falk linked the summer's experiences to education, democracy, and citizenship. "Working in Mississippi has given me a clarity about what I want to be learning in college that three years of studying in Widener Library could not give," she explained. "Now that I have helped people understand what it means to be a citizen in a democracy, I know things that I still have to understand. Now that I have worked with people to change the society in which they live, I know what I want to learn about societies and how other people have changed theirs." The Freedom Summer engaged Falk in a model of participatory civics that called into question certain aspects of her formal education at Radcliffe College. Yet, she maintained, Radcliffe College still offered an intellectual and educational resource to help her make sense of her political experiences in Mississippi.[14]

Falk was not alone in seeing civil rights activism and intellectual pursuits at Radcliffe as complementary. Ellen Lake, a fellow student at Radcliffe College, justified to her parents that the reason why she wanted to stay in the South after the summer was to continue her education. She explained in a letter home that she had spent most of her nineteen years "shuttled between Westchester, Martha's Vineyard, the Virgin Islands, summer camp, and Radcliffe," but she had gained a new perspective from Mississippi. Her experiences taught her that education "comes not so much from an evening at Radcliffe library" but rather from talking with a local Mississippian who details the "degradation of having to go to the other side of the bus station to buy a ticket."[15] Reflecting on the political goals of the summer, she argued further, "I have learned more about politics here from running my own precinct meetings than I could have from any Government professor." At the same time, Lake maintained that her academic education was valuable, as she saw the experiences she was having and the formal education at Radcliffe as complementary. "I'm sure that I will appreciate more the academic education which I will resume after the practical one I get here," she concluded in her letter home.[16]

While both Falk and Lake understood their activism in the South as complementary to their academic education, other students saw the two as being at odds. Harvard student Paul Cowan joined the civil rights struggle in 1963, when he worked with a SNCC project in Maryland. Working with the Black community in Chestertown, where he learned about local Black history and its relation to the struggle, Cowan concluded, "That summer I had found the American history I'd been looking for in my college courses."[17] When he returned to the classroom after working in Maryland, "the problems that were so immediate and compelling in Maryland suddenly became abstractions."[18] Cowan further built on this nascent critique of his education at Harvard when he joined the 1964 Freedom Summer. "The abstract questions that had haunted me [at Harvard]," he reflected, "seemed in the midst of the poverty, the energy, the concentrated intelligence that surrounded me now, sheer self-indulgence." In Cowan's view, the problem was that formal education treated political problems as abstract concepts for discussion rather than issues to act upon—an approach that created what he defined as a "lifeless education."[19]

But Cowan clarified his critique. His criticisms, he explained, "were more technical than moral." The role of Schlesinger and others as "scholar-activists in the Kennedy administration" put them in circles of power—a position that Cowan did not necessarily question. Indeed, he believed the connection between intellectual and political life was not itself the problem; rather, the predilection to connect intellectual life to *elite* political life left faculty disconnected from the people most affected by federal policy. Cowan argued that this was the product of how knowledge was produced within the institution. The political theories developed by scholars like Schlesinger and Hartz were "developed in libraries at Harvard" and were "not [based] on anything they had ever experienced." He thus sought an education rooted in "living with its least privileged people" so that he would develop a political sensibility more attuned to those marginalized communities. Even so, Cowan's key words are important to understanding his critique. He believed that such experiences would enable him "to govern them sensibly"—a view that reflected the ways that Cowan critiqued his formal education even as he maintained its design as a particular form of education for elite White students like himself.[20]

Other students likewise critiqued formal education, but unlike Cowan, they sought to challenge the elite class character of formal education at Harvard-Radcliffe. In the early 1960s, Bill Strickland, a Black student at Harvard, took on a prominent role in the civil rights struggle, both in the North and South. He not only joined the Freedom Summer but also played a key role in expanding the Northern Student Movement, an affiliated organization with SNCC. As the project director, Strickland expanded the group's tutorial projects to also include organizing rent strikes and encouraging voter registration. Strickland believed that the organization's narrow focus on academic tutoring assumed that the goal was to merely prepare a student for accessing middle-class life. But, in linking the tutorial to political organizing, he sought to teach both middle-class students who served as tutors and the tutees that notions of failure were just "as often from the inadequacies of the American economic and political system as from personal deficiencies."[21]

Indeed, Strickland aimed to develop a new political model of community education. The goal of the tutoring sessions was to use the question "Why do we need a tutorial?" as a way to discuss social problems within the community. Strickland believed this question enabled the tutees to be the firsthand reporters and the "experts" within the relationship, where the tutees' knowledge exceeded that of the tutors. By framing the sessions as reciprocal, Strickland flipped the student-teacher relationship. He envisioned these micro discussions of community problems as a means to develop new strategies to confront urban poverty and racial discrimination.[22] Rather than promote an education for individual or middle-class benefit, NSM sought to "bend education to the 'other America.'"[23]

The engagement of Harvard-Radcliffe students in the civil rights struggle extended beyond the relationship between formal education and the political experience of activism. It also raised questions about the political role of the institution. Harvard student John Perdew traveled South to support the civil rights struggle there. Participating in a sidewalk demonstration in Americus, Georgia, Perdew was arrested with four other SNCC students. Perdew was charged with a capital offense for what local Mississippi officials deemed an attempt to incite insurrection. The case raised the issue of what Harvard as an institution should do. Students argued that the college had a moral obligation to make a political statement. But Dean John Munro refused to issue a statement on Perdew's case. His reasoning reflected a common institutional logic employed by other academic leaders in the 1960s: he distinguished between the institution and the individual as political actors. Munro argued, "You have to make the distinction between Harvard as an institution and as a group of individuals."[24]

Similar to the argument made by John Hannah at Michigan State, the problem with Munro's stance was that it hid the institution's financial relationship to the structure of Jim Crow in the South. On the heels of the Freedom Summer, Moses sent a letter to the Harvard-Radcliffe community titled "Harvard's Responsibility to Mississippi." In the letter, Moses highlighted the university's holdings in Southern utilities and banks. Harvard was the largest stockholder in Middle South Utilities, which owned the Mississippi Power and Light Company. Through its financial support of these companies, Moses argued, Harvard was also connected to the Mississippi Democratic Party, the White Citizens' Council, and other dominant institutions that reinforced segregation and inequality in Mississippi. Moses believed that Harvard could not "disclaim responsibility for the 'goings on down there'" and hoped that the university would use its economic, social, and political roots in the state to change Mississippi. "But Mississippi is a profitable business enterprise," Moses admitted. "We wonder whether education is only incidental to the Board of Trustees of Harvard University."[25]

Munro's response to the Perdew case fragmented the original vision of Moses's efforts on the Harvard-Radcliffe campus. While drawing a distinction between Harvard-Radcliffe as a political institution and one of individuals, Munro did believe that the student body of Harvard and Radcliffe could support Perdew's case by raising funds. "The main thing to do now is to exercise his legal rights and get him out of jail," he explained. "I think this is a great cause for the Harvard student body to get behind in one way or another." Munro, in other words, deflected the political role of the institution while directing students to fundraise as an appropriate response. Indeed, he saw the Friends of SNCC as the appropriate place for student activism: in the extracurriculum.[26] Munro's reasoning shaped the institutional logic of disciplining democracy at Harvard-Radcliffe. Administrators and faculty affirmatively encouraged and supported students' participation in the civil rights struggle by developing a new E4A program while deflecting criticisms of the institution's role in American political life.

Interning for Citizenship

Radcliffe preisdent Mary Bunting never met Moses. But she was influenced by the atmosphere he helped shape at Harvard-Radcliffe in the 1960s. Bunting interpreted students' experiences in the civil rights movement as "an important dimension of liberal education." Indeed, Falk, Lake, and the cohort of volunteers from Harvard-Radcliffe who participated in the Freedom Summer inspired Bunting to establish E4A. Bunting framed the new program as being akin to the Freedom Summer in the way that the summer project and the civil rights struggle more broadly impacted students, faculty, and administrators. As she noted in her proposal, the program would have an "important influence on other students in their colleges and on faculty and administration as well as on their families and other friends as have so many of our young civil rights workers."[27]

Dennis Huckabay was excited when he learned about E4A. He saw similar elements of his varied political experiences in the E4A program. He organized projects with the American Friends Service Committee that involved students in migrant labor camps, worked with the World University Service, and volunteered as a Freedom Summer teacher in Mississippi. "Universities," he explained to Bunting, "have a way of closing students off from the outside problems. Education for Action is a door to the outside." While he recognized that the E4A program had potential for independent study and enabled students to define service on their terms, he also believed it held political possibilities. "My impression too is that the Education for Action Board is free to offer support to students who might wish to involve themselves in projects which might prove unpopular in some quarters—e.g. providing draft counselling service for ghetto youths (or at least letting them know that there are other ways to get job training besides joining the army), or helping to harvest sugar cane in Cuba—or in Haiti," he wrote to Bunting.[28] To Huckabay, the E4A idea offered an independent educational and activist outlet for students and held the potential to transform an elite institution like Harvard-Radcliffe similar to what Moses envisioned when linking the elite institution to the Freedom Summer.

Huckabay wrote to Bunting in hopes of becoming the director of the program, but he was not hired. This was partly due to the fact that Bunting defined the program differently than Huckabay did. Bunting described the program as a "citizenship internship," but the internship experience of "citizenship" was much more narrowly defined than what Huckabay imagined for E4A. Even as Bunting was inspired by the experiences of students in the civil rights movement, she interpreted the experiences not as a form of political activism but as an expression of volunteerism. What Bunting did in her proposal was make a political choice. She prioritized the type of learning expressed by students like Falk and Lake over the forms of political education envisioned by Cowan and Strickland. Indeed, the focus was on experiential learning over the political critiques of formal education and the institution that emerged out of student experiences in the civil rights struggle. This choice reflected Bunting's particular position—one that was critiqued by students like Cowan—in which she drew on the key ideas from her network within federal policy circles.

Indeed, Bunting's original idea for the E4A first took shape within the Peace Corps–higher education partnership. In the same year that Bunting developed the E4A program, she attended the Returned Peace Corps Volunteer Conference in Washington, DC, a gathering that brought together close to a thousand volunteers with representatives from higher education, business, and the public sector. She also attended a more intimate gathering of select volunteers and university administrators at the Brookings Institution that same year. At both conferences, a primary topic was the relationship between higher education and the Peace Corps. The theme of the Brookings Institution gathering, "The Peace Corps in an Educating Society," focused on three ideas—that "the Peace Corps should see itself as an educational institution"; that "colleges and universities should become more like the Peace Corps"; and that the "relationship between the Peace Corps and American higher education should move from a flirtation or collision to a marriage."[29] Bunting was inspired by the conference, so much so that she embraced the third component—a "marriage" between the Peace Corps and other volunteer programs with Harvard-Radcliffe. Roger Landrum, the Peace Corps volunteer who was trained at Michigan State University and expressed early ideas of service learning, wrote to Bunting about the E4A program. After learning about the effort from his colleagues in the Peace Corps, Landrum wrote, "It is good to see that some of the Brookings and conference of Returnees' thoughts led into this."[30] Susan Bartholomew, a former Peace Corps volunteer who served as part of the first cohort in Ghana, was hired as the director of the E4A program.

Like other university presidents and administrators, Bunting prioritized the way the volunteer experience enhanced students' technical and professional skills. As a trained microbiologist, she interpreted the volunteer experience as being similar to the science laboratory. "As a scientist quite used to giving credit for laboratory," Bunting explained, "credit for the Peace Corps seems to be analogous."[31] Her parallel to the laboratory was significant to her pedagogical and educational worldview. Indeed, Bunting emphasized that it was not just a training program for future volunteer work; rather, it would further enhance academic training. "They [the students] eagerly take advantage of the opportunity to deepen their volunteer experience with relevant academic preparation," Bunting explained, "at the same time making their academic preparation more immediately relevant and exciting." Her idea of E4A promoted experiential learning without the political commitment and broader political goals that initially inspired students at Harvard-Radcliffe. "The hope," Bunting further explained, was "that through summer service many students would discover problems and interests that would resolve their career decisions."[32]

Although operating in conjunction with the Phillips Brooks House (PBH), which had a long history of promoting volunteerism, the E4A program differed from PBH in the view of both Bartholomew and Bunting in terms of academic possibilities. Established in the first part of the twentieth century, the PBH focused on community service; it placed students at settlement houses, financed missionaries to serve in Asia in the first part of the twentieth century, and organized clothing and book drives. The PBH largely operated as an extracurricular program with very little relation to the general curriculum of Harvard and Radcliffe. In contrast, the E4A program was envisioned as an integrated component within the regular curriculum. "E4A offers a unique educational opportunity for students and faculty: they can bring their field experiences—confusing and chaotic as they often are—into the classroom for analysis under seminar conditions," Bunting wrote, "and then take their 'findings' back into the field for testing. The academic and field experiences revitalize each other in an on-going process."[33]

Integrated into the regular undergraduate curriculum, the E4A program represented one of the more radical pedagogical experiments in the Peace Corps–higher education partnership. Bartholomew and Bunting worked with deans and faculty from the School of Public Health and College of Education to identify courses that would supplement the service experience. Dean Theodore Sizer, from the Harvard School of Education, offered academic credit to students involved in community work with E4A. The two-year program consisted of three elements. The first year was a summer of service in VISTA or a related domestic program. After completing their service, students then took a range of seminars related to their service work. In their senior year, the students then did a second summer of service with the Peace Corps. In 1966 and 1967, the program sent students to work with Peace Corps volunteers in Togo, Ethiopia, Venezuela, and the Philippines.[34] E4A also acted as a granting agency. Students could develop their own proposal for some type of social service work in or outside the United States and receive funding from the E4A board made up of students and faculty members.

On paper, the E4A program maintained the political vision of the college articulated by Moses when turning to Harvard-Radcliffe to support the civil rights struggle as well as the tutorial projects promoted by Strickland. One E4A seminar was taught by Tom Wilson, a professor of education. The seminar's topic, "Teaching in Urban Areas," examined how the resources of the university could be used by students working in the community and how faculty could better connect their theories and research to problems in the world. But even as the seminar addressed ways to expand the intellectual resources, the primary focus was on how students learned from the experience over the political goal of such involvement. Indeed, students who participated in E4A opportunities framed their involvement through academic or personal-professional goals, including intellectual exploration, academic interests, and experiences to get into graduate school. After his summer in Togo, Harvard student Alex Hurder noted how he learned more about Africa and the many problems inherent in development work. His experiences also helped him better formulate his senior thesis on African cultures. "What I know of Africa from being there and what I know of it from reading in anthropology, government, French, African, and English African literature," he wrote in his final report, "are different realms of knowledge." He concluded, "Reading can certainly not replace being there." Hurder's report reflected the type of supplemental learning that Bunting envisioned in starting the program.[35]

Indeed, students were encouraged to see the political limitations or constraints of the program, especially in terms of addressing social problems and inequalities, as an element of learning. "At a time when students have been seeking a constructive means to real social change," Bunting explained, "E4A has provided a channel to learn about what is involved in this endeavor." Adopting this view, Maria Montamat, a Radcliffe student and Peace Corps intern in Tunisia, underscored the way she learned over the impact of her work. Since the Peace Corps operated in partnership with the Tunisian government, Montamat was unable to participate in any sort of social action or political work while there. Montamat's work was limited to academic tutoring as defined by the bilateral agreement. Although frustrated by these constraints, she wrote to Bunting that she was "learning a tremendous amount about Tunisia and the problems of a very poor developing country—and most specifically, about the education system, which is a major part of the national effort to modernize."[36]

Even as students adopted the academic learning goals of the program, the political potential of experiential learning was maintained within E4A. Indeed, some students critiqued the underlying assumptions of E4A and their roles in overseas work. In 1969, Kay Kreiss, a student at Radcliffe, worked in Guatemala as part of the San Francisco Miramac, a voluntary medical program. As soon as Kreiss landed in Guatemala, she was immediately troubled. Her service site was a military base. "In the following six weeks spent working in villages and on huge coffee plantations," she wrote, "it became increasingly evident that this organization was being used by the army to do grass-roots public relations and to redirect local farmers away from potential guerilla sympathies." She also noted that the organization was used "by local priests who manipulated some groups of volunteers in an attempt to extend church influence" and by "absentee landlords" who "took credit for the U.S. drug company–donated medicine and volunteer services of doctors and dentists." She linked her experiences to the other work being done through E4A, including tutoring programs and VISTA. Too often, she argued, education and literacy work, whether in the United States or around the world, were "assumed to be a good end in itself. But education is not a neutral force: it is education towards an end, towards certain values and skills."[37]

Kreiss's criticisms provoked a broader discussion among students and supporters about the form and nature of action in the program. Norm Diamond, a graduate student in government at Harvard and program participant, argued that the partnership with the Peace Corps meant that E4A also adopted the agency's political goals, which in his view was nothing but a "liberal form of control that directs change in underdeveloped countries which will not upset the social structure that is favorable to American business interests." Majid Tehransian, an international student from Iran studying at Harvard, disagreed with Diamond's interpretation. He approved of the "idealism of Peace Corps volunteers, of the transfer of technological aid and the educational component of volunteers' experience." Tehransian was more concerned about its affiliation with the US government, arguing, like other former volunteers, for an international version of the Peace Corps. Even as he defended the agency, Tehransian argued that if the goal was social change, one needed to engage in political organizing outside of the Peace Corps. The discussion revealed to students the limitations of only focusing on learning in the context of volunteerism without considering the politics of their engagement.[38]

The discussion and Kreiss's reflections pivoted on two ideas of neutrality associated with Harvard-Radcliffe that students increasingly challenged in the late 1960s. The first was whether a volunteer doing work in the community could ever be a neutral action. Kreiss noted that focusing only on the volunteer work narrowed the type of education into "an interesting personal experience." But she believed that the goal of the program should be an education in social and political activism. The problem, she concluded, was that "the Peace Corps does not seem to represent social service in the sense of social change." She said the student needed to acknowledge the very political salience of their volunteer work. "Social work," she concluded, "is not neutral or apolitical in either its means or effects."[39]

Kreiss's conclusion applied to more than just individual roles in volunteer or community work. It also included one's institutional affiliation. The second critique of neutrality centered on the institutional level. The primary criticism was of the Peace Corps' bilateral agreements and how those agreements shaped the boundaries of a volunteer's role overseas. Kreiss argued that the façade of neutrality of Bilateral agreements also applied to Harvard-Radcliffe. When discussing the relationship between the individual student and the college, she argued that "by being at Harvard, we are perpetuating apartheid in South Africa, and cheap labor in Mississippi where Harvard has extensive investments."[40] The reference to the financial role of Harvard-Radcliffe was important to the broader politics on campus, where students continued to challenge the college for its political role. Harvard-Radcliffe garnered national attention for both its anti-war activism and its efforts to combat the expansion of the campus into communities of color.[41] Kreiss's discussion of the political role of the volunteer thus concerned not only the type of action that Harvard-Radcliffe would support in its curriculum but also the action of elite colleges in American and global politics.

Reorganizing Student Activities

Kreiss's critique of the program's definition of action highlighted the productive tension within E4A. Kreiss at once criticized the narrow emphasis on volunteerism, even as the experience itself helped her experiment and evolve her political ideas in the world. The context of the program also provided further grounds for experimentation to evolve its primary mode of action beyond national and international volunteerism. But Kreiss confronted new institutional realities in the early 1970s. Indeed, as student leaders like Kreiss began to challenge the program's narrow emphasis on social service work, the initial Ford Foundation grant ended. Administrators at both Harvard and Radcliffe had to decide if and how the institution would continue to fund and support the program.

When the status of E4A as an institutional program was first raised, the main issue from the perspective of administrators was program redundancy. Charles P. Whitlock, the dean of Harvard College, interpreted the program as just another PBH. Both involved students in similar volunteer and social service programs, so to him, it made financial sense to consolidate the staff into one center that promoted volunteer service for students at both Harvard and Radcliffe. This view was also reflective of the hierarchy between Harvard and Radcliffe. Harvard deans had more financial and institutional power over programming than their counterparts at Radcliffe. In the context of E4A, where discussions critiqued social service efforts like those in PBH and connected social activism to formal education, student leaders worried that the program mission would be lost in the consolidation. Terry Rockefeller, a student at Radcliffe and member of the E4A board, argued that consolidating the two "would cause not only a loss of identity and individuality to E4A as a program, but also threaten its existence completely."[42]

In response to a student meeting where E4A students raised their concerns about the effort to consolidate, Harvard and Radcliffe administrators evolved their reasoning. Whitlock still maintained that the program could not be institutionally supported due to financial constraints. Whitlock's reasoning adopted the structure of the institution. Because the E4A program did not fit under a broader umbrella within the colleges, he argued that the program was not a traditional discipline that could be supported by the institutions. At the same time, he believed that the program was not a traditional student activity either. Whitlock and John Thomas Dunlop, the dean of the Faculty of Arts and Sciences, prioritized funding for what they defined as traditional student activities, including athletics, debate team, music, and drama. This was part of renaming the student center, where E4A was located, the Student Activities Center. In Dunlop's view, the issue was that E4A's philosophy of education—which combined formal education with volunteerism—did not fit within the institutional schema that maintained a sharp division between the curriculum and extracurriculum. Within this context, Dunlop encouraged students to embrace financial separation from Harvard-Radcliffe as a practical solution. While he recognized that, philosophically, it would have less of an impact on the core curriculum scheme as it was initially envisioned, he believed it would provide more programmatic and practical flexibility.

Indeed, at the core of efforts to consolidate the E4A program was a deeper division about the direction of elite education at Harvard-Radcliffe. Students interpreted the funding cuts and renaming as narrowing the meaning of student action—and, by extension, one's education. As E4A board member Laurie Oliver noted, "while the name Student Center maintians [sic] an open-endedness of possibilities for use of facilities and program, of ideology and meaning, the word activities connotes to me something on the order of fun and games, busy work of the sort that concerned our high school student councils, something very safe and restricted."[43] For students like Oliver, social action was more than a safe extracurricular activity. Rather, she argued, the various efforts of E4A were a fundamental part of education and the development of political awareness. In contrast, Whitlock and Dunlop interpreted such activities as supplemental experiences that were part of personal growth. Both had adopted the view of Derek Bok, the new president of Harvard in 1971. Professor David Riesman, a supporter of the Peace Corps and E4A, met with Bok in hopes that Harvard-Radcliffe would join the University Year of Action, but, as Riesman concluded, "Bok expressed reluctance to give academic credit [to community service], feeling although it may be valid for low income students, it certainly wasn't necessary for Harvard students."[44] Although supportive of community involvement and service among students, Bok believed such activities had very little relation to academic coursework or the perceived intellectual rigor of the Harvard curriculum. He believed it was only a concern for a select group of students rather than the student body as a whole.

Given the limited choice and support from the institution, E4A lived on but became an independent organization in the 1970s that was associated with Harvard-Radcliffe in name only. The change had a twofold effect on programming.[45] The shift disconnected the E4A program from the regular curriculum of the university. In the 1970s, students saw the program as a resource for finding opportunities and engaging with nonprofit and related organizations. As Connie Kreiss believed, E4A had a "dual front," serving "as a clearinghouse for ideas, projects, and people concerned with social change, and it served as a source of grants for students who need money in order to carry out projects."[46] At the same time that the program was marginalized to student affairs, it began focusing on more activist-oriented work in the community, as envisioned by earlier students. In 1971, the members of the E4A board expanded the mission of program. As board members explained in the new interpretation of the program and its history, "Begun originally as a social service program, the students increasingly defined our function in terms of social action. Our concern with social imbalances and injustices has led us to try to get at the structural roots of problems rather than merely provide temporary and superficial solutions to comprehensive problems."[47]

The program's activist mission reflected the backgrounds of those students who participated in the programs. In the 1970s, women and minority students oversaw the grant-making process of the program and the rearticulation of its mission, and many saw the program as an extension of the Feminist Movement and the Welfare Rights Movement, respectively.[48] While maintaining that students learned from community work, the new mission shifted the learning away from academic goals to what students believed was the more important process of "political development."[49] As Rockefeller explained, the center allowed students to build "a loose network of people engaged in various aspects of social change" and provided a space "through which people can share experiences, knowledge, and information."[50] Indeed, Shepherd Bliss, the new director of the program in the 1970s, was a staunch supporter of the dual mission as articulated by students. A trained minister, Bliss was actively involved in the anti-war movement in the 1960s, believing deeply that community work must be linked to broader efforts of social and political activism that challenged policy and institutional structures. At the same time, Bliss understood his task was to help guide the students into appropriate avenues for effective forms of social activism. Bliss believed the program provided "an ideal structure for many individuals—particularly women, minority students and others concerned with the shortcomings of our society—to work through and share ideas about these questions in a disciplined way and discover appropriate expressions and channels for their concerns."[51] In the 1970s, E4A efforts focused more on issue-based activism, including union organizing for waitresses in Boston, community organizing in Arkansas, organizing for tenants in Cambridge, and welfare advocacy.

A dichotomy reemerged between formal education and action that Bunting had hoped to reconcile when she started the program in the mid-1960s. Indeed, student participants in the 1970s contrasted the work and philosophy of the program with the regular curriculum. The program provided a resource and outlet missing in formal education, even if the opportunity was not integrated into coursework. As Dewey Hickman, an African American student at Harvard, explained, "A great many people here have had to take time off from school to satisfy their social consciences, when they shouldn't have had to." Indeed, Hickman recycled a view first expressed by Freedom Summer volunteers. "Sometimes you just can't stay in school and work on something you believe in," he argued. In the E4A, "we are trying to help those people keep from breaking up their education."[52] Hickman also believed E4A represented an important resource on campus that engaged students, as Bliss believed, in more disciplined forms of social activism. "We have been ready to help those that are ready to be helped, but we've never tried to force people," he explained. Through seminars, workshops, and reporting on their work in the community, E4A was more effective in raising political awareness, Hickman argued, noting, "we shouldn't have to take over some building before people stop and learn about a travesty."[53]

Fellow E4A member Rob Gips likewise interpreted the program as separate from the college's education. In 1974, E4A members implemented the East Boston's People's Rights Group, a project that not only demonstrated the program's issue-based form of activism but also further reflected the divergence of political action from the regular curriculum. The group's goal was to develop a recipient-run welfare advocacy project. The students worked with local citizens and others in the community organizing ethos of the Welfare Rights Movement, focusing on problems related to unemployment, medical care, housing, and schooling. By 1975, the center was run and directed by local residents and was financially independent. The university administration highlighted the effort, interpreting the project as a reflection of the ways the institution enabled students to learn through political involvement in the world. Gips was not impressed with the report and the institution's statement of support. In an editorial for the *Harvard Crimson*, he clarified the project's purpose and the role of the students. "While we did want to 'balance our Harvard view with reality,'" he wrote, "the main reason most of us became involved in welfare rights is our commitment to working toward a more just and egalitarian society."[54]

While appreciating such efforts, Eddie Quiñonez, another student board member, interpreted E4A's place on campus in the 1970s differently than both Hickman and Gips. He felt "alienated" by his "education" because it was disconnected from the concerns of his community. Quiñonez also believed his academic education taught the wrong lesson. "We find ourselves in an individual environment with little group experience, a great deal of competition and little community," he explained.[55] Working in the program allowed him to integrate his education with experience and community and political commitment. But he was also skeptical of its place in relation to Harvard-Radcliffe. Drawing on the history of activism in the 1960s, Quiñonez rightly noted that "E4A was created in '66 at a particular point in history when there was a large mass movement" and that "E4A was the result of this uprising." While acknowledging how E4A represented a legitimate institutional response to the movements of the 1960s, he wondered, especially as a student activist in the late 1970s, whether it was used more as a way to pacify student activists and direct their activism away from institutional involvement, education, and scholarly practices.[56]

Programs like E4A had a two-tiered effect on student activism. At Harvard and Radcliffe, the E4A program became an important resource for students interested in political and social action throughout the 1970s. In the E4A, students developed models of activism that, for Bliss and university administrators, were disciplined and focused and, for students, balanced their own political education with community empowerment. However, the efforts of E4A were largely marginalized to student affairs and disconnected from the regular curriculum, institutional funding, and student life more generally. The result was an activist clearinghouse that allowed students to get involved and take political stances in the world, but those activities had no relation to either the general patterns of the education or what Moses highlighted on the heels of the Freedom Summer.

The evolution of E4A and its position at Radcliffe and Harvard made clear that political activism as a moral commitment was an extracurricular activity that fell outside the institutions' intellectual pursuits and could not challenge the financial priorities of the board of trustees. The reasoning used by administrators provided political flexibility for the program, enabling students to engage more freely—and independently—in political action. But the flexibility rested upon a logic that reflected the pedagogical ideology of Harvard-Radcliffe. In light of the commitment to neutrality and disinterested judgment, administrators recategorized the program as an extracurricular activity unrelated to the regular curriculum and disconnected from the institutional mission.

Legacy

In her report to the Ford Foundation, Bunting expressed enthusiasm for E4A's potential. The concept of E4A, she explained, "has been useful and educational within Radcliffe and Harvard, and also beyond Cambridge." Indeed, she further noted, the E4A program garnered academic and political interest beyond Harvard-Radcliffe. Academic leaders increasingly reached out about the program after it was highlighted in the 1966 International Education Act and Nixon's Commission on Campus Unrest in 1970. In the Nixon report, the committee members noted that the E4A program represented "a model of student-community involvement" that could be replicated across American higher education.[57]

But as a model for other institutions, E4A as an integrated program in the curriculum was short-lived. Between 1966 and 1970, administrators like Bunting developed an experimental action program embedded within the regular curriculum that allowed students to take a course of study tied to international and domestic volunteer experiences. Even as students critiqued the limitations of the program's primary mode of action, they embraced its core mission to expand and reconstruct elite formal education at Harvard-Radcliffe. By the early 1970s, that program was not only disconnected from the curriculum, it was disassociated from the university as a financially sponsored program. On paper, the decision to do so was strictly financial. In the early 1970s, Harvard-Radcliffe administrators like Dunlop interpreted the program as a redundant opportunity with the presence of the Phillips Brooks House. Administrators deemed other, more traditional student activities to be those deserving of financial support.

The financial justification entailed more than just practical considerations; it also reflected a set of value judgments that were embedded in the program's founding and early history. When Bunting turned to volunteerism over other modes of political activism, she embraced an implicit—but strong—pedagogical belief that the university, like the curriculum, should be politically neutral. As students pointed out in the late 1960s, international and domestic volunteerism was no less politically neutral than other modes of political activism. Indeed, the critique of the program's primary mode of action echoed early criticisms of institutional neutrality: Harvard-Radcliffe was taking a political side in the civil rights struggle through its financial holdings. Disconnecting E4A from the regular curriculum revealed a particular pedagogical view about the relationship between action and education at Harvard-Radcliffe. A program of action could be a part of the curriculum if the primary focus was volunteerism or social service. If students wanted a mode of action that was political, the program could neither be integrated into the curriculum nor financially funded by the institution. The conditions of the program's transformation reflected the ways Harvard-Radcliffe promoted action insofar that it did not reveal the underlying politics of the institution. The process of disciplining democracy at Harvard-Radcliffe thus took the form of a financial decision that masked the institutions' own politics and values.

CHAPTER 5

Stanford University

Pursuing Objectivity

When Stanford University was established in the late nineteenth century, the first president and the board of trustees could not agree on the guiding motto of the educational mission. President David Starr Jordan called for the phrase *Die Luft der Freiheit weht*, which is often translated as "the winds of freedom blow." Jordan had taken the phrase from the German humanist and revolutionary Ulrich von Hutten, who famously defended Martin Luther's challenge to the Catholic Church. The phrase suggested a vision of the university as a space of open inquiry where students, faculty, and academic leaders had the autonomy to challenge prevailing political and cultural ideas. George E. Crothers, the board secretary, favored the motto *Truth and Service*.[1] He believed it better reflected the goals of the university. Indeed, Crothers objected to the German motto *Die Luft der Freiheit weht*, worrying that it would imply a degree of freedom not traditionally found in American universities, "both on the part of the student and the professor."[2] Initially, Crothers's motto won out—but only temporarily. By the mid-twentieth century, Stanford University embraced Jordan's phrase as its guiding principle.

The controversy surrounding the motto did not end there. Indeed, throughout Stanford's institutional history, the two mottos served as point and counterpoint between student, faculty, and administration when it came to the university's educational and social mission in the world. In the 1970s and 1980s, the competing visions signified different standpoints on the most prominent political issue on American college campuses: the anti-apartheid divestment movement. In putting pressure on the university administration and board of trustees, student activists at Stanford argued that the university should divest from holdings in companies that worked in South Africa because its role was to set a moral example for American society. On one level, the argument was a direct expression of the *Die Luft der Freiheit weht* mission. The university as a source of open inquiry should challenge prevailing policy—such as investment policy—that limited individual freedom. On another level, their argument took on elements of *Truth and Service*, as students asserted that the university's service was to the people of South Africa rather than American corporate interests there.

The administration argued that the university did not have the political or financial freedom to support divestment. This stance reflected the limits of the university as a space for free inquiry or Stanford's guiding motto. What emerged among students and Stanford officials concerned the perceived public role of the university that mapped onto the competing definitions of its original mission and motto of *Truth and Service*. Student activists understood their campus anti-apartheid activism as an extension of the university's service mission. Officials at Stanford believed such actions were outside the university, and, like their counterparts in the 1960s, they promoted volunteerism as the appropriate mode of service, recycling disciplining democracy as the primary logic in response to student challenges to the university's political role in society.

Stanford officials also extended the epistemological side of disciplining. Indeed, a secondary debate centered around the university's modern research mission or pursuit of "truth." Research was central to a student's education, especially in terms of cultivating the requisite attributes of modern citizenship. However, when students employed the research skills they had learned in the classroom to challenge the university—in particular, the university's investments in South Africa—the Stanford administration became less committed to the research mission. The campus movement revealed the inherent tension within the political logic of the university's pursuit of truth. The university supported student research and civic engagement, but only if the focus of both did not concern the university or the financial interests it depended upon.

Resurrecting Institutional Programs

In late spring 1977, Keith Archuletta and Chris Coleman participated in a sit-in at the Old Union Station of Stanford University. The purpose of the sit-in was to call attention to and protest Stanford's investment policy in apartheid South Africa. They were not alone. Throughout the day, over nine hundred students rallied at White Plaza. During the sit-in, Archuletta and Coleman were joined by 293 other Stanford students, all of whom were later arrested.[3] The sit-in was the culmination of a multiyear organizing process around divestment, a process that had generated broad support within the Stanford community. Coleman and Archuletta collected over three thousand student signatures, eighty faculty signatures, and backing from twenty campus groups, including the United Stanford Employees labor union, the Stanford Church, the YWCA, the *Stanford Daily*, and the student government.[4]

While the anti-apartheid movement served as the political inspiration for the actions of Archuletta and Coleman, the planning, organizing, and research for the demonstration was a direct product of the programs that grew out of student activism at Stanford in the 1960s. In drawing on institutionally sponsored programs, the anti-apartheid movement at Stanford resurrected an older dilemma that emerged on campus from the 1960s: the end goal of student-led education and research.

The first institutional hub of the divestment movement at Stanford was the Black Activities Center. Originally called the Black Student Volunteer Center, the center grew out of Black student demands in 1969 for an institutional home to support political action within the Black communities adjacent to campus. Indeed, in its formative years, the center operated under the theme *Hudumu Na Ujamaa*, a Swahili phrase that translates as "Service to the Community." By the mid-1970s, however, the center's original mission was replaced by a cultural focus, one captured by the center's name change to the Black Activities Center. The shift was rooted in the changing politics of Black students who focused on the cultural basis of Black Power combined with institutional policy changes that limited the type and form of political action within the community. When Archuletta enrolled at Stanford, he turned to the center, only to be dismayed by the lack of political commitment among his Black peers, especially those students within the communities near Stanford's campus. Archuletta resurrected the original mission of the center by linking the center's founding to the campus divestment movement. When he became the coordinator of the center after graduation, he renamed it the Black Community Service Center. In doing so, he reconnected the center to activism in the community. Research and education, Archuletta believed, "was not just in the classroom, but also engagement in the community."[5]

The second institutional hub was the Columbae House. The Columbae House was established in 1969 by David Josephson and other Stanford students who organized the April 3rd Movement (A3M), a coalition that

demanded an end to secret military research on campus. Set up as a cooperative house, it embraced a mission focused on social change through nonviolent action. The house also reflected the goal of the anti-war movement in
the 1960s: to create an institutional space for students to align their political
belief systems with both their educational and residential experience. One of
the central concerns of students within the A3M was how a student's education at Stanford was bound up with the violence of the Vietnam War through
the university's research.[6] When Coleman joined the Columbae House in the
mid-1970s, he sought to expand its mission by focusing on another moral
issue on campus: university investments in apartheid South Africa.

To expand the political mission of each program, Archuletta and Coleman drew on another institutional legacy from the 1960s: the Stanford
Workshop on Political and Social Issues (SWOPSI). The SWOPSI was first
organized by Stanford students in fall 1969 with the goal of reorienting the
general education curriculum. As students explained in their first series of
workshops in the late 1960s, "SWOPSI is a student-initiated and student-
led program to direct Stanford's curriculum to urgent social and political
problems." Like other programs that emerged on college campuses in the
late 1960s, the SWOPSI course had an explicit focus on translating ideas into
political action. The goal of the workshop, the students continued, was to
"seek ways of implementing proposed solutions through community education and political and social action."[7]

In his SWOPSI course, Archuletta facilitated a seminar titled "Black Leadership." The political meaning of the anti-apartheid struggle connected
closely with Archuletta's upbringing in the United States. Archuletta had a
mixed racial background: his mother was Latina, and his father was African
American. Although he was part of the first generation of Black students to
attend integrated public schools, Archuletta confronted the cultural legacy
of Jim Crow in his day-to-day encounters with local Whites. In Archuletta's
view, the divestment movement was an extension of the ongoing Black Freedom Struggle in the United States. The topical focus was key to his interpretation of the anti-apartheid movement. The seminar included student activists from the 1960s, such as Huey Newton and representatives from Stokely
Carmichael's All African People's Revolutionary Party. Archuletta combined
his SWOPSI experience with his work at the Black Community Service Center, linking the divestment movement in the 1980s to the political lessons
of the 1960s and their institutional legacies in ways that sought to connect
formal education to community activism. In the SWOPSI class, Archuletta
encouraged students to link the divestment struggle on campus to issues in
East Palo Alto, a predominantly African American community.

Like Archuletta in the Black Community Service Center, Coleman connected the Columbae House to a SWOPSI course that focused on the university's financial connections to apartheid South Africa. The product of Coleman's course was a position paper on Stanford University's investments in corporations operating in South Africa. The position paper reflected the ways that student activists at Stanford drew on not only institutional programs but also their formal educational training to support the campus divestment movement.

The purpose of the position paper, written in memory of Steve Biko, the renowned student activist who was killed by the South African government in 1977, was to challenge the "progressive force" argument about apartheid. This argument assumed that economic growth and American investment would undermine apartheid over time. Using evidence from United Nations and corporate documentation as well as scholarly works on the subject of the South African economy, the students argued that, rather than undermining apartheid, American investments in South Africa modernized apartheid as a political and economic system. They argued that the investments, which included Stanford's 1.6 million shares of stocks in companies that worked in South Africa—valued at $72.2 million—enabled the South African government to increase its wealth while regulating the labor and civil rights of Black citizens. The position paper demonstrated the hallmarks of research and education in the modern university. Students analyzed the sources and detected the underlying flaws of prevailing policy around South African investments.[8]

Despite these varied efforts from 1977 to 1980, university administrators and the board of trustees abstained from voting on investment policies. They recycled a familiar argument—they interpreted divestment as a political position that the university could not take. That university leaders had employed a similar argument in the 1960s was not a surprise. Richard Lyman, the president of Stanford in 1977, was the provost and president in the late 1960s, when Stanford came under fire by student activists for the university's research involvement in the Vietnam War. In response to the sit-in and the calls for an active role in investments concerning South Africa, Lyman argued that taking a political stand via investment was a "very risky matter for a university to become involved as a political spokesman on issues outside the institution" and that doing so would undermine the university as a space for free inquiry.[9]

In another parallel from the 1960s, student activists argued that the issue with this argument was that the claim to institutional neutrality masked the university's political position via investment. Indeed, the primary goal of student anti-apartheid activists in the late 1970s was for the university to live up to its stated mission of free inquiry. The focus of activists in the late 1970s was to push university officials and the board of trustees to take an active role in investment, develop a commission on investments with power that represented the different constituencies of the Stanford community, and compile a report that analyzed the costs and benefits of full divestment. In a letter to university officials, student organizers argued that refraining from debating investment policy was "morally and logically inconsistent." "The purposes of the institution," the students wrote, "are made hypocritical if the institution participates as a corporate shareholder in exploitation, illegal activities or other practices repugnant to the moral sense of the community."[10]

In both ways, the anti-apartheid movement resurrected the tension that initially emerged within SWOPSI courses and the university's research and education mission more broadly in the late 1960s. When the SWOPSI courses were first developed, the question of "action" was on the minds of students, professors, and administrators. Student director Nick Corff recognized that political action was a natural outgrowth of SWOPSI courses. Employing a logic similar to that of university presidents in the 1960s, Corff argued that whatever action was taken based on a SWOPSI course was an individual, rather than an institutional, effort. David Albernathy, a political science professor who also served on the policy board, held a different view on the relationship between research and action in SWOPSI courses. He distinguished between "proposing solutions, which should be a part of a SWOPSI," and political action, which should not be, even if he recognized "that might be a logical result."[11]

A similar dynamic thus arose in the late 1970s. The SWOPSI course on South Africa and its relationship to student activism on campus reflected what students of the 1960s envisioned in attempting to connect formal education to social and political concerns. The courses focused on a relevant political issue while providing students a set of intellectual tools and political strategies to address the issue at the institutional level. The problem, however, arose when students not only translated their research into social action on campus in the form of the sit-in but demanded the institution to similarly act based on the research findings.

Even if university administrators and students recycled familiar arguments and highlighted unresolved tensions, the institutional context was different at Stanford in the 1980s. University administrators did not simply rely on the claim of institutional neutrality. Lyman acknowledged that what the university confronted was central to its mission. He agreed with anti-apartheid activists that the university's policies regarding "educational and internal matters ought to be ethically well determined."[12] The ad hoc faculty committee on investment policy—a committee led by Albernathy—also highlighted this dilemma. While the primary fiduciary policy of the board of trustees was to ensure financial solvency and return on the endowment, Albernathy wrote, they also needed to consider the nature of the investment policy if it were to cause social injury.[13] Both views were captured by Rodney Adams, Stanford's director of finance. "A basic tenet of educational institutions is that there be freedom to express divergent views," he explained. But he also acknowledged that "the institution is expected, at times, to take a firm unilateral position on a particular societal issue." In the case of investment in South Africa, Adams concluded, the university confronted "a paradox that must be resolved."[14]

The paradox went to the heart of existing institutional programs and a student's formal education at Stanford. In three different programmatic contexts—the Black Community Service Center, the Columbae House, and the SWOPSI course—Stanford University provided institutional support and equipped students with tools of analysis to critically examine the question of investments in apartheid South Africa. This enabled students to reconstruct a dormant political culture that linked activism to one's formal education—only to confront an institutional culture that set limits on the application of the knowledge gained from their education and the programs that supported their activism. Indeed, the divestment movement at Stanford resurrected the political implications of and tensions within the university's culture of disciplining democracy. Influenced by the market logic taking shape in the modern American university in the 1980s, students, faculty, and administrators confronted how to ethically reconcile the educational and research goal of the university with an endowment policy that was vital to providing the very financial resources for an elite education at Stanford.

Debating the Morality of Educational Investment

When Mark Funk joined the 1977 spring sit-in, he was understandably nervous. Facing a large police force, Funk thought about the prospect of suspension. Even worse, he reflected, the possibility of arrest seemed "most unpalatable," given what it might mean for his job prospects. Despite these reservations, he stayed and was later arrested.[15] He believed that the commitment to the sit-in was vital to ensuring that his education was morally consistent. Indeed, the anti-apartheid movement at Stanford resurrected debates about the goal of an elite education. By sitting in, Funk grappled with his higher education pursuits at Stanford. In graduating from Stanford, Funk received what the market economy defined as an elite education that opened up new professional opportunities, even in a tightening job market. Yet, as Funk sat in the paddy wagon sent by university officials, he also recognized the failure of the university to take a moral stand against apartheid. Funk confronted what he and others of his cohort at Stanford interpreted as the moral costs of an elite education.

Although students embraced a moral argument about the university, the idea of moral concern took on different political meanings among student activists, illuminating a range of critiques that concerned not only the institution's role but a student's education within it. Indeed, the focus on institutional investment pivoted on divergent meanings of appropriate actions that also influenced how students interpreted the moral contours of their elite education at Stanford. The differences were represented by the varied organizations and backgrounds of students that made up the two key student groups in the 1980s: the Coalition Against Apartheid and Stanford Out of South Africa (SOSA). Both organizations brought together students from the Black Student Union, Asian American Students Association, and the African Student Association.

International students at Stanford, especially those from different countries in Africa, confronted the very political nature of education within the exchange programs that brought them to the university. A key organizer of the Coalition Against Apartheid was Vasavan Samuel, an Indian and South African law student and the treasurer of the African Students Association at Stanford University. Samuel was also a chair of a student council that represented close to five hundred South Africans who studied in the United States. Samuel attended Stanford as a participant in the South Africa Education Program—an opportunity that exemplified the political tension within his educational experiences. The target of student protests on American campuses like Stanford was the university investments in companies such as Exxon, Chase Bank, and IBM—the same corporate sponsors of the South Africa Education Program. At Stanford, Samuel worked with students from Kenya, Tanzania, and other parts of Africa in calling for university divestment, and all of them recognized that their presence at Stanford was a product of a global financial system that benefited from exploitation in South Africa.[16]

Students in the African Students Association interpreted the moral contours of the divestment movement as a material and structural legacy of colonialism. As Wunyabari Maloba, a Kenyan student at Stanford and a member of the African Students Association, explained, "foreign investment means the black man is being exploited. The economic position of the black man has not improved because of foreign investment."[17] For students like

Maloba, divestment was the best tool to challenge both apartheid South Africa and broader economic relations between Western countries and the continent of Africa. Indeed, students like Samuel, Maloba, and others who participated in the coalition through the African Students Association connected the divestment movement to the longer history and struggle against colonialism in Africa. In a statement written by the Stanford African Students Association, student members supported calls for complete divestment from South Africa, seeing it as the best means to challenge apartheid, or what they defined as the last "stubborn vestige of colonialism." "We consider the processes of colonization, of which apartheid is one particularly sinister form," they wrote, "to be immoral systems for the deliberate and systematic exploitation of human beings by other human beings for the greed of unbridled economic gain."[18]

The interpretation of institutional investment as but an extension of colonialism informed how students like Maloba interpreted their education at Stanford. Indeed, students connected US foreign policy and colonialism to Stanford's education and research. Two graduate students from Africa and members of the coalition—Charles N'Cho-Obuie and Mwesiga Baregu—argued that most "Africanist" scholarly work at Stanford and in particular the Hoover Institution reflected the ideological stance of the United States. Africanist scholars at Stanford supported investment policy, taking the "progressive force" position by arguing that the policy improved the economic lives of Black citizens in South Africa. N'Cho-Obuie and Baregu believed that the consensus among scholars at Stanford concerning South Africa did not provide students with a different political frame of reference. In their view, research on South Africa at Stanford largely assumed American foreign policy interests. "We consider it a fallacy and a deliberate obfuscation of the facts to suggest that disinvestment will hurt the colonized Africans more than the colonizing Europeans," they wrote. "We find the suggestion itself more painful than the purported actuality. Foreign investment aids all Europeans and a pitiably tiny minority of Africans."[19]

A moral education, Maloba, N'Cho-Obuie, and Baregu ultimately argued, required a commitment to anti-colonialism. The problem, however, was that students could not develop a moral commitment to anti-colonialism if what they learned merely echoed the prevailing policy of the country. In critiquing Africanist research at the Hoover Institution, they synthesized the anti-colonial goals of the divestment movement with the stated role of the university as a space for both free inquiry and civic development. Divestment, they argued, was central to the "decolonization process" and thus was important for all institutions, "especially those with a presumed and profoundly moral character or mission such as civic structures and universities of higher learning."[20]

While students like Maloba, N'Cho-Obuie, and Baregu critiqued the content of their education to make arguments about the moral role of the university and the need to divest, others connected the argument directly to what they learned in the classroom. Indeed, some students believed that the content of their education in the classroom taught a set of moral lessons that required them to demand the university to divest. Stanford student Jon Adelstein drew a direct parallel between what was expected of him as a student at Stanford to the role of the institution. He explained, "Stanford expects its students to observe the highest ethical and moral standards" based on what they learn in their classes, so "Stanford students expect the board of trustees to abide by exactly these same standards."[21] Phillip J. Ivanhoe, a PhD student in Chinese philosophy, also cited his coursework as a key factor in the evolution of his political views concerning the university investments and South Africa. At Stanford, he studied Chinese moral philosophy, an intellectual framework that led him to conclude what he perceived to be "the university's moral failure on the issue of divestment." He saw the university as a "force for good" but was "saddened to see it involved in a grave injustice" by maintaining investments in South Africa.[22] What both Adelstein and Ivanhoe confronted was the disconnect between the stated goal of their formal education as a source of moral and ethical development and an institutional context that seemed to disregard moral and ethical considerations.

Indeed, this dynamic was central to the experiences of Bill Cohn, a member of SOSA and the coalition. Like Adelstein and Ivanhoe, he linked the divestment movement to what he learned at Stanford while also confronting the institutional limits of applying what he learned. From July to November 1984, Cohn traveled throughout South Africa after receiving a grant from Stanford's International Relations Department. Cohn explained that his study-abroad trip gave him "a much clearer understanding of the realities and dynamics of social change in South Africa."[23] Like the SWOPSI course and earlier efforts at Stanford, Cohn's experiences demonstrated the embedded tensions of students' education in the 1980s. The university enabled him to develop a sophisticated understanding of South Africa and the political situation through direct experience, which he used to justify his activism and call for divestment. At the same time that the university facilitated his intellectual and political growth, it set limits on what he believed was the morally correct way to bring about change in South Africa. For Adelstein, Ivanhoe, and Cohn, divestment was a means to align the university's investments with the ethical lessons of their courses and programs.

Students within the Black Student Union negotiated and adopted both structural and educational arguments for divestment. While positioning the university as a central institution that could address social and racial injustice in the United States and around the world, they also questioned the content of their education like their international counterparts. A key leader in the Black Student Union and the anti-apartheid effort at Stanford in the 1980s was Amanda Kemp. Her identity and experiences as a student reflected the tensions within the movement and the university. Originally from Biloxi, Mississippi, Kemp felt insecure upon her arrival at Stanford. After attending an elite, predominantly White private institution, Kemp experienced the same doubts that other Black students reported concerning their identity, community, and education. "There's a contradiction (in my life)," Kemp explained. "I'm poor and come from the inner city—that's one part of me. But I did attend that elite school for four years and it was the most stable time of my life." She worried that at the same time her education at Stanford opened up new opportunities, the institution itself disconnected her from the political concerns of the Black community. "I have always felt a responsibility, an obligation and a link to the black community," Kemp said, but she feared her elite education at Stanford made many Black community members skeptical of her work and involvement in the community.[24]

Stanford University and in particular the Black Community Service Center provided an intellectual and political space for Kemp to reconcile the tensions within her educational journey. As the assistant director of the Black Community Service Center, she worked with Archuletta, who helped spark the divestment movement at Stanford in the late 1970s. Within that intuitional space, Kemp became one of the founding members of SOSA, an offshoot of the Coalition Against Apartheid. Kemp believed that her efforts in the Black Student Union and the Black Community Service Center were the "most valuable part of my education," as her participation allowed her to engage with issues relevant to her personal identity and develop friendships rooted in social and political efforts.

While Kemp navigated the possibilities and limitations of her education at Stanford, she believed deeply that another avenue for reconciling the competing impulses of her education was for the institution to take a political stand and divest. Kemp believed that when confronted by the situation in South Africa, one had a moral obligation to take a stand. She challenged the idea of institutional neutrality, arguing, "The bottom line is that there's a struggle going on. By not taking a stand, you are taking a stand. You're on the side that's not making it better, but making it worse." In the context of SOSA and the Black Community Service Center, she worked with Steve Phillips to expand on the moral and political implications of one's education if Stanford did not take a clear political position on investment policy in South Africa. "It is wrong to reap profits from a system that brutally represses and exploits the great majority of its population," they argued. "An education funded by this kind of 'blood money' is immoral; the buildings, books and faculty of Stanford University should not be built upon the bent backs of Black South Africans." Like their counterparts in the African Student Association, Kemp and Phillips argued that the university had a unique role to play in society, especially in relation to moral issues like apartheid. "The university should assume a role of moral leadership," SOSA activists wrote, "sending a message to other institutions and individuals that any sort of support for apartheid is unacceptable."[25]

Drawing on the lessons and efforts of students that came before them, particularly Archuletta and Coleman, Kemp and Phillips also held regular forums and produced research with students in the African Students Association on the effects of apartheid on Black life in South Africa. They also helped organize the National Anti-Apartheid Day at Stanford in the spring of 1985, bringing over a thousand students onto Stanford's main quad to demand for divestment. How new Stanford President Donald Kennedy responded to the campus-wide protest and efforts to reconcile different conceptions of moral education reflected the ways university leaders not only recycled but expanded disciplining democracy as an institutional logic to mitigate students' broader political visions of the university as a political actor.

Reconciling Moral Action

At the height of the anti-apartheid movement at Stanford, Kennedy met with students from SOSA. As a former student activist in the 1950s who challenged anti-Communist purges on college campuses, Kennedy recognized the importance of civil disobedience as a key element of democratic citizenship. He also agreed, at least in principle, that active citizenship included a combination of activism, service, and intellectual commitment. He disagreed with students as to what the university as an institutional actor could support. In Kennedy's view, the link between university investments and apartheid South Africa seemed tangential at best. Kennedy supported the Sullivan principles. In this way, Kennedy and the Stanford Board of Trustees largely adopted Ronald Reagan's policy of "constructive engagement." As he explained in his public statement in the fall of 1985, "Divestment by non-profit organizations will reduce the influence of those organizations most likely to exercise it in favor of the goal of ending apartheid."[26]

Kennedy, however, learned that the Sullivan principles and the idea of "constructive engagement" were also politically limited as a policy solution. In the late summer of 1985, a couple months after the National Anti-Apartheid Day rally at Stanford, Kennedy met with representatives from the Carnation Company, Ford Motor, Southern Cal Edison, Chevron, Amdahl, General Motors, and other companies that worked in South Africa. During the meeting, Kennedy explored the effects of American corporate roles and the Sullivan principles. He learned that most representatives took the stance that the companies were strictly in South Africa to do business. John Young, the CEO of Hewlett Packard and a Stanford Board of Trustees member, explained, "businesses provide jobs, products and services. We are not an agent for fundamental change. There are limits on what can be expected by businesses—they are an economic entity and not a social entity."[27] Even as executives like Young took this stance, most of the companies did attempt to align with the Sullivan principles. But, as Christopher Beirne of the Carnation Company admitted, when the company raised wages to conform to the Sullivan principles, they had to lay off people in order to "automize" more.[28] Kennedy learned that even those businesses operating in South Africa that committed to the Sullivan principles had very little effect on undermining apartheid as a political and economic system.

Kennedy's conclusions from the meeting demonstrated the institutional constraints of his politics—both the committed belief in the value of civil disobedience and the view of the Sullivan principles as a strategy to combat apartheid. Indeed, what the meeting revealed was Kennedy's intimate awareness of the university's dependency on external funding and investment from foundations and corporate donors. Rather than consider divestment as a political option, he concluded that the argument for divestment ignored the board's fiduciary responsibility to the institution. "Our judgment is that divestment of the kind proposed would entail significant losses to the University resources for which the Trustees are legally responsible. In effect, we would be moving resources from the purpose for which they were originally intended to another social purpose."[29] While maintaining a commitment to the Sullivan principles and strategic investment, he believed the anti-apartheid movement represented an important civic lesson on how institutions operated. Students needed to understand the economic reality of the situation, Kennedy concluded in his public statement, and the limited role of the university as a moral actor in political life.

Indeed, Kennedy believed that the task of the university was to teach students the perceived economic reality of South Africa and the political constraints of the institution. Divestment, he argued, ran "counter to our tradition of fair and rational processes for determining guilt. A wholesale condemnation of corporations for activities that are permitted under law strikes me as unfair."[30] Despite students' commitment to education and research, Kennedy also assumed that the students acted from emotion rather than "rational debate." In response to student activism, the Stanford administration published a small report defending the institution's stance on South Africa. As Kennedy emphasized in the introduction, the book was a reflection of "Stanford's responsibility as an education institution" to provide "the means for people to become more knowledgeable." The booklet presented the two arguments concerning South Africa: divestment or selective investment. Kennedy argued that divestment was but one "moral" approach. As such, "energy should be poured into trying to find ways to bring about fundamental change in a responsible manner" and to encourage students to "objectively" analyze the complex issues surrounding South Africa and American foreign policy.[31]

Ironically, students and faculty supporters of divestment found the report lacking "objectivity." Vladimir Matijasevic, a graduate student in physics and member of SOSA, argued that the book attempted to present the university as "above the issue itself" and sought to be "educational and objective." But, he wrote, "the administration finally has to see that it is taking a side on this issue," in the sense that "no decision on divestment is in fact a decision to continue investing." In Matijasevic's view, the book also had an analytical flaw in its attempt to be "objective": it overlooked the fact that most South African leaders called for divestment. Over the course of 1980s, South African leaders, ranging from Sipho Buthelezi, a cofounder of the South Africa Students Organization, to Bishop Desmond Tutu, called for university divestment, often helping to mobilize students in the United States. Given the support and advocacy for divestment by Butheleze and Tuto, Matijasevic argued, the belief that university leaders like Kennedy held—that is, that elite leaders in the university knew what was best to combat apartheid in South Africa—was but an extension of the "white man's burden."[32]

Faculty members also supported the students' critique of the pamphlet, focusing on the report's stated objectivity. A panel sponsored by the African and Afro-American Studies Association concluded the pamphlet was misleading. One invited panelist was Kennel Jackson, an African history professor at Stanford. He called the pamphlet a "provocative act," adding that it represented at best "a kind of propaganda."[33] Many student activists ultimately believed Kennedy and the institution's response created false categories. Baregu, the coalition activist who challenged Africanist work at Stanford, argued that "the choice is not between moral urgency and rational discourse, as Kennedy would have us believe. It is between resistance and collaboration." In Baregu's view, Stanford was a collaborator, and he wondered if university officials had the "moral courage to face up to this truth."[34]

The pamphlet was part of Kennedy's broader strategy of teaching what he believed were more effective forms of civic engagement, most prominently public service and volunteerism. Amid campus unrest around the divestment movement, Kennedy created a new Public Service Office that supported student work in legislative processes in Washington, DC, among many activities. He envisioned the program as a way to educate students about the policy debates and legal procedures, with a particular focus on those concerning US–South African relations. SOSA activist Cohn drew on Kennedy's call for public service, developing a proposal for students to work in DC for the summer. He saw the opportunity as part of the broader divestment effort. "My proposal, based primarily on President Kennedy's statements," Cohn wrote, "seeks to diversify Stanford student anti-apartheid efforts with an emphasis on the legislative perspective."[35] Kennedy believed Cohn's proposal was a legitimate use of university finances, and the Public Service Office supported Cohn's work in Capitol Hill.

The DC program attempted to channel the activism of students like Cohn into more acceptable activities, but his experiences also demonstrate the ways students co-opted those programs to support the divestment movement. Indeed, like the legacy programs that served as the basis of the anti-apartheid movement at Stanford, the DC program accommodated competing tendencies. It was designed to support a set of learning experiences within certain boundaries even as the experience provided political knowledge that extended beyond the mission. After spending the summer in DC learning about legislative processes and debates, Cohn recommitted to calling for university divestment. In an op-ed for the *Stanford Daily*, he explained, "In examining the economic sanctions legislation on Capitol Hill over the summer, I found anti-apartheid movers in Congress expressing deep gratitude to students for our divestment activity on college campuses." The lesson he took from his experience was that there was a need for continued pressure on the university to divest from South Africa. After all, Cohn asked, "would powerful people like Derek Bok [Harvard president] and Donald Kennedy have publicly supported economic sanctions legislation against South Africa if it weren't for the demands being made upon them to divest?"[36]

Like Cohn, other SOSA activists utilized the Public Service Office as a resource for political organizing. Like Archuletta, both Kemp and Phillips interpreted the divestment movement as an extension of the Black Freedom Struggle in the United States. Indeed, they took direct inspiration from the 1960s by planning and coordinating Project Democracy, a voter registration drive modeled off of the 1964 Freedom Summer. "Inspired by the example of students in the Sixties who participated in Freedom Summer in Mississippi," they explained, "this project is designed as our generation's contribution to the struggle to extend the blessings of democracy to all U.S. citizens." They justified the project based on Kennedy's new public service effort. "We also see this experience as part of our responsibility as concerned citizens"; the experience will educate students and "lend a needed sense of urgency to the task for supporting the ongoing struggle for justice and equality."[37]

For students like Kemp, Phillips, and Cohn, public service and activism were complementary civic activities. The public service projects, whether they involved learning legislative processes in DC or conducting voter registration drives in Alabama, were a political education process connected to transforming institutions like the university. Indeed, activists associated with the divestment movement sought to expand the original mission of the Public Service Center. Along with Lisa Neeley, a member of the Third World Coalition, Phillips connected political activism and public service in the handbook for Stanford's Public Service Center. "Given the abundance of problems in the world one can literally start anywhere," they noted. "Some people choose to comfort the afflicted" through food drives and visiting the sick, all of which "are valuable and immediate forms of public service." But, they argued, activists needed to "go beyond treating the symptoms to dealing with the root causes of our social condition (social discrimination, economic exploitation, lack of democracy and political power)." In their view, this type of commitment also included addressing the need for divestment.[38]

Indeed, student activists also challenged Kennedy on a related public service initiative: You Can Make a Difference conferences. Held from 1986 to 1990, the conferences sought to encourage and develop mechanisms for students to get involved in social and community issues, similar to the DC program. The conferences had wide-ranging support from the Stanford student community. The *Stanford Daily*'s editors—Beth Klein, Allison Hartwell, and Mark Lawrence—supported the conferences. "Given the gravity of the issues confronting us today—hunger, poverty at home and abroad, concern over the quality of our education, the escalating arms race, and the rising federal deficit," they explained, "this conference served a very important function."[39] They believed the conference provided students a mechanism to engage deeply with what role they might play in addressing the issues plaguing American society.

In fact, the editors further argued, students had been active. They high-lighted SOSA students who challenged the university on its investment poli-cies related to companies working in South Africa. "Indeed, students have taken to heart the now oft-heard slogan, 'You Can Make a Difference,'" they argued. "The University has been quite successful in encouraging students to take initiatives and become involved in certain public service activities, but Stanford *as an institution* has itself not heeded the call for public respon-sibility." They framed their critique around engaged citizenship. "We must take action both as citizens and as an institution to be a real force for social responsibility." The students called on Kennedy and the board of trustees to take up a resolution to divest. "Students have taken the lead in making con-tributions to the public welfare through numerous activities. Now it is time for Stanford to translate its talk and advice into action. Only in this way can we really make a difference."[40]

To the dismay of students, the university never took a broader institu-tional stance on South Africa, and the Stanford board of trustees determined that selective investment was the best means to address the institution's role in South Africa. In this context, Kennedy also prioritized volunteer service over dissent as the preferred way of reconciling the relationship between moral concern, formal education, and the role of the university. While dis-agreeing with students' call for divestment, Kennedy supported and funded Project Democracy and expanded the Public Service Center. He saw the project and the new center as appropriate forms of citizenship at the uni-versity. Students, he believed deeply, should be involved in community and public service. "Civic responsibility," Kennedy stated, was central to citizen-ship. By supporting Project Democracy and expanding the new center, he encouraged a notion of citizenship that aligned with institutional norms of providing public service. By dismissing calls for divestment, Stanford discour-aged an activist form of citizenship that sought to reimagine the university's role in political life.

Kennedy's programmatic efforts to teach students what he thought were the institutionally appropriate forms of political involvement also had a long-term effect: they drove a wedge into student efforts to integrate local community service with a broader global student politics that sought to transform institutions like the university. As the debate around divestment subsided, students interpreted the meaning of public service differently than Phillips's initial framing of the Public Service Center, raising a much broader debate about appropriate forms of activism and citizenship on cam-pus. Mark C. Estes, an engineering student, also drew inspiration from the You Can Make a Difference conference, highlighting a range of activities at

Stanford—including Reach Out Today, the Stanford Volunteer Network, and Bike Aid—to demonstrate the varied ways that students made a difference. He contrasted these activities with the work of SOSA, in particular the construction of shanties that sought to build social awareness among students. These forms of activism—among others—put too many political and moral demands on the university, he argued. As he explained, "students can make a difference. We must also realize that there is a fine line between making a difference and just making noise."[41]

Andrew Shields, a student activist who supported the divestment effort, responded to Estes, arguing that "the methods of volunteerism proposed by 'You Can Make a Difference'—'student planning, dedication, innovation, and cooperation help[ing] to improve the lives of others'—while friendly, do not and cannot lead to a better society.' They are band-aids for society's self-inflicted wounds. They treat symptoms, rather than causes." Shields believed that Estes's solution of "remaining within the bounds of politeness" also meant "remaining within the already existing social structures." As such, Shields concluded, maybe Estes would "understand the value of 'noise.'"[42]

The political value of "noise" was also marginalized in the new Public Service Center. A particular historical amnesia informed the center's expansion in the late 1980s and early 1990s. At Stanford University, when Archuletta was included to discuss the new Public Service Center, the conversations centered on what it would do rather than on the insight and experiences of the Black Community Service Center or the perspectives of students who mobilized the campus community around divestment. Archuletta saw the effort as a form of institutional colonialism. He believed deeply that service must be linked to social movements and political struggles that challenged the status quo. Like many students in the divestment movement, he worried that the Public Service Center promoted a particular kind of service that tended take the approach that the student's moral role—like the university's—was to provide charity and service.

Legacy

Over the course of the 1970s and 1980s, a broad coalition of students challenged Stanford University to divest its holdings in companies working in South Africa. The student efforts grew out of the institutional legacies of the 1960s, reflecting the persistent tensions within the programs. In taking the position to divest, the students again raised questions about the moral contours and implications of their education at Stanford in light of university investments in companies that worked in South Africa. Could my education be morally and ethically sound, the students asked in different ways, if it was partly or fully funded through investments that reinforced a system of racial injustice and inequality? Students ultimately took the position that their education could not be morally consistent unless the institution itself also acted in morally consistent ways by divesting from its holdings. Indeed, students argued that in the same way they sought to relate their education to political action, the university needed to align its research and education with its actions as an institution.

University leaders, including Lyman and Kennedy, agreed with students that investments in apartheid South Africa raised ethical questions about Stanford's role in the political economy. However, they worried that divestment would undermine the very mission of the university. They argued that the institution and the board of trustees had a financial responsibility to ensure a return on investment to continue to provide an elite education for students. They thus turned to the logic of disciplining democracy to reconcile the moral disconnect in one's education. Believing that students did not understand existing institutional arrangements, Kennedy promoted, developed, and expanded a series of public service opportunities that he believed would support students' moral and ethical development as citizens in ways that helped them better understand the limits of the university as a political actor.

What emerged in Public Service Center programming was a pedagogical approach that synthesized moral consideration with public service. In 1990, Kennedy convened a meeting to explore the status of public service and its place within the university. The committee defined public service as participation in university-sponsored service projects, work sponsored by community service agencies such as Big Brothers/Big Sisters, events organized by for-profit organizations and churches that sought to meet a community need, government-supported volunteer service, and independent service projects. Nonpolitical public service, Kennedy believed, represented the best way to reconcile the moral gaps in one's education in a way that aligned with the structure and logic of the modern American university. Kennedy and others in the meeting argued that the public service experience integrated the development of academic skills with the development of ethical considerations. In the view of Kennedy and other faculty participants like Terry Karl, one of the important components of ethics was the ability to practice empathy—a trait that they believed was necessary for public service. "In the sense of good scholarship, empathy," Karl argued, "is the ability to move outside what you understand from your own experience or your own training, and to be able to move into and put yourself in the place of others who come from very different settings and have different problems."[43]

Efforts like Stanford's Public Service Center maintained important discussions about the place of moral and ethical considerations within one's education that grew out of the anti-apartheid movement. It also enabled students to apply what they learned to a social context in ways that expanded the initial vision of SWOPSI courses and other institutional legacies from the 1960s. As Goodwin Liu, a Stanford student who participated in the 1990 meeting, explained, "What is unique about public service is that there is a social context to what you do. You affect populations; you affect people. And that's where its value is."[44] In both ways, the center represented the ways that university leaders at Stanford reconciled what students interpreted as the moral conundrums of their elite education. But the context in which students could explore and act on moral concern was limited to nonpolitical public service. Much like what occurred in the 1960s, the focus on public service disciplined the mass student politics that emerged from the anti-apartheid movement. The Public Service Center limited the goal of a student's education and research in the community to individual and scholarly development, which had the effect of deflecting the broader critiques of the university's political role.

The divestment movement on campus and Kennedy's response in the form of public service efforts across Stanford reflected what South African student Jonathan Jensen saw as the university's competing impulses. Jensen grew up in Western Cape, the Black township of Cape Town, South Africa. A precocious student, Jensen was one of the lucky few Black students to attend college in South Africa in the late 1970s. At the University of the Western Cape, he majored in science education and, after graduation, became a teacher. Through the South Africa Education Program, he then attended Cornell University, where he obtained a master's degree, before pursuing a PhD in International Education Development at Stanford.

Jensen was not politically involved in the movement until arriving in the United States. The program and the university provided a space for Jensen to meet with and learn from different groups in ways he had not been able to in South Africa. "Something happened to all of us—particularly those of us who weren't . . . full blood activists," Jensen explained about the meetings. "And that is you found yourself . . . being addressed by leadership of the groups demonized at home."[45] The leaders from the African National Congress and the Pan Africanist Congress engaged the students as active and vital participants in the political struggle. After those meetings, Jensen noted, "many of us got involved full time." Over the course of his four years at Stanford, Jensen also found a supportive environment for both his political goals and educational pursuits. He worked with American activists as president of the African Students Association, developed new education programs for South Africans in the international office, took courses that exposed him to the history of South Africa, and used the newly established Public Service Center to raise funds for Ethiopia.

Jensen's experiences reflected the ways Stanford played a key role in the broader anti-apartheid struggle in South Africa, similar to how the SWOPSI courses and the Black Activities Center served as the basis for the divestment movement in the late 1970s. But Jensen was also disappointed with Stanford for its failure to take a clear moral stance by divesting holdings from companies working in South Africa. Jensen's experiences at Stanford shaped his understanding of education and knowledge. "Knowledge is not neutral" and often "acts as an arm of the state," Jensen came to believe. He also maintained that knowledge and the university could be used to develop grassroots political power. In the context of the anti-apartheid movement, university leaders chose to act as an arm of corporate interests even as they promoted efforts that seemed to support local and global grassroots efforts. The university, Jensen ultimately concluded, had "two faces."[46]

CHAPTER 6

Brown University

Updating the Liberal Arts Tradition

Brown University's founding motto is *In Deo Speramus*, which translates as "In God We Hope." But, in the university's modern institutional history, the motto was understood to have a different meaning by the Brown Corporation Board: "In the market we hope." Over the course of the 1970s, the Brown Corporation turned its attention to market investments to address the institution's poor financial health. This strategy paid dividends. Market investments transformed Brown from a small, poorly funded liberal arts college to a financially endowed university on par with other Ivy League schools. As students wrote in the *Brown Daily Herald* in the mid-1980s, Brown was transformed "from a poor college to a hot college."[1] To a growing contingency of students at Brown, however, the financial success came with moral costs: twenty-three million dollars of those investments were in companies that worked in South Africa, an amount that accounted for 10 percent of the total endowment.[2] Student activists at Brown argued that the failure to address the moral quandary of investments undermined the university's distinct role as a liberal arts institution.

Unlike other university leaders, who acknowledged that investments in South Africa brought a limited financial return, the Brown Corporation Board and academic leaders maintained that those investments were vital to the financial solvency of the institution. Shaped by the institution's history of poor financial planning, they worried that divesting from holdings in

South Africa also meant limiting the financial success of the institution. As a result, Brown never fully divested from investments in South Africa. Unlike both Stanford and Georgetown, both of which adjusted investment strategies much earlier, Brown maintained its investments until the late 1980s. In 1986, when many other universities and Leon Sullivan himself concluded that the Sullivan principles did not work, Brown changed its investment strategy to a selective investment approach aligned with the Sullivan principles. The Brown Corporation Board retained hope in the market.

Of course, board members and the university's president, Howard Swearer, did not defend their decisions in terms of market returns for the endowment. Rather, in their public statements, they concealed the economic calculus behind a defense of traditional conceptions of the university. On the institutional level, board members and university leaders defended an orthodox conception of institutional neutrality, even as they acknowledged Brown's embeddedness in the market and political economy. In their public statements to defend continued investments, they argued that divestment was an institutional action that the university could not take. Their orthodox conception of institutional neutrality informed what they interpreted as appropriate forms of civic deliberation and action among students. In response to student efforts to organize rallies and publicize the issue of investments, Swearer asserted that student activists failed to commit to civil responsibility and respectable debate. University leaders employed older traditions to delegitimize and limit students' political actions on campus.

The problem with the argument made by Swearer and other university leaders—at least to student activists—was that the institution itself did not live up to its own traditional ideals by encouraging honest debate on the issue of investments. Indeed, even as university leaders referenced these ideals to defend their stance, they also utilized institutional mechanisms of disciplining developed in the aftermath of the mass student politics of the 1960s to limit how the campus community deliberated on investments. Joining Georgetown President Timothy Healy and Stanford President Donald Kennedy, Swearer took a prominent role in promoting public and community service. He highlighted students engaged in volunteerism as the appropriate models of civic engagement while simultaneously dismissing the public commitments of anti-apartheid activists and regulating the type of political action on campus. But Brown was also unique in the ways its leaders employed the ideological side of disciplining by broadly defining what was and was not political—a move that enabled the university to limit the political terrain of debate on institutional investments. What emerged in the aftermath of the divestment movement at Brown was an updated educational mission that hid the internal disciplining mechanisms behind the promotion of public and community service as core commitments of the liberal arts.

Defining the Issue

In the fall semester of 1977, Shaun Brown, a young African American activist at Brown, traveled to the United Nations in New York, where she met with and learned from other anti-apartheid student activists from the United States, Canada, the United Kingdom, Nigeria, and Haiti. At the gathering, the international group of young activists came to a clear consensus. The continued investment by Western—particularly American—businesses in South Africa reinforced rather than challenged the system of apartheid. Drawing on her experience, Brown concluded that her university also had a role to take: divest from all corporations working in South Africa. As a member of the Undergraduate Council of Students at Brown, she encouraged her fellow board members to critically examine the university's investments in South Africa. In the spring 1978, the Undergraduate Council of Students at Brown voted for divestiture. At the core of the decision was the view that moral stances required moral action. As council member Nanci Maclean explained, "If you're going to say something is immoral, than it's immoral. You have to take that to the limit and do something about it."[3]

While making a broader moral argument, the decision to support divestment was based on extensive research by students that highlighted the political implications of investments and what they saw as the university's direct support of apartheid. With other members of the council and the newly formed Southern Africa Solidarity Committee (SASC), Shaun Brown wrote and published a range of pamphlets titled "What's the Word?" The pamphlets focused on the relationship between the American corporate role in South Africa, Brown University's investments, and the economic and political conditions of apartheid. One pamphlet issue focused on Brown University's $3.2 million investment in IBM stocks.

The hyperfocus on IBM was significant for two reasons. First, students highlighted that IBM technology was an integral part of the apartheid system. Starting in 1952, IBM was the largest computer supplier in South Africa, where government officials used the technology to modernize the pass system that tracked and limited the movements of Black South African citizens.[4] Second, and even more significant to students, a prominent board member of the Brown Corporation was Tom Watson, the CEO of IBM.[5] This direct relationship between the Brown Corporation and the technological system used in apartheid South Africa demonstrated to the students that the university was far from a complacent actor there. In the view of students, Brown University was playing an integral role in the perpetuation of the apartheid system both through investments and membership on its corporation board.

As a member of the Brown Corporation, however, Watson was not going to outwardly defend the institution's investments based on his company's bottom line. Rather, members like Watson took it as an opportunity to teach civic lessons that contained a set of assumptions about the market, the role of business, and the position of the university. Foremost, the corporation board argued that university investments were the product of the modern global economy. "The division of labor has been carried so far in the modern economy that it would be almost impossible to find a public corporation that does not derive at least some income from sources which are repugnant to some within the university," the board explained in its "Statement on Investment" in 1971.[6] The economic entanglement of the university with the modern market economy, they further argued, made it difficult to take a clear moral position on investments. Central to their argument was an analytical distinction between business practices and the university. "The dilemma we face in the South African question is not a clear-cut issue of high morality vs. [sic] financial profit," the board wrote. "Brown, as a non-profit institution whose resources are devoted to teaching and research, is not in the same category as an individual or corporate investor whose main motive in maintaining a large portfolio is the accumulation of wealth."[7]

Indeed, the distinction between the mission of business and of the university was vital to the board's evolving argument on maintaining investments. In response to appeals to divest in 1978, Brown Corporation members shifted their focus away from an economic lesson to a defense of traditional ideas of institutional neutrality. Foremost, they argued, the role of the university was to function as a space for open debate on political issues. "From a philosophical standpoint," they wrote, "not enough has been said about the need for Brown and other great U.S. private universities to encourage diverse viewpoints within the academic community." The university could not take "'institutional' positions on issues," they continued, without running counter to institutional commitments to neutrality. Brown Corporation Board members believed that the institution should not take a political position via investments. As they explained in the 1978 "Statement on Investment," "from a practical standpoint to the University, we reject the notion that our portfolio—through the wholesale divestment of a large number of securities—can or should be used as a means in support of social change."[8]

The value claims made by the board concerning how the market operated, the role of business, and the position of the university obfuscated not only the financial interests of members like Watson but also the primary motivation for continued investments. Swearer and corporation members were concerned with the financial health of Brown and its related position as an elite institution. In its 1971 statement, corporation board members worried that "total abstinence from participation in corporate sources of income would severely curtail the vital educational functions of the university." They expanded on this view in their 1978 statement, focusing in particular on the financial health of the institution. "Brown is currently operating on its first break-even budget in a decade after a long battle to stabilize our expenditures and increase our revenue," the corporation underscored. As a result, "a precedent-setting action to divest would also have a major effect on our ability and flexibility to reinvest. That is a price we cannot pay at the very time we are attempting to increase our endowment in the early stages of the larger capital campaign in Brown's history."[9] The financial benefit of investments, especially in terms of funding and supporting education at the institution, the board concluded, was more important than a broader moral claim about the university's public mission.

The decision to maintain investments was supported by select faculty at Brown in 1978, who, like the board members, drew on traditional ideas of the university and academic culture to defend continued investments. In a letter to Swearer, math professor Walter Freiberger defended the corporation's decision to maintain investments by inverting the idea of academic freedom. While acknowledging that "both—teaching and investment—have moral overtones," he believed that how individuals made decisions based on their position in the institution mattered more. "I expect the trustees not to advise me how to teach my courses and conduct my research. I should therefore be inconsistent were I to presume advising them on investment policy." He continued, "I have full confidence in the ability of our trustees to solve their moral dilemmas, as they have shown their confidence in my ability to solve mine."[10]

Other faculty members at Brown offered a different civic lesson that directly challenged the claims made by the corporation board and thus articulated a more progressive vision of the university's role. In the view of David Buchdahl, a professor of anthropology, Swearer and the board's presentation of the issue was misleading. "We are not confined to two alternatives, an all or nothing choice between complete and immediate withdrawal of investments on the one hand, and a continuation of all our investments on the other," he argued. Rather, "conceiving and debating the choices in this manner only appears as a misplaced effort to avoid the real issue, namely—is symbolic moral action less important than responsible fiscal action, both generally and in this particular case." In his view, the "facts of this particular case demand a strong moral response on the part of the University." To support his position, he drew a historical parallel. For the United States to be involved in South Africa, he argued, "is merely a repetition of the same tragic mistake made recently in Vietnam." As such, Buchdahl called for a "gradual divestiture" so "that the position of Brown is clearly evident." Indeed, the general view of faculty was that divestiture was more about its symbolic meaning for the university's mission than its immediate effect. But, he worried, "apparently it is nearly impossible for the United States business community and its government allies to learn from the lessons of the past."[11]

Arguments for symbolic action by faculty were also supported by Brown alumni. After graduating from Brown University, Monica Ladd worked for the United States Mission to the United Nations. In her view, the economic argument for continued investments, especially in terms of challenging apartheid policy, ignored the legal context of corporate investments in South Africa. "Foreign investment is always required to obey local laws," she wrote to Swearer, "and in South Africa this amounts to participation in and furtherance of apartheid." Moreover, she continued, Brown's own investments were insignificant to the companies themselves. When understood in this way, Ladd argued, divestment was the morally right decision to make, especially for the university: "It is my contention, then, that for the university to pass up the opportunity is to shrink the responsibility that the university has to the society in which, and for which, it operates."[12]

The different political positions and interpretations of the university demonstrated what Brown professor and African American Studies scholar Dean E. McHenry saw as the competing impulses within the institution itself. McHenry understood the dilemma as reflective of the gap between theory and practice when applied to the institution. In theory, he argued, the university was against any form of injustice. The university's primary education role was the theoretical engagement with ideas to develop thoughtful and critical thinkers. He believed that the research and organizing efforts of students in SASC and the arguments made by alumni like Ladd exuded the hallmarks of a liberal arts education at Brown. However, McHenry continued, the university rarely put those ideas into practice. Nowhere was this more clear, in McHenry's view, than in the ways the university perpetuated injustices in South Africa through its investments. "There is a divergence," he explained, "between Brown's objective of not aiding racism and her practice of supporting it through her investment policy." Like student activists at Brown, McHenry linked the financial investments in corporations that worked in South Africa to the university's role as an institutional actor.[13]

Even as faculty, students, and alumni alike made arguments about expanding the very idea of the university's role when it came to apartheid South Africa and grappled with the implications of those investments to a student's education, Swearer interpreted the situation differently. Throughout the late 1970s and into the 1980s, Swearer remained skeptical of divestment. "There is something very appealing and simple in washing one's hands of complex moral and practical problems," Swearer wrote in his public statement to the Brown community, and "at the present time, there are too many unanswered questions."[14] But he was not dismissive of student efforts or the wider views shared by those associated with Brown, at least not initially. Indeed, he read the alumni and faculty letters sent to him and the efforts of student activists as evidence the university served as a space of public debate. He also saw SASC efforts as a reflection of the liberal arts tradition, even as he ignored the students' critique of the political implications of a corporate-sponsored education. In this reading, he concluded that the university must maintain institutional neutrality. This conclusion supported his political position on divestment but was also demonstrative of how institutional culture shaped his educational worldview.

Swearer thus focused his attention not on the issue itself but on how the university should appropriately debate the problem of Brown's financial relationship to South Africa. As he explained in a letter to SASC, "There is no disunity among us—the trustees, the faculty, the students, and the administration—on the repugnance of apartheid policies of the South African government." However, he argued, "The only disagreement we have is over what to do about those policies."[15] In the late 1970s, as Brown students organized to highlight the issue of investments, Swearer underscored the disagreements to defend the need to remain institutionally neutral. In doing so, he built upon the corporation board's argument. He recast the anti-apartheid campus movement as a civic problem to be addressed through the teaching of appropriate forms of debate and deliberation.

Narrowing the Political Issue

In late spring of 1978, SASC organized an anti-apartheid protest that attracted over three hundred students. A prominent figure at the protest was Barney Mokgatle, a leader of the 1976 Soweto Student Uprising. He supported Brown students' political demands while also challenging the logic of Brown leaders. Mokgatle argued that "the money from U.S. corporations does not go to improve our lives"; rather, "it goes to buy guns to kill us." While supporting students' demands, Mokgatle also resurrected the political salience of "action" that initially grew out of the mass student politics of the 1960s. He called on students to "take uncompromising action. We want to see action!"[16] Mokgatle's appeal was central to SASC's argument about the role of students and the university. SASC student leader Ruben Cordova believed that students needed to maintain and act on their own individual moral conscience in order to transform the conscience of the institution. As Cordova argued, "We students cannot allow ourselves to become morally bankrupt because we are the conscience of the university."[17]

While SASC activists used the rally to demonstrate that divestment concerned the moral conscience of the university and required action by both students and the institution, Brown academic leaders and other students believed the rally represented SASC's disregard for free speech and public deliberation. Swearer attended the divestment rally, hoping to present the university's position on continued investment. SASC leaders voted to deny Swearer the chance to speak at the rally. In response, Thomas Bechtel, the associate dean of student affairs, concluded that the decision to deny Swearer the opportunity to speak was "an issue of free speech."[18] The news of SASC students' decision to deny Swearer the chance to speak did not just pit students against university leaders, either. Other students, some of whom sympathized with the cause of divestment, also called out SASC activists. In the *Brown Daily Herald*, the editorial board argued that the actions of SASC at the rally "indicate that group members are more eager to chant slogans on the Green than to rationally exchange information with university officials. Regardless of whether divestiture is the right course of action to take, the group's methods are unquestionably wrong."[19]

The decision to deny Swearer the chance to speak at the rally shifted the political focus away from institutional investments and the moral conscience of the university toward questions about appropriate forms of civic deliberation. The rally thus supported Swearer's initial interpretation that there was a need to promote debate. In the aftermath of the rally, Brown leaders interpreted the issue more in terms of teaching appropriate citizenship than of addressing the underlying moral dilemma of the university. Richard A. Marker, the university chaplain, suggested setting up forums to discuss the issue in order to diffuse and redirect student energies. "While students claim that they want a specific leadership response, in fact, I think they simply want to feel enfranchised," Marker wrote; "the most appropriate leadership position may be to add dignity and direction to the questions."[20] In the context of the SASC-sponsored rally, Marker called for a strategically structured approach to create a venue in which Swearer's position was presented as a response to the student position and a model of appropriate deliberation.

University leaders also argued that the rally did not represent the diversity of views present at Brown. On the same day the rally was held, the Undergraduate Council of Students recognized Students for Rational Action (SRA), an organization that challenged calls for divestment. The organizer of SRA, Victor Houser, echoed the views of Swearer and other university leaders. The SRA is "disgusted by the racist behavior of the South African regime," he argued, "but we didn't think divestiture . . . was the best way."[21] Students who took this view also raised issues with the approach of SASC. Julie A. Shapiro, a student at Brown University, agreed with the efforts of SASC in principle but worried about the implications of the institution divesting from corporations working in South Africa, especially in regard to the operation of Brown. "The consequences of any action on Brown's part are questionable," she explained in a letter to Swearer, "and the probable adverse affects [sic] on Brown's financial situation could impair the diversity of the student body and the academic quality here."[22] Shapiro made this argument in a letter to Swearer because she worried that her views were often marginalized at Brown. "Such opposition" to SASC, she wrote, "is the deterrent to people in my position to voice an opinion on this issue in light of the certain misunderstanding and attack which would result." Shapiro's letter reinforced Swearer's stance on the issue of divestment and his interpretation of the university's role as a space for public debate.

Indeed, Swearer used Shapiro's letter to delegitimize the modes of action employed by SASC activists. After receiving the letter, Swearer forwarded an excerpt to Shaun Brown and Cordova, the two students who oversaw SASC. In particular, Swearer underlined the reason why Shapiro sent the letter—concern that her views were dismissed on campus. Swearer believed the concern raised by Shapiro reflected a twofold problem. Foremost, he argued that dissenting views like Shapiro's were marginalized by SASC's actions. He had experienced this himself at the 1978 rally. He also extended his interpretation of Shapiro's experiences to his understanding of the university's role. He believed her letter demonstrated further evidence of the problem with taking moral stances as an institution. If the university took such a stance, Swearer argued, the institution would exclude views like Shapiro's and thus constrain open debate.[23]

In the view of SASC activists, however, the response to SASC's actions was contradictory. SASC leaders argued that denying Swearer the opportunity to speak was merely an extension of the same logic of the university's position on SASC. As Adam Max explained, "Howard Swearer doesn't yet recognize SASC, so we won't recognize Howard Swearer and we won't let him speak."[24] Indeed, Swearer and the associate dean of student affairs did not recognize SASC as a university-associated student organization. As an unrecognized organization, SASC was denied the right to participate in any deliberations related to university investments. "The administration has not recognized them [SASC] in that they were never invited as a group to speak with the administration," Shaun Brown argued.[25] SASC leaders also noted that their political rights to action were already limited by the institution itself. In organizing the rally, students had to notify the university in advance of when and where the rally would take place at Brown University, a policy they interpreted as an existing constraint on their political right to action on campus.

Brown University leaders adopted the policy guidelines of the American Council on Education that emerged from the mass student politics of the 1960s, recycling the ideological side of disciplining to constrain the political actions of SASC activists on campus in the late 1970s. University leaders maintained that the institution was to function as a neutral actor. Indeed, the first guideline, which supported the right of student and faculty action, also maintained that such rights were only protected "PROVIDED that it is made clear they are not speaking for or in the name of Brown university." But, in the view of SASC leaders, the university's position through existing institutional policies masked two key issues. First, the problem with the guidelines to students—especially in the context of the anti-apartheid movement—was that they concealed the existing political positions of the university itself. In one guideline, university leaders underscored the use of funds for political activities: "Funds or contributions may not be solicited under any circumstances in the name of Brown University for use by or in any political activity."[26] But, in the view of SASC members, Brown University leaders were using funds and investments to take a political position. As student activist Pedro Noguera argued, "the university makes clear its political values in the stances it has taken on South Africa."[27] The 1978 rally was an attempt to offer a different political position for the university to take, especially in its use of funds. However, university leaders interpreted divestment as contradicting the guiding principle of the use of funds.

Second, the guidelines provided leeway for university leaders to interpret what was and was not political. While supporting the right of students and faculty "to express their individual and collective political views," the policy guidelines also defined politics in a way that gave university leaders broad discretion. "'No substantial part of the activities' of the university, as an exempt institution, may be used for 'carrying on propaganda, or otherwise attempting to influence legislation.'"[28] Indeed, Swearer employed this definition of politics to limit the type of student organizing, actions, and public events on campus. He drew a distinction between "avowedly political organizations," such as SASC, and "organizations whose actions occasionally and inevitably have political consequences," such as the church or local human relations board.[29] In his interpretation of the guidelines, Swearer believed that church activities were allowed functions of the university in ways that SASC's activities were not. In the view of student activists, Swearer's interpretation of the guidelines enabled him and the university to make political decisions behind the façade of institutional neutrality.

When taking into account the policy guidelines and Swearer's interpretation of politics, SASC leaders concluded that Swearer's commitment to public debate masked the ways that debate and political action were already limited on campus. Indeed, they argued that Swearer's idea of public debate was narrowly defined and served to reiterate the university's position. In the fall semester of 1978, university leaders sponsored a debate about the institution's investments and South Africa on the university radio channel. But, as Cordova noted, "the so-called WBRU 'debate' was merely a question and answer session" and "concerned parties had no input and could neither ask questions nor express their viewpoint." The debate, Cordova continued, also only presented the Sullivan principles and continued investments as the two possible actions by the institution. In addition, given the board corporation members' political power within the university, their policy statements had the effect of shutting down genuine public deliberation. Cordova thus argued that the problem was the university itself in how it conceived of public debate and deliberation. "In light of this," Cordova concluded, "the 'careful and reasoned consideration by the community of the various factors and arguments' that you claim to be more 'appropriate' is rendered difficult, if not impossible."[30]

The 1978 rally thus shifted the political terrain of the divestment issue on campus. Initially conceived as a rally to motivate political action among students and challenge the university's continued investments, it was recast as an effort to promote appropriate public deliberation within the university. Brown student activists in SASC maintained a focus on the moral problem of continued investments but argued that the institution itself limited genuine democratic debate and engagement on the issue of university investments. This position rested upon a view made clear at the 1978 rally: the civic role of the student was to serve as a moral conscience for the institution. Activists demanded institutional flexibility for constant and open deliberation on campus, which would serve as a core teaching practice of the university itself. Swearer and Marker also emphasized civic debate and deliberation but argued that Brown's goal was to teach a particular kind of citizenship that helped students understand what they interpreted as the limited role of the university within prevailing national and economic policy. Ignoring critiques of prevailing institutional policy, they treated existing policies and their own views as descriptive truths of the university rather than political positions. This approach also informed how university leaders and students defined education when responding to efforts by Brown Divest in the 1980s.

Promoting the Liberal Arts

In 1982, a new class of students formed Brown Divest, an organization that sought to carry on the legacy of SASC. Two key leaders of Brown Divest had deep connections to the civil rights movement and SNCC in the 1960s. The first was James Forman Jr., the son of SNCC field-worker James Forman. When he helped form Brown Divest, he believed the student organization was embarking on something new in the broader Black Freedom Struggle in the United States and around the world. He changed that opinion when he spent a summer working in the archives at the Martin Luther King Jr. Center for Social Change and listened to a recording of Julian Bond and his father, James Forman, discuss their protests against South Africa. He found the conversation inspiring. Listening to the tape, he remembered, "forged a connection between what he was doing and previous generations."[31] Rachel Harding also made those cross-generational connections. As the daughter of Vincent Harding, the prominent Black historian and activist, Harding interpreted the divestment effort at Brown as an extension of the Black Freedom Struggle in the United States. At campus rallies and within the Brown Divest organization, she called on students to address "the South Africa within us."[32]

The study of history and institutional memory became a key guidepost for Brown Divest's educational efforts. Collete Mattzie, who took on a leadership role within Brown Divest, learned from her peers like Forman and Harding to see the divestment effort as tied to issues in the United States. As Mattzie explained, the process of coming to terms with issues concerning US relations to South Africa inevitably led to "our own coming to terms with racism and our own role in the world." The anti-apartheid struggle, she noted, "resonated with our own history" and "felt like the next chapter of that story." This included the next chapter in the history of Brown. Indeed, on the ten-year anniversary of when student activism helped form the Third World Center at Brown University, Brown Divest activists planned an Alternative Day of Education. Organized as part of the National Anti-Apartheid Day, the gathering brought close to six hundred students together to participate in a range of workshops focused on African American history and

South Africa.[33] The workshops were also linked to direct action on campus, including a sit-in that called on the university to divest. The combination of the workshops, South Africa protest, and sit-in resurrected efforts from the 1960s that sought to integrate political action within formal education. As Lauren Christman, a Brown Divest member, explained, "we have always stressed education and action."[34]

In response to the Alternative Day of Education and the National Anti-Apartheid Day, Swearer addressed the Brown Community concerning the university's role in relation to apartheid South Africa. He asked, "What can we do as citizens and as members of the Brown Community to help achieve an early end to the system of apartheid in South Africa?" In the same way he challenged the tactics of SASC in the late 1970s and 1980s, he was critical of the ways that students expressed their views as citizens of the university as part of Brown Divest. Swearer criticized the anti-apartheid protests, sit-ins, and Alternative Day of Education in the spring as devoid of purpose, believing that they could have been expressed in more "constructive ways." "There are many mechanisms for discussing and reaching decisions," Swearer explained. "In too many instances last year the established mechanisms were by-passed in favor of the politics of confrontation."[35] Swearer's public statement not only dismissed the educational commitment of the campus protest, it also recycled a familiar argument: the approach by Brown Divest activists was not a constructive form of civic engagement.

Brown Divest activists argued that Swearer's views reflected three key issues with the university itself—issues that were already raised by the generation of Brown activists associated with SASC. First, in response to the university's call for students to utilize existing campus mechanisms, Brown Divest activists countered that those very mechanisms entailed restrictions that limited debate. Indeed, as Eric Widmer, the dean of student life, explained in a letter to divestment advocates about their campus activism, "we will decide what is disruptive and what is not, following University rules."[36] Second, the statement ignored students' commitment to education and research. In the public letter, Swearer identified several points that student activists had already addressed in their mobilization effort, including the views of South African leaders, discussions of the role of the university, and the impact of divestment both on the university and South African society. In the view of Richard Gray, a member of the campus Organization of United African Peoples and organizer of the Alternative Day of Education, the fact that Swearer suggested that students needed to study these factors demonstrated not only the need to "educate the educators" but also the value of the Alternative Day of Education.[37] Third, Brown Divest activists again reiterated an older argument about investments. Forman argued that university officials interpreted investment strategies as "apolitical" and assumed that calls for divestment would politicize not only the portfolio but also the institution. Forman countered that Brown was already taking a political position through its investments. Sustaining investments, Forman and others argued, meant taking a political position.[38] In all three ways, supporters of divestment illuminated the implicit and explicit political positions of education at Brown in the 1980s.

Although familiar arguments re-emerged, the campus climate of the 1980s was different. In the late 1970s, university leaders could draw on students' skepticism of divestment, but the political context was different in the 1980s. Divestment was more widely supported among students at Brown. Over the course of the 1980s, Brown Divest garnered wide-ranging support among students and staff; a student referendum on divestment was backed by 83 percent of the undergraduate body, the Graduate Council, and Local #134 of Brown staff. A year after the Alternative Day of Education, in 1986, the faculty voted in full support of divestment. Reflecting the impact of this broader political shift, students who were not involved in Brown Divest or did not consider themselves activists made similar arguments about the politics of the endowment. As Brown student James Karb wrote, "I contend that it is impossible to hold apolitical investments in South Africa."[39]

Moreover, student activists now had further experiential evidence of institutional constraints. Brown Divest members and student supporters utilized university mechanisms, only to be stymied by their processes. In the aftermath of anti-apartheid activism in the late 1970s, Brown University established the Advisory Committee on Corporate Responsibility in Investment. The committee included representatives from across the university, including students. However, committee members found that their recommendations on investment had very little impact on the Brown Corporation Board's decisions. In a meeting with Swearer, committee members noted that the committee only disagreed on two recommendations, but the corporation overturned eight. The process demonstrated to the members the limited power of the committee—a limitation that also suggested to the students that the committee deflected rather than enhanced genuine deliberation on the university's actions as it related to investment.[40]

With increased support for divestment and the use of existing institutional mechanisms, university leaders again changed their response, focusing less on pushing for honest debate between different alternatives and more on the nature and form of education itself. After a range of debates and forums, Brown Corporation members voted to take a "selective" investment approach in 1986. Over the next four years, Brown would sell all stock in companies that did not comply with the most stringent Sullivan principles for doing business in South Africa.[41] Defending the stance taken by the corporation, Duncan MacMillan, an emeritus corporation member, told students that their purpose on campus was to be devoted to "scholastic concentration." As such, he continued, "I am strongly opposed to anyone using Brown University Campus as a platform for social or political purposes. You are encouraged to express your viewpoints, but care should be taken to not interrupt the educational process for any reason." In defining Brown Divest's efforts as political, MacMillan deemed the activities as falling outside the educational function of the university.[42]

Students from Brown Divest and other organizations responded to MacMillan's editorial, labeling his "perception of 'education'" as "both patronizing and frightening." In MacMillan's view, they argued, the ideal campus would be characterized by "5200 young automatons demurely scribbling regurgitated discourse." While MacMillan narrowly defined education as occurring in the classroom, the students argued that education also included "theater, music, art, community service and yes even (shudder) social and political activism" as "valuable, and more importantly, *educational*." They also argued that civic education must be rooted in political commitment, thus resurrecting a key argument from the mass student politics of the 1960s. "'Scholastic concentration' is absolutely useless," they wrote, "without active application to a very real issue." They believed that divestment activists were not, in the words of MacMillan, bringing ruin to the university. Rather, if they remained silent, "what they are bringing ruin to is Brown's [sic] concept of a liberal education."[43]

While the exchange between Brown Divest activists and MacMillan focused on the character of the American liberal arts tradition, South African students at Brown highlighted the underlying financial logic of the liberal arts and its relationship to the struggle in South Africa. Lunga Madlada, a student from Lamontville, a Zulu-speaking township outside of Durban, attended Brown as part of the South African Education Program. Madlada recognized the value of his education at Brown. "Compared to Zuzuland," Madlada noted about Brown University, "it is great. There we had no choice. Here, I have access to so much information." Although he appreciated the opportunity to study at Brown University, Madlada questioned the underlying motives of the program and the implications of his American education in South Africa. Madlada knew that his education in the United States was funded by Mobil and Shell, two key supporters of the South Africa Education Program that also worked with the apartheid government in South Africa.

Corporate support of the program, he concluded, was intentional. The companies wanted Blacks educated through the American university so that they returned to South Africa and helped lead the Black population in "evolutionary" change along American lines rather than revolutionary change.[44]

By focusing on the corporate funders of his education, Madlada navigated the political implications of his education at Brown. He worried that his education might hinder the liberation struggle. "For [the corporations], human rights isn't the only priority," he argued. "They are also interested in securing their investments," which included developing educated Black citizens to maintain those investments. Having an elite education from the United States, he would be able to return to South Africa and join the Black middle class, a prospect that concerned Madlada. "You become part of the very system you've been oppressed by and fighting against," he worried.[45] Madlada joined and became president of Brown's African Student Association, believing that the only way that his education could support the liberation struggle was if it was connected to the campus movement to divest. Working with American students, Madlada became a prominent activist who pushed the university to divest its financial holdings in companies working in South Africa. Madlada's experiences as a student—as someone who benefited from corporate investments in the program that made his education possible and as someone who participated in campus activism with his American counterparts—captured the competing impulses at the heart of Brown's liberal arts education.

Indeed, Madlada's reflections and the exchange between Brown Divest activists and MacMillan revealed how campus debate had further evolved to include the appropriate form of education and what it meant to be educated. In the late 1970s, the focus was on what Swearer defined as proper civic debate. In the mid-1980s, with Brown Divest's efforts that combined formal education with direct action, Swearer focused on what he deemed to be appropriate forms of action as part of a student's liberal arts training. In addition to implementing a selective investment policy, the Brown Corporation increased funding for South African exchange and volunteer legal programs. As Vice President Robert A. Reichley explained, funding for these programs reflected what he believed the university could do based on its institutional mission. "There was also a recognition that universities should do what universities are specially equipped to do, and that is to use their knowledge and experience to assist South African students and educational institutions." The new programs in South Africa, which included scholarships, research, and education, fell under Swearer's emphasis on community service and volunteerism.[46]

Swearer adopted educational language that was reminiscent of anti-apartheid activism but stripped of its political goals. Indeed, amid the anti-apartheid movement at Brown, Swearer became a leading figure in promoting national service as part of one's higher education pursuit. He viewed community service as vital to a liberal education. "A liberal education encourages awareness of the responsibility that individuals bear toward the society to which they belong," Swearer noted when establishing the C. V. Starr Fellowship. Indeed, he believed the program, which linked formal study to volunteer service, represented the new liberal arts education at Brown. He emphasized that "service to the commonwealth deepens the understanding of social and economic conditions, human needs, and political issues in contemporary society" at the same time that the "experience complements and enhances formal education." Echoing claims made by Brown Divest students, Swearer noted that community service would "awaken a deeper awareness of the moral relationship between University education and social obligation."[47] While dismissing the type of civic commitments by anti-apartheid activists, Swearer promoted civic action through community service.

The emphasis on volunteerism as Brown's commitment to updating its liberal education served as bulwark against the educational efforts of the divestment movement. In a 1986 editorial titled "The Age of We," the *Brown Daily* editors argued that recent promotions of volunteerism and service by Swearer represented more effective forms of activism. They stated that Brown needed more "doers not talkers" and wondered whether "instead of rallies on the green this year, we can concentrate on rallies to build parks in South Providence." James Berson and Bryant Walpert agreed, challenging Brown Divest and other students' ideas of civic activism and its place in the university. In response to an editorial by Forman, who lamented the lack of political activism on campus, Berson and Walpert argued, "We're trying," although in a different way. "We're not getting arrested. And our names are seldom in the paper," they explained. Rather, students in the "Brown Community Outreach and the newly created Center for Public Service sacrifice both their mental and academic health spending hours helping others, organizing service projects, and just plain getting involved because they want to make a difference."[48]

Like their peers at Stanford, other student activists and Brown Divest members argued that community service and political activism were not mutually exclusive. As they wrote in response to the editorial, "Service may prove to be a double-edged sword if it becomes a pretext for government inaction, or fuel for someone's hidden agenda." The students supported community service and volunteer programs on campus, as many were deeply involved in these efforts. But they believed that such work should either be a means to broader political education or be connected to other forms of activism that challenged institutions and how they operated. They argued, "It is true that volunteerism can build parks and clear abandoned lots, but it is only economic and political empowerment that can erase blight."[49]

In responding to new institutional efforts to promote public service, Brown Divest activists also navigated internal tensions concerning appropriate modes of action, especially in light of the corporation board's decision on selective investment. Indeed, with the decision by Brown administrators to commit to selective investment, students differed on the most effective methods to respond. Some advocated for more direct action, believing that confrontation "is the only logical next step" and that Brown Divest was "past the stage of education. People are as educated as they want to be."[50] In the spring of 1986, a couple months after the Brown Corporation decided not to divest its holdings in South Africa, Brown Divest members constructed a shanty on campus. When Brown Divest was supposed to take down the shanty, however, some student members refused, leading to mass arrests that divided both the community and Brown Divest members. Some believed such confrontational approaches alienated the broader campus community. As Brown Divest member Eric White explained, "I didn't see what immediate goal [a confrontational action] would accomplish. It didn't seem a logical action."[51]

In this context, the promotion of service represented an alternative form of action that better aligned with academic culture and opportunity. In the process, the arguments made by some Brown Divest activists on the need to connect community service to a broader set of politics were increasingly marginalized in Brown's promotion of volunteer service. Students who engaged in public protests, rallies, and other forms of activism that challenged the institution faced academic probation and arrests, like those associated with the shanty sit-in. In contrast, students involved in the new social volunteer programs supported by Swearer were rewarded for their "activism" with financial support and institutional recognition. In the fall of 1986, Brown gave a scholarship to Jon Rubin for his work as a legal aide in South Africa, only a couple months after Brown University leaders arrested students for the shanty sit-in on campus.[52] University officials supported students' moral commitments by encouraging them to engage in action that served the world as is but pushed back against the educational models of Brown Divest that attempted to change the institution's economic and political relationships at home and around the world.

Legacy

In 1987, when Swearer inaugurated the Center for Public Service as part of his wider promotion of national and community service, he drew on Arthur Schlesinger's book *Cycles of American History*. In the book, Schlesinger developed a theory of American history, what he saw as the cycles of private and public interest constitutive of the American political tradition. In his speech, Swearer employed Schlesinger's theory of history to make sense of the decade of the 1980s. "What we witness on the evening news and the front pages of the newspaper is, in simplistic terms," he argued, "the playing out of a cycle of dominated by private interests." As a result, he continued, "it is no wonder that the current generation of college students is caricatured as self-interested and more concerned about their financial security and career prospects than about the welfare of their community." In the new Center for Public Service, he saw "the beginnings of a turn of the cycle, in Schlesinger's words, away from private interest toward greater levels of public concern and involvement."[53]

Swearer's use of Schlesinger's theory of cycles reflected what he defined as genuine public interest. Between the late 1970s and the early 1980s, Swearer responded to a range of cycles of genuine public involvement among students in the divestment movement. Indeed, over the course of the 1970s and 1980s, Brown student activists demonstrated wide-ranging commitment to public debate, deliberation, and action that transformed the political community of the university. Yet, at each stage of those efforts, Swearer mitigated and disciplined their forms of public engagement while adopting the private interests associated with university investments. In drawing on Schlesinger's theory of history, Swearer ignored the role of the university itself in promoting or limiting public interest. Indeed, his promotion of community service as an expression of public involvement merely masked the private interest of the university. In the context of the anti-apartheid movement, Swearer's use of Schlesinger's theory reflected a broader worldview that narrowly defined student and institutional agency.

Swearer's efforts extended beyond Brown's campus. He became the head of the Campus Compact, the national organization that promoted community service. He also worked with Susan Stroud, the first director of the Center for Public Service, to create a marketing campaign around community service. In a letter to Swearer, Stroud underscored the ways the "Media Relations Task Force has acted as a catalyst for media coverage of student public service and community service on campus," referencing coverage of Brown's community service efforts in the *New York Times*, the *Chronicle of*

Education, and other media sources.[54] While Brown's efforts to promote its institutional reputation in media resources reflected new marketing trends in higher education, it also had the effect of marginalizing other forms of public interest on campus in the 1980s. Indeed, when promoting Center for Public Service and combating the image of the "me generation," Swearer referred to the one thousand students who volunteered in public service and did not mention the students associated with the anti-apartheid movement. Swearer's efforts enabled him to speak widely about Brown's promotion of civic engagement in public life in a way that masked the university's role in limiting other forms of civic engagement.

CHAPTER 7

Georgetown University

Redefining Jesuit Service

On Georgetown's original college emblem is a scroll with the Latin phrase *Utraque Unum*, or "Both Are One." In the context of Georgetown, the phrase encapsulated a core institutional belief: there was no conflict between education and religion. Yet, there was a conflict between the finances of the university and the institution's commitment to religious morality and Jesuit service. When Georgetown University was established in the eighteenth century, it struggled to survive due to its limited financial resources. The Maryland Society of Jesus, the founding religious community of Georgetown, used slaves to financially and physically build the university. The institution also participated directly in the slave trade economy. To raise money for Georgetown in 1838, Maryland Jesuits sold 272 slaves to two plantations. In this context, Jesuit service masked the university's financial exploitations.[1]

The university's relationship to slavery was far from unique among the early colonial colleges. After all, these colleges were deeply intertwined with the formation of a nation economically reliant on slavery. In the case of Georgetown, the conflict between the institution's finances and its religious, moral, and service commitments persisted well into the twentieth century. This chapter examines the modern iteration of this institutional conflict within the anti-apartheid movement at Georgetown. Like Stanford, Georgetown emerged as an elite institution within *U.S. News* rankings. Between the mid-1970s and 1980s, the board of trustees and President Timothy Healy capitalized on the perception of Georgetown as an elite institution, increasing the university endowment from $38 million to nearly $228 million.[2] But university leaders and student activists increasingly worried that financial comfort came with a moral cost. Indeed, the anti-apartheid movement revealed the implications of the institution's commitment to Jesuit service and morality when its finances were tied up in corporations that operated in apartheid South Africa. What emerged at Georgetown University in the 1970s and 1980s was a modern iteration of an older moral conflict within Georgetown's Jesuit tradition.

Like Stanford and Brown, Georgetown experienced two waves of anti-apartheid activism—one in the late 1970s and one in the mid-1980s. However, unlike what occurred at the other institutions, there was a political shift among Georgetown student activists and administrators between these two eras. In the late 1970s, the focus of activists and administrators alike was ensuring that university investments aligned with the Sullivan principles. This commitment changed by the mid-1980s, when student activists called for complete divestment. Administrators agreed, albeit more slowly. After multiple years of protest, Healy and the board of trustees fully divested in the academic year 1986–1987.

The evolving political alignment around the institution's investment strategy concealed the tense relationship between student activists and the university administration, especially as it pertained to the appropriate form of action for students to critically engage with the issue of apartheid South Africa. Healy and the board promoted the traditional service commitments of the Jesuit university—teaching, research, and community service—as the most suitable way for both students and the institution to engage with the political issue of South Africa. Students supported these efforts, but they also included protest and dissent as necessary forms of action for the university to support. The differences centered around competing personal and institutional memories of student activism in the 1960s. Indeed, how participants remembered the legacy of student activism at Georgetown informed both their moral position and whether protest and dissent were components of Jesuit service.

In 1986, the competing views—and different historical interpretations of student activism—converged at the student-led Freedom College, when university leaders called in campus and DC police to arrest and discipline participants. The decision by university leaders to arrest students recycled a core component of disciplining: regulating the type of student action on campus. In the context of a broader agreement on investment strategy, the decision also contained an epistemological position. In deciding to support divestment, university leaders cited the influence of US bishops while ignoring the efforts of students—a strategic move that again sought to constrain the memory of student activism as a source of moral guidance and Jesuit service. The combination sent a clear message to students: the political knowledge of university leaders or those with more authority took precedence on campus.

Historicizing Campus Activism at Georgetown

"Does anyone care about apathy?," asked Georgetown student Bartholomew Edes in an editorial for *The Voice*. The lack of political engagement among his peers, he believed, contradicted what he interpreted as the unique position of Georgetown within both the political world and the American higher education landscape. "It is very sad," he continued, "that at one of the country's most prestigious educational institutions located in the capital of the Western world, too many just don't give a damn about matters that concern them in the most profound ways."[3] But Edes was only partly right. Students were engaged, but in a way that administrators and students believed aligned more closely with Georgetown as an elite institution that served a predominantly middle- and upper-class White student population. In the late 1970s and in the 1980s, Georgetown students turned to a range of programmatic opportunities, including the D.C. Action Project, a living-learning community focused on service; Community Action Coalition (CAC), a clearinghouse for volunteerism; and Sursum Corda, a tutoring project in the DC neighborhood of the same name. While the programs—most prominently the D.C. Project and CAC—grew out of student activism in the 1960s, the mission and character mirrored the student culture and administration in the 1970s and 1980s. The programs encouraged Georgetown students to connect their education to a broader service commitment without political activism.

When university leaders spoke of the CAC and related service programs, they linked the initiatives to its Jesuit tradition, ignoring its roots in the mass student politics of the 1960s. In 1981, the Georgetown Board approved a new set of goals for the Jesuit university. These included a recommitment to not only the liberal arts tradition but to the continued dedication to serve others. They believed that supporting volunteer programs was part of "preparing citizens and leaders to serve Washington, the Nation, and the International Community."[4] University leaders saw service programs as a cohesive part of a liberal education. Healy connected the idea of volunteerism to the faculties of the original liberal arts—what he saw as "political citizenship training ground." He believed volunteerism represented "one of the integrators in a very fragmented and disintegrated world."[5] In the new goals for the institution and the subsequent statements of support, the board and Healy made a historical argument that presented service—and community engagement in the DC community—as a deeply embedded institutional commitment rather than an initiative that developed out of mass student activism in the 1960s.

University leaders framed community service programs within Georgetown's elite academic culture. Indeed, the view of university leaders like Healy was that community service represented the Jesuit supplement to a student's elite education at Georgetown. Yet, Healy's rhetorical support of community service was secondary to his deeper commitment to what he defined as "academic maintenance." Like his collegiate peers across the country, Healy adopted the view that his primary function as president was fundraising. He understood his role as a figurehead that promoted Georgetown as an elite academic institution to both preserve and expand its financial endowment. "Without that," he wrote referring to his phrase of *academic maintenance,* "everything else becomes a waste of time."[6] Despite his position as a leader of a Jesuit institution and his rhetorical support for Jesuit service, his primary concern was on building the endowment to ensure that Georgetown maintained its academic reputation—one that was tied to the new collegiate ranking system.

This combination—the promotion of Jesuit service within Healy's "academic maintenance"—shaped how students understood the goal of service and community involvement. Students involved in community service programs at Georgetown, like many of their peers who participated in these programs in the 1970s, adopted the outlook that involvement served academic and professional goals. Ed Deberri, a Georgetown student who participated in the CAC, called on his fellow students to get involved in efforts to meet the needs of the city's poor. But engagement was not for political goals or to address the structural problems of inequality. Rather, he made a twofold argument that focused more on the individual student than the concerns of the community. First, he argued, such experiences in the community would be beneficial for one's education. By getting involved, he wrote, students would enrich their education. "We get things like experience for a career, personal fulfillment, and pride in a job well done," he wrote. Second, volunteering in the community would provide a social context for one's intellectual pursuits. The experience, he further argued, "is also an essential facet of our learning experience because it presents an opportunity for understanding of the human dimensions of the major problems facing the world."[7]

The presence of the programs and promotion by students and administrators alike produced a campus culture that defined service as an alternative to political activism. Over the course of the 1970s and 1980s, students and administrators wrote a range of articles in the *Hoya* and the *Georgetown Voice* that defined community service as the primary form of political engagement that fit within one's Jesuit and moral education at Georgetown. Titles included "The New Activism," "Community Action Coalition: Tutors Learn as They Teach," "CAC Offers Alternative," and "Meet the Less Fortunate." Lisa Ferdette argued that the five hundred participants in CAC programs represented the strength of what she defined as the "positive attitude and activism" of Georgetown students who shared "the fruits of a Georgetown education with the less fortunate" through tutoring and volunteer service at food pantries. While quoting directly from students involved in the CAC, Ferdette also cited other editorials within the campus newspaper to demonstrate the new activism culture. She drew on a column by fellow Georgetown student Colman McCarthy, who argued that the CAC is "the most noticeable and enduring gift of Georgetown" because it provides a space for "young idealists who refute the misperception that college students are into self absorption and indifferent to the work of peace and justice."[8]

The interpretations by both university leaders and students reflected the politics of memory and the political uses of the history of campus activism at Georgetown. As Ferdette understood it, the CAC was continuing the legacy of earlier forms of activism that focused on students doing community service work in the DC area. But, like the spate of articles promoting community service, a similar set of articles published by former and current students of Georgetown in the alumni magazine and the university newspaper focused on the activism of the 1960s. In "Where Did the Activism Go?," the editorial board of the *Georgetown Voice* highlighted the protests and organizing of the late 1960s and early 1970s—the political context in which the CAC was established. The editorial board highlighted the mass student-led sit-in against Three Sisters Bridge, a beltway project near campus that displaced thousands of families; the mass student rally against the Vietnam War and weeklong student strike; and the arrests of Georgetown students who held a sit-in at the Capitol. In highlighting the examples of the late 1960s, the editors contrasted this type of mass student action with the new activism of the late 1970s and early 1980s. "We may individually support causes such as Oxfam or ERA [Equal Rights Amendment]," they noted, "but mass demonstrations have become rare."[9]

Students and administrators from that era of mass protest also noted the political differences but took away widely different lessons for Georgetown University in the 1970s and 1980s. Dan Kerrigan was a student leader who helped organize the weeklong strike at Georgetown in 1970 to protest the

university's involvement in the Vietnam War. Interviewed as part of an article memorializing student activism for the *Georgetown Voice Magazine*, Kerrigan noted, "There was a realization on the part of the students that they
can act, that the university doesn't have to be this way. The status quo can be
changed." He worried that student culture at Georgetown had slipped back
to its pre-sixties state.[10] In contrast, Georgetown leaders expressed relief that
students were turning to community service as the new form of activism.
Reflecting on the broader challenges to the university in the 1960s, Patricia
Rueckel, the vice president for student development, noted, "We can't be
in that dynamic tension all the time." She hoped more students would get
involved in community service programs because they allowed students to
make value commitments in ways that aligned closely with institutional and
Jesuit notions of moral commitment.[11]

   The divergent interpretations of the history of student activism and its
institutional legacy at Georgetown shaped how students understood the
reemergence of such activism as part of the anti-apartheid movement.
Georgetown students interpreted the anti-apartheid movement based on
their understanding of the history of activism at the university. In his article
"Protesting '80s Style," Jason Warburg argued that the Georgetown student-
led protests at the embassy were a direct legacy of the civil rights activism led
by students in the 1960s. The challenge, however, was that the cultural and
political context was different. "Once upon a time college students would
have joined a protest such as this with alacrity," he wrote, "but today we're
too busy pursuing our American Dream or we want to maintain our post-
'60s equilibrium so badly that we block out the concept of protest."[12] Warburg argued that the protests represented a similar moral commitment to
that displayed by earlier generations of student activists. In contrast to the
1960s, he argued, students had to consider the increased cost of higher education and the narrowing job market—a social calculus that limited a more
expansive commitment by students.

   Char Welse disagreed with Warburg's interpretation that drew a direct line
between civil rights activism and the protest at the South African Embassy.
"To call the protests at the South Africa embassy an exercise in civil disobedience" and "return to the spirit of the sixties," she argued, "is to misuse the
term and forget the real meaning of the sixties protests." In Welse's view,
there were two issues with this historical claim. First, unlike students in the
1960s who committed to nonviolence, there was "no such philosophical justification for breaking the law" at the South African Embassy. Rather, the
approach was merely to capture media attention. Second, the hyperfocus on
just garnering media attention transformed the protest into a coordinated

affair. People who volunteered to protest were "told when to be civilly disobedient and exactly what to do," and, she further noted, "the police are on the side of the protesters this time, and play their part by arresting the protesters (to give the exercise that authentic sixties touch)." Both factors, Welse believed, reflected the fact that the protests were organized by those with power in Congress or the very establishment that student activists challenged in the 1960s. As such, Welse concluded, "Georgetown's neo-sixties rads have been co-opted, and they don't even know it."[13]

Both Warburg's and Welse's reflections contained kernels of historical truth. While Warburg focused on the political and cultural context of the 1980s, with its pressure for students to see higher education as a market commodity, Welse highlighted differences in political tactics and what it meant to commit to the philosophy of nonviolence. Historical interpretations thus pivoted on diverse views on the appropriate political actions of students and the university. When applied to anti-apartheid activism and Georgetown, they also pivoted on varied ideas of the right moral action of the university. The different interpretations of the historical legacy of student activism and the institutional programs they produced informed how students and administrators understood the university's education mission and how they sought to address the moral dilemma of Georgetown's portfolio of investments in companies that worked in South Africa.

Developing a Philosophy of Moral Action

In a 1977 report for the *Hoya*, Georgetown student Kevin Mager highlighted the institution's investments in companies that operated in South Africa. The university's investments included Chase Bank, Honeywell, and General Electric and totaled six million dollars.[14] Mager argued not only that investments sustained apartheid in South Africa but that Georgetown, a Jesuit institution committed to justice, was complacent through its investment portfolio. In response to the report on Georgetown investments, the Student Senate at Georgetown voted on a resolution that called on students and the university officials to openly discuss investments in South Africa. Scott Ozmun, a sophomore who submitted the proposal, argued that "Georgetown did not square with what I perceived to be the values of a Jesuit University."[15]

George Houston, Georgetown University's treasurer, responded to Mager's report. While acknowledging that Mager's research was accurate, Houston argued that the university's social responsibility did not apply to its finances. In his view, "financial return must be the primary criterion for University investment."[16] Houston responded with a narrow financial interpretation—

a view that was important to the institutional logic of the university but did not reflect the full stance of university leaders. Healy and the board of trustees took their guidance on the issue from the United States and South African Roman Catholics. The bishops argued that US corporations were more morally responsible actors, especially when they committed to the Sullivan principles. The South African Roman Catholic Bishops requested that Healy and Georgetown keep investments because, in their interpretation, the "United States corporations are much more concerned with the social issues than are non-American corporations."[17] Taking into account the views of the bishops, Houston believed that continued investment was not only financially sound but also the morally right action of Georgetown as a Jesuit institution.

Houston recast what Mager saw as the ethical dilemma of investment as a reflection of the moral commitment of the university. Indeed, Houston framed the university's investment as a moral lesson in Jesuit education. He cited the New Testament story of Pontius Pilate, who washed his hands when he disapproved of Jesus's sentence. This decision, Houston argued, symbolized the unwillingness to do anything to correct the wrong except disassociation. Likewise, he argued, "We could wash our hands like Pontius Pilate and walk away, and what good would that do? If we divest, what effect will we be able to have? The only way corporations will listen to you is through stockholder resolutions."[18] In drawing on a biblical reference, Houston aligned financial investments with Georgetown's identity as a Jesuit institution and the Catholic Church.

Like Kennedy at Stanford, university leaders at Georgetown believed that students who called for divestment needed to better understand investments as a moral commitment. Healy and the board of trustees recognized that, like the students, the institution had "an obligation and an opportunity to contribute in affirmative ways to the long-term prospects for South Africa," but they framed such involvement through the "university's mechanisms: teaching and research." In response to student efforts to raise the issue of investments in South Africa, the board agreed to fund "lectures, panels, and other forums for ongoing discussion and exploration of these issues." In particular, they emphasized that "faculty members shall . . . help students explore the complex issues of South Africa; the University shall provide resources for individual faculty members to engage in research activities related to the problem of apartheid." The focus on faculty expertise was not just an effort to respect academic cultures—what the board described as "the autonomy of their disciplines and academic freedom."[19] They also believed turning toward faculty would reinforce its existing argument on maintaining investments. Georgetown University had become a respected academic force in international relations and foreign policy, especially during the Reagan administration. Chester Crocker, an international relations faculty member at Georgetown, helped formulate what became Reagan's policy of constructive engagement.[20]

The history of academic tradition and a particular interpretation of the Bible informed the moral position of university leaders. Indeed, the stance of these leaders mixed a particular moral interpretation of the Jesuit tradition with the realist politics of the school of international relations. It was also a view held by some of the early student activists who drew inspiration for their work from the Sullivan principles. When Georgetown Law students learned that Marriott Hotels failed to align with the Sullivan principles in South Africa, they led a boycott of the hotel in the Washington, DC, area. As a result of the protests and publicity, the hotel chain signed onto the Sullivan principles.[21] The principles enabled the university to maintain investments while also giving the impression that it supported the political activism of students who pressured the Marriot Hotel chain.

Rejecting the view that maintaining investments was morally sound, student activists and faculty members who supported full divestment understood the anti-apartheid struggle—and the issues they raised for the university— as part of a longer historical movement led by students to transform the university. The Georgetown faculty member and veteran activist Richard McSorely took Mager's position, focusing on the ways that investments were far from a financially neutral position. To justify his position, McSorely cited his experiences working with students to end racially discriminatory practices at Georgetown's medical and dental clinics in the 1960s. While the university had overcome those overt forms of racism, he believed the "economic entanglement may be just as murderous." He directly challenged the narrow financial logic of Houston by focusing on the broader Jesuit and educational mission of Georgetown. "If the purpose of Georgetown is the 'Greater Glory of God,' (the Jesuit motto), or if the purpose is to fully educate, or to make the truth known, then financial return can not be a primary concern of any aspect of Georgetown which is subordinate to the whole." Indeed, McSorely took the position that education extended beyond just what was taught in the classroom; it also included the corporate actions of the institution. "We teach that racism is evil and contrary to the belief that we are all children of God," but, McSorely argued, Georgetown's teaching "also concerns the actions of University officials, and the use of University money."[22]

The student organization that organized the divestment movement at Georgetown likewise defined the campus movement as part of a longer historical struggle. In 1983, Georgetown student Marty Ellington formed the DC Student Coalition Against Apartheid and Racism (SCAR). The inclusion of *racism* in the organization's name reflected the students' historical understanding of the anti-apartheid struggle. In the view of African American students like Ellington, the global anti-apartheid movement was directly connected to the Black Freedom Struggle in the United States.[23] Students in DC SCAR planned a protest outside of the South African Embassy in Washington, DC, on the twenty-fifth anniversary of the Greensboro sit-in. They placed their organization in the context of the efforts of earlier student activists, explaining, "we today, as students, Black and White, Asian, Hispanic, and Caribbean, are the beneficiaries of sacrifice. We stand here today in front of the South African Embassy, the embodiment of injustice and evil, to dedicate ourselves to freedom at home and abroad."[24] Similarly, when SCAR planned a campus meeting the following year, they did so on the anniversary of Martin Luther King Jr.'s death to draw a direct connection between his lifework and that of the anti-apartheid movement. As SCAR activist Mary O'Brien explained, "Wednesday, April 4, is the anniversary of the death of Martin Luther King, and at a service in the evening we will be reflecting on his philosophy of non-violence in relation to the injustices in South Africa."[25]

Like university leaders, SCAR coalition activists focused on the university as an intellectual resource, but they believed the institution had to also cut its investment ties to fully serve as a resource for public debate and deliberation. Ellington and Wally Packard, another SCAR member, outlined a broad vision of the university in relation to South Africa. They called on the university to connect the resources of the African Studies Program, the School of Foreign Service, the Center for Strategic International Studies, and the Center for Peace Studies to examine US involvement and make policy recommendations, create a scholarship fund for South African students, and develop a partnership with a Black university in South Africa to which students could send books and related educational materials. These different forms of university involvement, they argued, had to be linked to institutional divestment. Starla Washington, a member of both Georgetown NAACP and SCAR, argued that "we reap a benefit at the expense of our fellow humanity." Washington connected the university's "moral obligation" to divest to its standing as a Catholic institution. "The issue that will be decided is what price will Georgetown put on its moral and spiritual soul—how cheaply can our morality be bought."[26]

What emerged were different understandings of the role of the university that pivoted on whether the struggle was interpreted as part of a historical movement that stretched back to the issues that arose on campus in the 1960s or a unique challenge to the late 1970s and early 1980s that required a response aligned with perceived institutional traditions and a particular interpretation of Jesuit moral action. The significance of the differences was made apparent in the context of new service programs that Georgetown leaders developed as part of their effort to support the anti-apartheid struggle. The first programmatic effort was a service program, run under the Volunteer and Public Service Center, that sent Georgetown students to work as teachers in South Africa. John DeGioia, the dean of student affairs and the special assistant to Healy, explained that the purpose was to "expose Georgetown students to the third world and especially what the Catholic Church is doing there."[27]

In the context of this program, students confronted the political limitations of narrowly focusing on education and tutoring. Despite being placed in Catholic schools, the volunteers in the program were required to teach their classes according to standard government syllabi and textbooks. This requirement restricted the content of discussion that Georgetown students could have within the context of the classroom. Relatedly, the focus on education—in particular, teaching from South African government-sponsored textbooks—treated the students' situation in a political vacuum. Bo Martin, who attended Georgetown, was one of the first students to participate in the program in South Africa. After a student missed a class, he inquired as to why, seeing poor attendance as a reflection of bad behavior. In response to Martin's complaint, the principal told him that the student had missed the class because he was still recovering from losing his brother to government violence.[28] The response by the principal demonstrated to Martin that the program's emphasis on education and attendance ignored the broader political reality of Black students' lives in apartheid South Africa. Martin's experiences reflected what many anti-apartheid student activists concluded about programs in South Africa that narrowly focused on education and service. Such efforts, they argued, tended to serve the status quo rather than challenge the political and economic system

Indeed, Georgetown administrators used the Harvard teaching volunteer program in South Africa as a model, one that was critiqued by student activists and South African leaders. In a wide-ranging report on the Harvard program shared with students within SCAR, student activists on the Harvard-Radcliffe Southern Africa Solidarity Committee found that the internship program only served White student populations in South Africa and had no representation from Black South African students studying in the United States. In their research, the students contacted representatives from the United Democratic Front, the African National Congress, and the South-West African Peoples Organization, all of whom argued that they did not want Americans to participate in volunteer programs because "such involvement, in their opinion, damages the cultural boycott of South Africa and legitimizes the South African educational system." As Neo Mnumzana, chief representative of the African National Congress, told the students, the South African volunteer program only served to fill the vacuum of students and teachers' boycotts of the system. "Those people who claim they are going to South Africa in order to change its educational system," he explained, "wittingly or not, only succeed in sabotaging the cultural boycott and helping apartheid to break its international isolation." More worrisome, the student activists noted, education internships in South Africa were "part of a national effort to establish such programs in American universities, an effort which has some links to universities' efforts to contain protest and activism relating to divestment from South Africa. It also has links to South African government-run universities." While students had found these programs admirable, they ultimately concluded that they tended to serve the South African apartheid system and redirect student political energies in the United States.[29]

The differences between SCAR students' vision of moral action and that of university leaders were also apparent in the efforts in the DC area. One of the major initiatives of the CAC at Georgetown was tutoring in the local community neighborhoods as part of a program called For the Love of the Children. Cesie Delve, the coordinator of the effort, believed these programs gave students an opportunity to "experience the other side of Washington D.C." and to "provide service" to that community. She translated this idea through the conception of citizenship that Georgetown supported through its Jesuit Mission. Working in community service, she explained, "is recognizing that as a citizen there is more to being human than amassing prestige."[30]

Student activists in SCAR agreed, seeing their service as a way to act as citizens in the world. Many SCAR members linked the anti-apartheid struggle to their service work in the DC community. SCAR activist Ellen Lake volunteered with Sursum Corda, a community service effort at Georgetown that involved work in the Sursum Corda neighborhood of Washington, DC. Meaning "lift your hearts," the name of the neighborhood came from a large public housing unit. Lake saw her service work as intimately linked to her campus activism against apartheid. She noted that the kids of the neighborhood were "Sharpesville kids" who faced the same set of political disempowerment and poor living conditions as those in South Africa. In contrast to CAC initiatives, their service work did not end with learning about the "other side" of Washington, DC. Rather, they saw their service work as a means to broader efforts of community organizing and political activism that included the transformation of institutions. Drawing on their work in the community, SCAR members also organized a march and protest at the Department of Education, where they focused on economic, ethnic, and racial barriers to education.[31]

In linking the political demand for divestment to service work both in DC and South Africa, SCAR activists made a larger argument regarding Georgetown's actions and identity as an institution. Student activist Dan Burke argued that Georgetown suffered from an "identity crisis" as a Jesuit institution. Shifting the focus away from the individual student and toward "corporate actions" or the "actions with which Georgetown is identified as a cohesive whole, as an institution," Burke contended that the "aggregate picture is muddled and murky." While Healy and board members made rhetorical calls for social and racial justice, the university's actions as a corporate entity perpetuated apartheid, he asserted. Specifically, Burke turned his attention to poverty within the DC area and the institution's investment practices in South Africa. "While six million dollars of our investment capital supports firms in South Africa," he noted, "very little investment goes into our own city's neighborhoods." The issue, he believed, was Georgetown's close affiliations with corporate money and the military defense, both of which ran counter to his understanding of Christian justice and action. In his view, the first action that the university had to take to more closely align its corporate actions with its Jesuit identity was to publicly condemn apartheid and fully divest from corporations working in South Africa.[32]

Burke's argument resurrected the broader concern about the university as an institutional actor but was largely confined to the pages of the student newspaper. Indeed, over the course of the late 1970s and well into the mid-1980s, the interpretative differences concerning the appropriate moral action of Georgetown were largely abstract and academic: they concerned either the numbers and reports around the university's investment portfolio or programmatic efforts in South Africa and the DC area. The implications of the differences took on greater significance in the mid-1980s, when SCAR activists shifted their political actions away from the South African Embassy and toward Georgetown's campus. University leaders were then directly confronted with whether political action in the form of protest was part of Jesuit service, resurrecting the more fundamental question about the role of the university that emerged out of the mass student politics in the 1960s.

Freeing the College

In 1985, SCAR activists had gathered over two thousand signatures in support of divestment. Despite the broader support for divestment, university leaders maintained that their appropriate moral action was to continue with selective investments. "We disagree with the Committee [of students] that the response [to apartheid] should be absolute divestment," the board of trustees concluded, "because we believe that the Sullivan Principles and other efforts to influence the South African government carry promises of success." University leaders also maintained that student activists should continue to engage with the issue within the context of what they deemed were appropriate institutional processes. "The university should assume a leading role in the education of citizens generally," the board's committee members explained, "so that public debate will be provided with a reliable and full foundation."[33] Indeed, as DeGioia noted, "Georgetown continues to address these investment issues in the framework appropriate to an institution of higher education."[34]

SCAR activists did commit to the institutional processes that university leaders believed were necessary to engaging with the issue of South Africa while focusing their political actions off campus. They worked with the Coalition for Responsible Investment to review Georgetown's investments. Protests focused on the South African Embassy. Organizing centered around public events. But, frustrated by what they saw as the tepid response by university leaders, the students challenged the continued emphasis on "the framework appropriate to an institution of higher education." SCAR activists took inspiration from students' aspirational visions of the university that grew out of the 1960s, believing that such visions better represented the university as a space for education and open debate. They organized a campus sit-in and teach-in. Highlighting the historical connections to the student activism of the 1960s and the Black Freedom Struggle in the United States, the students named the college the Jimmy Lee Jackson Freedom College, in memory of the SNCC activist who was murdered while working in Alabama in 1965.[35]

The campus sit-in—and the Freedom College in particular—revived one of the central questions that emerged in the 1960s: To what extent, if at all, can the university explicitly support students' political actions? But, in the 1980s, there was an important difference. SCAR activists had to align their campus political actions to ensure they complied with the regulations that grew out of the 1960s. Indeed, DeGioia's framework also applied to the form and nature of student political action on campus. Prior to the national anti-apartheid protest in the spring of 1985, SCAR activists were required to meet with representatives of student affairs to clarify the time and day of the gathering. In a meeting with Marguerite Fletcher, a SCAR activist, student affairs representative Phillip Inglima said that there were only certain places where students could hold the gathering. "I also reminded her," Inglima noted on an internal memo, that "I did not think it would be possible to have such a protest on the first or second floor of the Healy building because of classes and administrative work going on during the daytime." Moreover, when Fletcher expressed the plan to present student signatures directly to the board of trustees, Inglima responded "that it would not be possible for all of the protesters to be present at such a presentation." Inglima informed her that if the signatures were brought beforehand, he would share it with the board.[36]

Similarly, when students organized the Freedom College, they had to follow strict guidelines. DeGioia told students that they were required to follow two regulations. First, he explained, "the demonstration cannot disrupt any function of the University," particularly classes and administrative meetings. Second, "the demonstration cannot threaten the safety and security of this community," This rule gave university leaders extensive interpretive flexibility on what constituted safety and security.[37] Inglima and DeGioia supported students' right to political action, but such action could not disrupt regular functions of the university, as defined by DeGioia.

At the heart of the Freedom College was one component of the institutional legacy of disciplining democracy adapted to the particular context of Georgetown and anti-apartheid activism in the 1980s. DeGioia was supportive of the idea of the Freedom College, but his affiliation with the institutional culture of disciplining limited how he could support the political action. Throughout the divestment effort, DeGioia was the main contact person between students and the university administration. At the Freedom College, DeGioia ran a seminar with the student activists and explained that their efforts, both in the community and at the university, exemplified the meaning of "godliness" and spiritual commitment in the world. At the same time, DeGioia's professional position limited the ways he could support the students and their commitments to their ideals. When students sought to expand the Freedom College to include a shanty as a symbol of South African Black poverty, DeGioia interpreted such an action as being counter to the institutional regulations on political action. DeGioia called on the police to dismantle the Freedom College after a week of operation, and the thirty-five students who stayed to protect it both as a symbol and site of community were arrested.

The arrest revealed the competing notions of appropriate education and action at Georgetown in the 1980s. To student activists, the sit-in and the Freedom College represented a different kind of education. Fletcher resurrected the older vision of action education, focusing on the sit-in as itself a form of education. "This is part of your education," she emphasized, referring to the sit-in. "All of you are better educated."[38] In taking this view, students argued that the university-sponsored arrest and dismantling of the Freedom College contradicted Georgetown's education mission. Christian Driscoll argued, "It is the very nature of protest to confront, disturb, and raise unsettling questions. It is the very nature of a university to allow these questions not only to be raised, but also debated." But the moment the university took down the Freedom College, she wrote, it "displayed its misunderstanding of the notion of University." Indeed, Driscoll focused on university leaders' persistent calls for the institution to serve as a space for open debate. "When challenged by the students, the administration showed what they thought of open debate and protest in a university," she further argued. "Municipal police were called in to assist GUPS [Georgetown University Protective Services] in the removal of the challengers." Like their counterparts in the 1960s, students were disciplined for attempting "to speak for an ideal, to do what they thought they could do to lash out against injustice," Driscoll argued.[39]

Arrested students interpreted Georgetown's decision as an expansion of the disciplining apparatus of the university in a way that would further limit a core component of their education—political action. Prior to their arrest, students rightly noted that the administration never made any efforts "to negotiate or discuss the ramifications of their protest." Moreover, they were never made aware "of any official university statement explaining the rationale behind the disciplinary actions taken against us." Despite statements that said otherwise, university leaders decided "to use force before dialogue," they concluded, fearing this would have long-term implications on students' political action. "We interpret the disciplinary actions taken by the Administration to be an attempt to stifle nonviolent student protest on campus through intimidation."[40]

The debate about the educational meaning of political action and the Freedom College did not just pit university leaders against student activists. Rather, the issue went to the heart of institutional policy, faculty governance, and the university's educational mission. The first issue that emerged centered around the rationale and legality of the arrests. DeGioia's main reason for ordering the arrest was the perception of possible violence. Citing other incidents of violence that emerged from the construction of shanties on college campuses across the United States, he argued that his decision had been made to protect students. "I have a fiduciary responsibility to protect the members of this community and it was my judgment that if the shanty went up I would no longer be honoring that responsibility."[41] In a meeting with DeGioia, Law Professor Michal Seidman reminded him that freedom of expression was protected and that his rationale—what was known as "protective arrests"—had been declared unconstitutional in the civil rights movement.[42]

The arrest had direct implications on the type of civic lessons it taught students. Indeed, faculty member Phil Herzbrun raised a set of more pointed questions that went to the heart of the issue. Was the reason, he asked DeGioia, really just about protecting students, or was it to "cause them to take the consequences for their actions?" If the latter, university leaders could take the position that the goal was to teach the implications of what it meant to commit to political and moral action. However, when asked this, DeGioia said he had acted *in loco parentis* and emphasized the need to protect students. Herzbrun and other faulty members thus worried that the arrests sent a troubling message about students' political actions. In their view, the university made a value judgment as to what were appropriate forms of Jesuit action and what were not. As faculty members in the meeting agreed, the arrests and the subsequent "disciplinary probation will curtail the rights of some of the most concerned students to express their views."[43]

To faculty members, it was, in other words, both a troubling civic and Catholic lesson. John Pfordresher, another English professor, framed the issue in terms of what kind of lesson it taught students about the university. "It was clear," he explained to Healy, that the students who were arrested last Friday "are idealists who care deeply about human justice, and Georgetown's relationship to matters of right and wrong." But the arrests taught students that their actions—and political commitments—were outside the periphery of the university. "Their occupation of University property has ended; their shanty has been pulled down. I am sure that whatever their personal reaction to the experiences of the past few days, they now know how seriously the University's administrators regard their actions."[44] Pfordresher's faculty colleague, John Glavin, argued that the arrests shattered the Catholic educational ideal of Georgetown. "I am shocked and deeply angered that the Administration of a University that prides itself on its Catholic and Jesuit heritage should not only cooperate with, but actively invite the arrest of its own students who were harmlessly standing witness against a grave evil," he argued. "Surely," he continued, "Georgetown must be a place that does not simply tolerate, but actively encourages the public demonstration of conscience."[45]

Glavin's assertion related to statements made by Healy about his vision of the university's role. In the first part of the 1980s, Healy publicly argued that the university must be a place for dissent. He believed that critics misunderstood the university by assuming that institutions "are orderly places, and if they aren't, presidents and trustees ought to make them so, even by force." Healy emphasized, "Force is, however, our last and least resource."[46] But this principle was largely ignored. During the faculty meeting, he was noticeably silent about the arrests of the students associated with the Freedom College. The silence suggested that the type of actions that students engaged in did not align with his understanding of Jesuit values and service commitments. When pressed by the faculty member William McElroy about the relationship between protest and "a campus that encourages students to question values," Healy responded that he assumed "no one at Georgetown defended apartheid theoretically but that the appropriate means of challenging it are a matter of judgment." His response was instructive. Moreover, he countered that the university did allow students to question values in the world, citing the Georgetown Law and Graduate school programs that trained students to work in South Africa.[47]

In referencing the service opportunities, Healy clarified his view that the political actions of students associated with the Freedom College did not align with his vision of the university—a view that also disappointed Georgetown's campus ministry. In a letter to Healy, the campus ministry wrote:

The real issue, as we see it, is the breakdown in communication resulting in actions which contradict your own vision of what a university like Georgetown should be, as stated in the 1985 Annual Report, a "quiet space where we, faculty and students, deal with each other, where our shared citizenship in a commonwealth called a university makes us neighbors, colleagues and friends." You even seem to concede a potentially healthy role for occasional dis-quiet caused by "the turmoil and din outside the gates, not to mention the turmoil and din of growing up." We submit that the real underlying issues here center around the failure of all of us (for each of us, according to his/her own role and function, has a stake in this "commonwealth") to live up to this vision. We sense that what might have been a genuine search for truth, an educational praxis for all of us, degenerated for whatever reason into a power struggle, a tug o' war, a flexing of muscles, that not only fails to do justice to the vision that we share with you, but also leaves a number of casualties in its wake: alienated faculty and students who should be "neighbors, colleagues, and friends."[48]

Legacy

Georgetown University divested from all holdings in late winter of 1986. But the chronology of the decision revealed the institution's stance on political action. In the spring of 1986, when DeGioia called in the police to arrest students, the board of trustees maintained that investment was the right moral action of the university. However, over the course of the spring, political developments increasingly supported the arguments made by SCAR student activists. In the fall of 1986, the House of Representatives passed a blanket bill ruling out all investment and business relations with South Africa. That same year, Leon Sullivan concluded that his principles did not have any effect on South Africa, let alone their intended effect. Most importantly for Georgetown University, the US Catholic Conference, the national action arm of Roman Catholic bishops, divested $5.3 million in investments in American firms doing business in South Africa.[49] Healy and the board of trustees decided to follow suit and divest.

Georgetown's decision to divest was not just a product of shifting political winds. Throughout the anti-apartheid campus movement, university leaders were not dismissive of calls for divestment. Those on the investment committee acknowledged that "the University must reflect upon the nature of its associations, including its revenues." Moreover, the board chair, Donald Donahue, publicly stated that the university would give the divestment issue "very careful study."[50] Likewise, Healy did not rule out divestment, especially if the conditions in South Africa continued to deteriorate. Healy was willing to engage with the evidence that demonstrated the limitations of selective investment or the Sullivan principles. Healy was also privy to congressional hearings and debates. As a member of the Secretary of State's Advisory Commission on South Africa, Healy engaged with other members, such as the labor union organizer Owen F. Bieber, who argued for the original house bill, and Sullivan, when he changed his stance and called "for the withdrawal of all U.S. companies and a total U.S. embargo against South Africa."[51] Unlike Kennedy at Stanford and Swearer at Brown, Healy did engage with the mounting evidence that demonstrated continued university investment had any effect on undermining the system of apartheid.

Yet, Healy also ignored students' arguments throughout—a point made by South African leaders during the Freedom College. Indeed, South African leaders closely followed the political efforts of students on American college campuses. In hearing about student actions at Georgetown, Twiggs Xiphu, who helped form the South African Student Organisation with Steve Biko, wrote to Healy at Georgetown: "As a South African and leader of one of the organizations opposed to the apartheid regime of South Africa, I have nothing but praise for the stand that the students have taken against the unjust policies of the racist Pretoria government." Moreover, he argued that "investing in Apartheid South Africa is investing in slavery, at best, and genocide at worst." He offered to testify before a Georgetown committee about his experiences as a Black person in South Africa, the impact of Bantu education, and being an employee of a US company.[52]

The decision to divest was noticeable not only because Georgetown University leaders took a political position on the issue, but also because they were explicitly silent on the role of students. When Healy participated in the faculty meeting concerned with the arrests of students associated with the Freedom College, he remained silent on his stance about the arrests. While he refused to take a public position on the arrests, he staunchly supported DeGioia's decision. DeGioia also remained steadfast in his position to arrest the students, even after dropping the charges against them. "I believe I made the correct judgment last spring, and I also believe I made the correct judgment in dropping the charges. I believe the shanty had to come down."[53]

Though Healy was silent and DeGioia remained committed to his initial position on the political action of students, they both celebrated the work of students associated with the CAC. Indeed, what emerged in the aftermath of the anti-apartheid movement was an explicit effort to promote community service while disciplining of other forms of political action. With Kennedy at Stanford, Healy took a leading role in the formation of the Campus Compact. Likewise, DeGioia became a leading figure in promoting and expanding community service on campus. "Community service is a critical commitment: it allows the students to know and share something together that they could never get alone," he emphasized. "It fosters an understanding of a way of life that students from predominantly upper-middle class homes would never be exposed."[54] At the same time that DeGioia celebrated the commitment action of students associated with the CAC, he also led efforts to develop stricter protest policies. In the new policy guidelines developed after the Freedom College, any individual or group seeking to host a public event for the exchange of ideas had to reserve a space and get prior approval by the university—in some cases at least ten days in advance.[55] The *Hoya* editorial board noted the implications of this new policy: "The very nature of protest is to defy rules like this that may inhibit the protesters' ability to hold any kind of sustained demonstration." They concluded, "DeGioia's committee has produced yet another law to limit and regulate the behavior on campus."[56]

In the context of efforts to promote community service and develop new policies on student political action, student veterans of the Freedom College published an op-ed to remind others of the critical role of students in pushing Georgetown to take a position of moral clarity. "We remind the administration," wrote Maria Rodriguez and Beth Knight, "of the significant role students have played in divestment." They further argued that despite Georgetown's decision to divest, it was important to remember that university leaders had not taken a proactive stance. "We regret that Georgetown, a university respected among the intellectual and religious worlds," they wrote, "was so slow in acting and missed the opportunity to lead in this moral and responsible position." The students published the article to ensure that the memory of the Freedom College and student activism in the divestment movement—and the vision of the university it produced—remained as a source of inspiration. In their view, this was especially important to challenging Georgetown's explicit recycling of disciplining that mitigated the value of student protest and political action on and off campus during the anti-apartheid movement. The article represented the persistent politics of memory at Georgetown and the ways such politics informed what the administration deemed as appropriate moral action in and beyond the university.[57]

Conclusion
"To Channel Off Discontent"

In the early 1960s, Paul Potter helped develop leadership institutes for students involved in civil rights activism across the South. The seminar largely took on key characteristics of the university's traditional disciplinary culture: expert lectures with discussions. In the leadership institute report for 1962, Potter wrote that the seminars were effective because many participants had been on the front lines of the sit-ins and freedom rides. Thus, he explained, when they attended the seminars, they could connect the discussions to their activist experiences. However, in his 1963 report, Potter expressed concerned about this model. The participants in the 1963 program, he noted, did not have the same political experiences as the previous cohorts. In Potter's view, the lack of experiences demonstrated the limitations of the leadership seminar model. "We moved from an anticipated group of experienced and tested leaders whose work in and around decision-making situations would have led them to appreciate the need for the study of certain subjects and problems," Potter wrote, "to a group of relatively inexperienced, untested young leaders whose lack of experience with or responsibility for larger problems of the movement on a community or national level had kept them from developing sophisticated interests in the material planned for the Institute." Potter argued that future institutes needed to include some sort of "systematic community work or action program" for students to make connections between the material in the classroom and the community context.[1]

As the new president of SDS, Potter expanded on this idea in a white paper titled "An Action Education for the Southern Civil Rights Movement." He remained committed to developing particular programs of study that would directly support the civil rights struggle. The exigencies of day-to-day organizing and the geographical spread of student civil rights activists, he worried, prevented activists from engaging with formal education and research that would provide context for their social and political challenges. He believed that the creation of action education centers on college campuses would provide leadership training, research, and other educational support. Potter also remained committed to developing "systematic community work or action program." Indeed, he later concluded that "the community may prove a more effective place in which to educate students as radicals than is the insulated university." The challenge—and the core tension within his idea—was how to best integrate formal education with activism. As Potter argued, the goal was both "dropping out" and "hanging on" to the university.[2]

The concept of action education centers was not a fleeting idea heaped onto other stacks of SDS white papers. Along with fellow SDS member Rennie Davis, Potter reached out to the University of California, Berkeley. To Potter, the University of California seemed like an ideal place. He had been inspired by the student sit-in and its critique of the modern American university. He was also familiar with the efforts of Martin Meyerson to develop a new community program in the aftermath of the 1964 campus protest. But when Potter asked the University of California administration to support its action education in the Bay Area, he was disturbed by what he interpreted as the administration's tepid response. In a letter to Davis, Potter wrote, "They are trying to buy us off." He explained that Meyerson "wants a program to send students into the slums for credit" but did not want to be affiliated with the political goals of either SDS or the local civil rights struggle in the Bay Area. Some in SDS, Potter noted, believed the programmatic effort was an attempt "to channel off discontent."[3] He worried the new program would attract students with social or political concerns but funnel their commitments toward community service, not political activism. He was concerned that this mode of disciplining would mitigate rather than enhance student activism.

Potter's efforts and the new program at the University of California was but one instance of a broader campus debate that reshaped civics across American higher education in the late 1960s and early 1970s. In 1969, university leaders, representatives from federal volunteer programs, and former volunteers gathered at a conference in Atlanta, Georgia. The sponsors were the Peace Corps, Volunteers in Service to America, and the Southern Regional Education Board. Robert Sigmon, a returned Peace Corps volunteer, helped organize the gathering. Sigmon called for "service learning"—a model of civic education that connected formal education to domestic and international volunteer service. He and other attendees defined *service learning* as "the integration of the accomplishment of a needed task with educational growth." The combination, advocates like Sigmon believed, would provide "breadth and depth and relevance to students' learning" and "assist in assuring disciplined learning as part of this service."[4]

But others, like Potter, called for a different model. Paul Lauter and Florence Howe, both of whom worked with SNCC, argued that the program models for national service on campus—proposals that aimed to make education "more relevant"—sought to absorb the energy of youth "without disturbing or altering the nation's basic political, economic, and social arrangements."[5] Government- and university-defined ideas of service masked what they believed was the key lesson of students' various forms of social activism in the 1960s. "What young people discovered in the Peace Corps as well as in Mississippi or northern ghettos," they wrote, was "to eliminate the sources of misery, they would have to begin to challenge American institutions." They explained that students and young people in the 1960s had experienced a "process whereby 'involvement' in the lives of poor people" had led "to consciousness about, then confrontation with, such institutional causes of poverty."[6] In contrast to service learning, they called this educational process "service for change."[7]

The different visions of the university's civic mission— service learning and service for change—converged in the Nixon administration's Commission on Campus Unrest. The authors of the report—a committee that included university officials and college students—identified the contradictory demands for and definitions of service in American higher education as a central issue of campus unrest. While government and industry officials turned to the university for research for military and market needs, students, faculty, and citizens urged the university to develop action programs to tackle racism, housing, unemployment, and other related issues that plagued American society. To address demands for rethinking the meaning of service in American higher education, the committee called on universities to support programs that promoted service projects and fieldwork at the local level, albeit with one caveat: "Universities should avoid actions that will aggravate existing local problems or create new problems."[8] Universities should support community service and volunteerism, according to the report, but eschew efforts that were deemed political and outside the service mission of the university.

Service learning provided academic and political leaders with a civic model that reconciled the critiques of the university that inspired campus movements while also fitting with the new political culture of Nixon's New Federalism. Indeed, the emphasis on the "accomplishment of a needed task" lent itself to broader political shifts across the nation in the late 1960s and early 1970s. University-sponsored community service aligned with New Federalism, a policy proposal that relied upon volunteerism to replace federal programs and address gaps in social services and public goods. When university officials and policy makers defined and promoted service learning in the early 1970s, they thus did so in a way that underscored how it would fill in the service gaps not met by the reduction of federal social programs. By 1973, the National Student Volunteer Program—a new agency within the Nixon administration—listed 565 programs on college campuses that linked a student's coursework to volunteer service.[9]

The political and economic logic of service learning also informed the new culture of educational "relevance" reshaping the American university. In 1971, a year after the Nixon administration released its report on campus unrest, Frank Newman, the secretary of Health, Education, and Welfare, shared his findings on reforming higher education in his *Report on Higher Education*. The report was wide-ranging. Newman analyzed access, cost of education, and credentials. But a common theme in the report was the need for the university to extend education outside of the classroom to make it more relevant to students' professional and civic development. "We often lose sight of the enormous amount of teaching and learning that goes on outside of colleges," Newman wrote. Like Meyerson at the University of California and those in the Nixon commission, Newman prioritized the learning that occurred "in business, government, voluntary service organizations, military organizations."[10]

The learning in voluntary service organizations in particular became a primary focus of Newman's thinking on higher education reform. His main policy effort in the 1970s was the GI Bill of Community Service, a policy proposal that offered students tuition credit in exchange for volunteer service. Newman believed the GI Bill of Community Service would give students intellectual direction that would enable them to develop as citizens. Noticeably absent in Newman's proposal was any reference to the other modes of action education that emerged out of the student movements of the 1960s. Newman, like others before him, embraced the educational value of action in public life in a way that aligned with the prevailing disciplining culture in the American university.

Newman's report had the effect of further narrowing the possibilities of the new civics in the university. He presented service learning not as one option among others but as the model of the new civics in the modern American university. His vision came to fruition in the 1980s. In his 1985 report, *Higher Education and the American Resurgence*, he argued that the issue universities and colleges confronted was how "to restore to higher education its original purpose of preparing graduates for a life of involved and committed citizenship." Again, Newman emphasized community service and volunteerism as the primary means of learning civic responsibility. He also prioritized how students would learn from service over the ways it would benefit the community. "I would say that the first and foremost purpose is not to serve the communities," Newman explained, "but I think that the first thing would be to educate students in ways that their responsibility to see the larger issue as a citizen is the first task of the institution." He believed that community service offered a way to teach students a set of professional skills. Thus shaped by the new market ethos of the university in the 1980s, Newman summarized, students would learn "intangible skills" through service that would prepare them for professional success in the new economy.[11]

Newman's framework for service learning shaped the contours of civics in American higher education since the 1980s. He played a central role in the first meeting of the Project for Public and Community Service, or what became the Campus Compact. He invited Howard Swearer, Don Kennedy, and Timothy Healy, the three presidents who came under fire for their roles during the anti-apartheid movement on campus, to the gathering. The funding streams for the 1985 meeting and project also came from the foundations of corporations that were criticized by student anti-apartheid activists in the 1980s, including the Ford Foundation, Exxon Education Foundation, and Hewlett-Packard.[12] At the 1985 gathering, Newman and the university presidents focused on public service in higher education. Despite the rhetorical shift to "public" service, the type of action remained the same. University presidents defined *public service* as work in nonprofit and governmental agencies. They prioritized volunteer service as a "powerful educational tool" that would be a key component of "training for citizenship" in American higher education and would "infuse altruism into the ethic of the institution as a whole." "We call for steps," they further explained in their public statement, "to be taken now to recapture higher education's legacy of preparing students for service to others."[13]

In the 1960s, Newman chose to highlight students engaged in volunteerism over other forms of activism while developing his conception of civics. He did so again in the 1980s. At the same gathering where they outlined the service and volunteer components of learning citizenship and civic responsibility, Newman, Swearer, Kennedy, and Healy identified the Campus Outreach Opportunity League (COOL) as the model for the Campus Compact. At the first Campus Compact meeting, Newman invited Wayne Meisel and Robert Hackett, two Harvard students who helped start COOL, seeing in their work a range of examples that exemplified "constructive student activism."[14] Meisel called the COOL organization the "student service movement." As outlined in the "Durham Statement," Meisel, Hackett, and others in the COOL organization defined their work as "service activism," which took on three different practices. The first was "direct action"—working in soup kitchens or shelters for the homeless. The second was "education action"—students served as tutors for adults in need of living skills or for elementary students needing reading help. The third was "enabling action"—teaching "people to help themselves" and become self-sufficient. In all three ways, COOL participants envisioned transforming the university through volunteer service work. By the end of the decade, they hoped that every college and university designed new programs that enabled students "to make concerted service efforts in their communities." They believed that such involvement allowed students to explore public service careers and learn to "become leaders." As they explained, "By helping students to become involved in community service, we are supporting that kind of leadership and citizenship now and for the future as well."[15]

The Campus Compact reflected the triumph of service learning as the prevailing educational model of the modern university's civic mission. As it was in the 1970s, the emphasis on service learning was also politically flexible. Service learning garnered support from the former civil rights activist John Lewis and the former Peace Corps associate director Harris Wofford as well as from conservative commentators like William F. Buckley. As Buckley argued, "Common service," such as "helping to care for old people in homes or teaching ghetto children to read or shoring up security in the subways or helping to maintain the parks and museums and libraries would add up to a little but an indelible contribution to society that permits us so much by giving us freedom and sovereignty."[16] Community service also made political sense among American policy makers in the 1990s. Federal efforts like the Points of Light under George H. W. Bush and the Corporation for National and Community Service Act under Bill Clinton also promoted community service among college students, demonstrating the political ambidexterity of service learning as the new civics in American higher education. The Bush and Clinton administrations connected their efforts to the idea of social capital. First articulated by sociologist James S. Coleman and made popular by Robert Putnam's *Bowling Alone*, social capital encompassed the nonmaterial elements of civic life—the circles of trust and community relationships. In the context of American higher education, student volunteer service was promoted as a means of rebuilding social capital among communities.[17] As a 1989 Campus Compact report explained, the purpose of community service was to "nurture a sense of human community and social responsibility in our college students, and contribute to the quality of life for individuals and groups in the community."[18]

By the 1990s, appeals to action no longer appeared as a model for political education or a means to transform the university but as a new source of charity work and a more relevant professional education. In the transition from action education to service learning, the political goals were largely gutted. Of course, the ideals lingered on in the educational rhetoric of the new service learning and civic engagement centers. University officials, often citing the presence of those centers on campus, boasted about civic engagement opportunities that enabled students to be actively involved in the social and political world. At the same time, university civic and service learning programs tended to prioritize the ways the experiences enriched learning and enabled students to "do good" rather than how those commitments might address structural inequalities embedded both within and beyond the university. Martha Prescod, who was a student activist in both SNCC and SDS, believed what triumphed in the university was a far cry from the ethos and commitments of student activists in the 1960s. "I get a little upset when I see the Martin Luther King Jr. holiday turned into clean-up, sweep-up activities," she wrote. Activism and civic participation in the 1960s, she argued, "was not about 'giving back' or 'helping those less fortunate' or doing something for other people. It was about making social change with the understanding that we are all linked together on this earth. It was a 'doing with'—not 'doing for'—people who were not treated fairly."[19]

The political triumph of the Campus Compact did not mean that the debates as to how best to integrate social action into the university disappeared. Rather, those debates moved into the context of the emergent scholarly literature that grew out of the Campus Compact. In early scholarship, service learning practitioners largely adopted the engaged learning approach normalized by the Newman reports. The focus on charity-based civics was practical, so argued Edward Zlotkowski, the founding director of the Service

Learning Center at Bentley University in Waltham, Massachusetts. He worried that focusing on what he interpreted as the ideological aims of political advocacy would inhibit the adoption of service learning across American higher education. He argued that advocates of service learning in the 1990s needed to see "'enhanced learning' as the horse pulling the cart of 'moral and civic values,' and not vice versa." Zlotkowski's views represented those who saw service learning in the 1990s as a movement of socially and pedagogically concerned academics.[20]

In both Newman's initial framing and Zlotkowski's article, the priority was student learning. Other scholars who supported service learning worried that the tendency to prioritize it marginalized community needs and perspectives. John W. Eby, a professor of sociology and the director of Service Learning at Messiah College in the mid-1990s, was a regular contributor to and supporter of the Campus Compact's efforts to infuse higher education with a broader public purpose. Despite recognizing its value to student learning, especially in terms of developing social responsibility, Eby concluded that "service learning is bad" because "the demands of a learning orientation places on service limits its effectiveness and its ability to address community needs at a structural level." He argued that the problem with service learning was that it prioritized institutional and student needs over those of the community. Service learning programs were designed for "the needs of an academic institution which sponsors it, the needs of students, the needs of an instructor, the needs of a course."[21] Herman Blake agreed with Eby. A prominent Black sociologist at the University of California, Santa Cruz, Blake was a leading voice in reminding service learning scholars and practitioners to consider the perspective of the community. Like Robert Green at Michigan State University, Blake worried about the effect of "service" and instrumental research on communities. "My strongest criticism is that practitioners do not look at the community as a place of integrity," he explained. They "start out with a deficit approach" and ignored the distinct and valuable knowledge within communities on the receiving end of service.[22] From the perspective of both Eby and Blake, the challenge was to update the service learning model to better serve the community and not just the students.

While Blake and Eby sought to reorient the programs toward community need, they nonetheless maintained a focus on service and volunteerism. Scholars from the new disciplines that grew out of the 1960s critiqued prevailing models for their myopic focus on community service, a criticism that echoed the views of early activists who initially helped establish the programs. Although supportive of efforts to encourage volunteerism because the experience exposed students to community knowledge and issues, Kathryn Forbes, Linda Garber, and other feminist scholars in the women's studies program at Fresno State University worried that such efforts tended to reinforce relations of subordination rather than transform them. "Community service," they argued, "is at best an exercise in observing otherness and at worst a missionary expedition." Moreover, they wrote, community service requirements tended to only occur in courses focused on diversity, leading students to equate difference with deficiency. "If community service cannot incorporate students, professors, and organizations as partners with similar vested interests," they wrote, "then it will reinforce volunteer work as observation rather than activism." The university, they believed, should develop students who "integrate activism into their lives rather than be weekend volunteer warriors."[23]

Indeed, a growing set of scholars associated with the Campus Compact increasingly critiqued prevailing service learning models for the singular focus on volunteer and community service as the prevailing form of action in public life. One of the more prominent voices in the 1990s was Harry Boyte. Boyte was drawn to the work of public service programs in American higher education from his work as a student activist in the 1960s. As the director of the Unitarian Service Committee in Atlanta and a field-worker with Robert F. Williams in Virginia, Boyte organized students and local community members to desegregate education and set up alternative schools. He also joined Martin Luther King Jr.'s staff at the Southern Christian Leadership Council, where he helped organize community workshops that directly challenged political and economic institutions. Like others who worked with King in the 1960s, Boyte saw service as an inherently political act. Writing in the early 1990s, he criticized prevailing conceptions of service associated with the Campus Compact and other programs because they prioritized "personal relevance and a sense of membership in a community" and led students to see "service as an *alternative* to politics."[24]

By the 2000s, the growing criticism of prevailing models of service and civics led some scholar-practitioners to delineate between "traditional" and "critical" service learning. In traditional forms of service learning, argued Tania Mitchell, the focus is on student learning in which the service experience enriches the classroom content. Emphasizing the connection between content and experience, advocates of traditional service learning, she explained, enabled students to become "active learners, bringing skills and information from community work and integrating them with the theory and curriculum of the classroom to produce new knowledge." In contrast, Mitchell wrote, critical service learning programs "encouraged students to see themselves as agents of social change and use the experience of service to address and respond to injustice in communities." She called on administrators and educators to implement a more "critical" service learning in their practice and outlook, which often involved embracing a progressive political agenda.[25] Despite efforts to promote more critical forms of civic engagement in American higher education, prevailing models continue to prioritize community service. In their study on contemporary service learning, Anne Colby, Elizabeth Beaumont, Thomas Ehrlich, and Josh Corngold show that among the six hundred service learning programs, only 1 percent included "a focus on specifically political concerns and solutions such as working with groups to represent the interests of a community," and about half focus only on direct service, such as tutoring and food pantries.[26]

What scholars of service learning are confronting—that is, the tensions within and limitations of institutional civic engagement programs—is not something new. Indeed, what is surprising about scholarship on service learning is how little acknowledgment has been given to the models in the 1960s and the institutional debates and programs that predate the Campus Compact. It appears that most scholarly writing on service learning and civic engagement have been in response to the ideas associated with the Campus Compact.[27] Efforts by students to reimagine the university and the new civic programs they helped establish have largely been forgotten. Ironically, the amnesia has been aided by historians. With a few exceptions, the tendency among historians has been to treat education policy, intellectual transformations in the university, and student activism as separate categories of analysis.[28] It should not come as a surprise, then, that civic and service learning scholars today, when looking at the historical record, find no precedent. Prevailing scholarly approaches to the history of the university and activism thus leave civic scholars, academic leaders, and students interpretively impoverished.

Contemporary interest and writing indicate that civics is still an important mission of American higher education, but scholars continue to express ambivalence about its practice, place, and purpose on college campuses. This is especially the case when student activists attempt to translate their civic lessons on and off campus. Over the course of my writing this book, student activism captured national and international headlines. Concerned with issues related to police violence, economic inequality, and climate change, students challenged the priorities of American universities. University administrators and social commentators have responded in a range of different ways, from focusing on free speech to seeing activism as antithetical to the pursuit of truth. Even those who are strong advocates of civic education in the university have expressed consternation about institutions explicitly supporting student activists, let alone advocating a particular political position associated with a social movement.[29] What lessons, then, can be drawn from this history—and the legacy of disciplining democracy—especially for contemporary debates on civic education and the role of the university?

One way of reading this history is in creative terms. In the original version of this book, I defined students' visions as expressions of "civic intellectualism." Although the label did not stick, as the book's title suggests, the formulation captured the broad vision of student activists and faculty supporters who articulated a different idea of what it meant to pursue knowledge and education in and beyond the university. This vision of "civic intellectualism" produced new civic engagement programs in higher education that provide an important outlet for students to learn and engage through public participation in community life. Moreover, the presence of such centers also reflects the creative approach by university leaders. When faced with the political aspirations of their students, they responded by supporting new institutional homes for civic engagement. From this perspective, then, service learning and new civic engagement programs reflect not only the pedagogical possibilities of campus activism but also the ingenuity of campus leaders that brought about significant educational reforms within universities.

Another way of reading this history is in terms of political limitations. The triumph of service learning within civic engagement programs demonstrates the dilemma of turning toward the university as a source of social transformation. At different historical periods, student activists and their supporters expressed an intense faith in the university as a source of not only truth but political change in wider society. But that utopian faith often met an institutional incrementalism that limited students' political actions both on and off campus. In today's higher education context, practitioners and scholars associated with the civic engagement centers and programs, like the students and faculty members of the 1960s who helped lay the groundwork for those programs, also confront the institutional regulations that limit the type of opportunities and actions that students can engage in as representatives of the university. From this perspective, service learning and civic engagement programs demonstrate not only the constraints of the programs as a source for political transformation but also the unintended ways they have functioned to deflect and co-opt student political energies away from the university.

Both readings hold kernels of truth. However, the lessons miss the larger and more persistent problem. The university's mode of disciplining—that is, the very regulations that limited student political actions and determined what was appropriate civic engagement—was concealed by a common refrain embedded in the culture of the university: the institution is a neutral actor. Indeed, most university leaders from the 1960s to the 1980s adopted the argument made by Harry Kalven in what became the Kalven report at the University of Chicago. In response to the mass student politics of the 1960s, Kalven underscored the vision of the university as a community of scholars and source of dissent. "By design and by effect," he wrote, "it is the institution which creates discontent with the existing social arrangements and proposes new ones." Yet, he maintained that the institution itself must remain neutral, arguing, "The instrument of dissent and criticism is the individual faculty member or the individual student. The university is the home and sponsor of critics; it is not itself the critic."[30] Academic leaders today have likewise returned to the logic of the report to deflect criticisms of the university as an institutional actor.[31] The problem with this reading of "the University's role in political and social action"—the topical focus of the Kalven report—is that the university was rarely just a "home and sponsor of critics." If there is a common theme throughout this book, it is that the institution, through its leadership and boards but also its internal mechanisms, also made direct value judgments that impinged and limited the actions of critics, whether student or faculty.

Indeed, institutional neutrality was one of the primary issues of the sit-in at the University of California, Berkeley, where this book began. Throughout the campus movement, Mario Savio consistently emphasized the ways the university was deeply involved in military and corporate research and dependent upon military and corporate funding. This connection, he argued, demonstrated that not only was the university far from a neutral actor when it came to its research and teaching activities, it also lacked the institutional independence and autonomy required for it to be a space for debate, civic action, and the pursuit of truth. However, Savio did not dismiss the ideal of neutrality altogether. Rather, he asked an important question that went to the heart of this institutional ideal. "Don't you think," Savio asked, when considering the university's role in the development of military technology, "in the spirit of political neutrality, either they should not be involved or there should be some democratic control over the way they're being involved?"[32]

The second part of his question reflected Savio's political vision of the university associated with his appeal to action. When he argued that "action and knowledge cannot be separated," he made a claim on how we come to know ourselves as citizens in a democracy and how we might develop new political knowledge for building consensus. Indeed, Savio envisioned collective action as the educational practice for building consensus on political and social issues in and beyond the university. In response, university leaders maintained a commitment to an orthodox conception of institutional neutrality and promoted service learning as the appropriate form of action education. The combination shaped the contours of disciplining democracy. If we want to think beyond the logic of disciplining democracy, taking Savio's question seriously—and the other political visions articulated by the historical actors in this book—might be a helpful starting point for remaking the university into a genuine space for public deliberation and civic engagement.

NOTES

Introduction

1. Mario Savio, Speech at Sit-In, Sproul Hall, September 30, 1964, in *The Essential Mario Savio: Speeches and Writings That Changed America*, ed. Robert Cohen (Berkeley: University of California Press, 2014), 114.

2. Mario Savio, Speech at FSM Rally, November 20, 1964, in *The Essential Mario Savio: Speeches and Writings That Changed America*, ed. Robert Cohen (Berkeley: University of California Press, 2014), 163.

3. "Kerr Condemns Politicking," *Daily Californian*, September 28, 1964.

4. "Chancellor's Committee for Community Service," September 10, 1965, box 57, CU-149, University Archives, Bancroft Library, Berkeley, California.

5. "Chancellor's Committee for Community Service," September 10, 1965, box 57, CU-149, University Archives, Bancroft Library, Berkeley, California. A couple of months before the Meyerson report came out, Sargent Shriver, the director of the Peace Corps, visited the University of California. In his speech, he equated the campus activism at Berkeley to international volunteer work in the Peace Corps. The initials "FSM," Shriver explained, stand for the "free service movement." Speech by Sargent Shriver at the University of California, Berkeley, March 31, 1965, box 22, Personal Papers of Sargent Shriver, Subject File 1961–1966, series 2.1, John F. Kennedy Library and Archives, Boston, MA.

6. Savio, "Speech at FSM Rally on Sproul Plaza," November 20, 1964, in *The Essential Mario Savio*, 164.

7. On the effects of traditional forms of disciplining on social movements, see Ellen Messer Davidow, *Disciplining Feminism: From Social Activism to Academic Discourse* (Durham, NC: Duke University Press, 2002); Fabio Rojas, *From Black Power to Black Studies* (Baltimore: Johns Hopkins University Press, 2007); Roderick Ferguson, *The Reorder of Things: The University and Its Pedagogies of Minority Difference* (Minneapolis: University of Minnesota Press, 2012).

8. On education for the nation and leadership, see Bernard Bailyn, *Education in the Forming of American Society: Needs and Opportunities* (New York: Vintage, 1960); and Mark R. Nemec, *Ivory Towers and Nationalist Minds: Universities, Leadership, and National Development* (Ann Arbor: University of Michigan Press, 2006). On education and the liberal state, see Christopher P. Loss, *Between Citizens and the State: The Politics of American Higher Education in the 20th Century* (Princeton, NJ: Princeton University Press, 2014); and Andrew Jewett, "Naturalizing Liberalism in the 1950s," in *Professors and their Politics*, ed. Neil Gross and Solomon Simmons (Baltimore: Johns Hopkins University Press, 2014). Other historians have focused on the gender and racial components of citizenship. See Craig Steven Wilder, *Ebony and Ivy: Race, Slavery, and the*

Troubled History of America's Universities (New York: Bloomsbury, 2014); Andrea Turpin, *A New Moral Vision: Gender, Religion, and the Changing Purposes of American Higher Education, 1837–1917* (Ithaca, NY: Cornell University Press, 2016); Leigh Patel, *No Study Without Struggle: Confronting Settler Colonialism in Higher Education* (New York: Beacon, 2021).

9. Most work on the rise of the modern university argues that moral concern was marginalized on campus, but scholars disagree on factors that led to the marginalization of morality. Some scholars focus on the rise of industrial capitalism and the administrative state. See Clyde W. Barrow, *Universities and the Capitalist State: Corporate Liberalism and the Reconstruction of American Higher Education, 1894–1928* (Madison: University of Wisconsin Press, 1990). Others identify science's naturalism as the source of value-neutrality in the university. See especially George M. Marsden, *The Soul of the American University: From Protestant Establishment to Established Nonbelief* (New York: Oxford University Press, 1994); and Julie Reuben, *The Making of the Modern University: Intellectual Transformation and the Marginalization of Morality* (Chicago: University of Chicago Press, 1996). Other historians argue that "value disengagement" was a result of shifting political cultures and ultimately the Cold War. See Andrew Jewett, *Science, Democracy, and the American University: From the Civil War to the Cold War* (New York: Cambridge University Press, 2012). This intellectual transformation was an important trend in the rise of what some call the "Cold War" university. On this, see Rebecca S. Lowen, *Creating the Cold War University: The Transformation of Stanford* (Berkeley: University of California Press, 1997). Ethan Schrum sees the Cold War university as a prominent offshoot of what he calls the instrumental university. Schrum, *The Instrumental University: Education in Service of the National Agenda after World War II* (Ithaca, NY: Cornell University Press, 2019).

10. For conservative criticism of the university's responses post-1960s, see Allan Bloom, *The Closing of the American Mind: How Higher Education Has Failed Democracy and Impoverished the Souls of Today's Students* (New York: Simon and Schuster, 1987); for its liberal response (and defense), see Lawrence Levine, *The Opening of the American Mind: Canons, Culture, and History* (New York: Beacon, 1997).

11. The notion of disciplining as an institutional logic takes inspiration from Pierre Bourdieu and Jean Claude Passeron's idea of "pedagogic action." See Bourdieu and Passeron, *Reproduction in Education, Society, and Culture* (New York: Sage, 1990).

12. I am indebted to the excellent scholarship on student activism in the 1960s, in particular the works that focus on Students for a Democratic Society (SDS), the Student Nonviolent Coordinating Committee (SNCC), and the Peace Corps. On SDS, see James Miller, *Democracy in the Streets: From Port Huron to the Siege of Chicago* (New York: Simon and Schuster, 1987); Jennifer Frost, *An Interracial Movement of the Poor: Community Organizing and the New Left in the 1960s* (New York: New York University Press, 2002); and Martin Klimke, *The Other Alliance: Student Protest in West Germany and the United States in the Global Sixties* (Princeton, NJ: Princeton University Press, 2011). On SNCC, see Clayborne Carson, *In Struggle: SNCC and the Black Awakening of the 1960s* (Cambridge, MA: Harvard University Press, 1981); Charles M. Payne, *I've Got the Light of Freedom: The Organizing Tradition and the Mississippi Freedom Struggle* (Berkeley: University of California Press, 1995); and Wesley Hogan, *Many Minds, One Heart: SNCC's Dream for a New America* (Chapel Hill: University of North Carolina Press, 2007). On the Peace Corps, see Gerald T. Rice, *The Bold Experiment: JFK's Peace Corps*

(Notre Dame, IN: University of Notre Dame Press, 1985); Elizabeth Cobbs Hoffman, *All You Need Is Love: The Peace Corps and the Spirit of the 1960s* (Cambridge, MA: Harvard University Press, 1998); Fritz Fischer, *Making Them Like Us: Peace Corps Volunteers in the 1960s* (Washington, DC: Smithsonian Institution Press, 1998); Molly Geidel, *Peace Corps Fantasies: How Development Shaped the Global Sixties* (Minneapolis: University of Minnesota Press, 2015); and Jonathan Zimmerman, *Innocents Abroad: American Teachers in the American Century* (Cambridge, MA: Harvard University Press, 2008).

13. Some scholars defined this model as "modernist citizenship." See William Talcott, "Modern Universities, Absent Citizenship? Historical Perspectives" (working paper 39, Center for Information and Research on Civic Learning and Engagement, September 2005). An early iteration of this project employed a similar conceptual framing; see David S. Busch, "Service Learning: The Peace Corps, American Higher Education, and the Limits of Modernist Ideas of Development and Citizenship," *History of Education Quarterly* 58, no. 4 (November 2018): 475–505.

14. The new general education curriculum was initially formulated by academic leaders and policy makers on the Truman Commission on Higher Education and popularized by scholars in the newly established *Journal of General Education*. Earl McGrath, a member of the Truman Commission and founding editor of the journal, articulated the core tenets of this vision when describing what a student needs to know to a citizen in a democracy. The new general education model outlined in the Truman Commission, wrote McGrath, "provides youth with a knowledge of the origins and meanings of the customs and political traditions" of American democracy. In the process, the curriculum introduces "the student to the moral problems which have perplexed men" and acquaints that student "with the solutions they have devised" as a way to "instill attitudes and understandings which form the essence of good citizenship." McGrath, "The General Education Movement," *Journal of General Education* 1, no. 1 (October 1946): 3–8. For more on the history of general education and its transformation, see Gary E. Miller, *The Meaning of General Education: The Emergence of a Curriculum Paradigm* (New York: Teachers College Press, 1988).

15. Tom Hayden and Students for a Democratic Society, The Port Huron Statement, 1962, 10, 61, Online Archive of California, California Digital Library.

16. For an excellent and honest overview of Dewey's ideas, see Robert B. Westbrook, *John Dewey and American Democracy* (Ithaca, NY: Cornell University Press, 1993); Westbrook, *John Dewey and American Democracy*, 549.

17. The Peace Corps' emphasis on community development represented the other side of Gandhian nonviolence. For more on Gandhi and community development, see Daniel Immerwahr, *Thinking Small: The United States and the Lure of Community Development* (Cambridge, MA: Harvard University Press, 2015). For more on Gandhi's emphasis on both civil disobedience and constructive service, see Dennis Dalton, *Mahatma Gandhi: Nonviolent Power in Action* (New York: Columbia University Press, 1993).

18. Due to the Peace Corps' place within the US State Department, volunteers had to avoid certain forms of political advocacy, especially those efforts that ran counter to American foreign policy interests. The most prominent example was the Bruce Murray case. See Cobbs-Hoffman, *All You Need is Love*, 204–206. On community development and modernization theory, see Immerwahr, *Thinking Small*. On modernization, expert knowledge, and American exceptionalism, see Michael E.

Latham, *Modernization as Ideology: American Social Science and 'Nation Building' in the Kennedy Era* (Chapel Hill: University of North Carolina Press, 2000); Nils Gilman, *Mandarins of the Future: Modernization Theory in Cold War America* (Baltimore: Johns Hopkins University Press, 2003); Bradley R. Simpson, *Economists with Guns: Authoritarian Development and US-Indonesian Relations, 1960–1968* (Palo Alto, CA: Stanford University Press, 2008); David Elkbadh, *The Great American Mission: Modernization and the Construction of an American World Order* (Princeton, NJ: Princeton University Press 2010); and Mark Solovey, *Shaky Foundations: The Politics-Patronage-Social Science Nexus in Cold War America* (New Brunswick, NJ: Rutgers University Press, 2015).

19. In regard to the Peace Corps and SNCC, the historian Brenda Plummer argues that a "comparable implicit set of values underlay their respective missions." Plummer, *In Search of Power: African Americans in the Era of Decolonization, 1956–1974* (Cambridge, UK: Cambridge University Press, 2013). For more on parallels between SNCC and the Peace Corps, see Julia Erin Wood, "Freedom Is Indivisible: The Student Nonviolent Coordinating Committee, Cold War Politics, and International Liberation Movements (PhD diss., Yale University, 2011). On community "development" and empowerment, see Alyosha Goldstein, *Poverty in Common: The Politics of Community Action During the American Century* (Durham, NC: Duke University Press, 2012).

20. This is part of the shift in what the historian Jon Shelton argues is the political formation and triumph of the "education myth" within American policy making. Shelton, *The Education Myth: How Human Capital Trumped Social Democracy* (Ithaca, NY: Cornell University Press, 2023).

21. These policy changes fall broadly under what scholars have defined as the making of the "neoliberal university." See Christopher Newfield, *Unmaking the Public University: The Forty Year Assault on the Middle Class* (Cambridge, MA: Harvard University Press, 2008); and Sheila Slaughter and Gary Rhoades, *Academic Capitalism and the New Economy: Markets, State, and Higher Education* (Baltimore: Johns Hopkins University Press, 2009).

22. On the limitations of the Sullivan principles, see Zeb Larson, "The Sullivan Principles: South Africa, Apartheid, and Globalization," *Diplomatic History* 44, no. 3 (June 2020): 479–503.

1. Howard University

1. W. E. B. Du Bois, "The Talented Tenth," in *The Negro Problem: A Series of Articles by Representative Negroes of To-day* (New York: James Pott and Company, 1903). On Howard University as an expression of Du Bois's "Talented Tenth," see Zachery R. Williams, *In Search of the Talented Tenth: Howard University Public Intellectuals and the Dilemmas of Race, 1926–1970* (Columbia: University of Missouri Press, 2009). On Howard University as a global institution and hub of transnational race politics, see Jason C. Parker, "'Made-in-America Revolution'? The 'Black University' and the American Role in the Decolonization of the Black Atlantic," *Journal of American History* 96, no. 3 (December 2009): 727–750.

2. Richard I. McKinney, *Mordecai, the Man and His Message: The Story of Mordecai Wyatt Johnson* (Washington, DC: Howard University Press, 1997), 60–61.

3. In its development in the twentieth century, Howard University depended on the financial support of the Rosenwald Fund, Phelps Stoke Fund, and Rockefeller Foundation, among many others. See Williams, *In Search of the Talented Tenth*, 52.

4. Henry "Hank" Thomas participated in the first sit-ins in Virginia. Thomas also joined fellow Howard Students Muriel Tillinghast, Jean Wheeler, Dion Diamond, John Moody Jr., and Stokely Carmichael as they risked their lives in the freedom rides in 1961. Other Howard students, like Courtland Cox, Charlie Cobb, Travis Britt, Michael Thelwell, and Bill Mahoney, were prominent figures both in the organizing of the 1964 Freedom Summer and the national chapter of SNCC in Washington, DC.

5. "Call Out for New Leadership," *The Hilltop*, November 10, 1961.

6. "Demonstrators State Their Position on Rally: Ask Policy Clarification," *The Hilltop*, March 23, 1962.

7. "Call Out for New Leadership."

8. "1500 Hear Integration-Non Segregation Debate," *Tri-State Defender*, November 18, 1961, 6.

9. "Address by Dr. James M. Nabrit, Jr., President of Howard University, Formal Opening Exercises, September 16, 1963," 1–2, James M. Nabrit Papers, Moorland-Spingarn Research Center, Howard University, Washington, DC (hereafter, Howard University Archives).

10. For more on the roots of the policy and debates in the 1940s, see David S. Busch, "To the Students: Education for Nonviolence in the World," in *India in the World: 1500–Present*, ed. Rajeshwari Dutt and Nico Slate (New York: Routledge Studies in Modern History, 2023).

11. Rayford Logan, *Howard University: The First Hundred Years, 1867–1967* (Washington, DC: Howard University Press, 1968), appendix B, I, 589–591; Charles E. Williams, comp. *The Howard University Charter: Upon the Centenary of Howard University* (Washington DC: Howard University, 1967), 29–33.

12. Interview with Ekwueme Michael Thelwell by Emilye Crosby, August 23, 2013, Civil Rights History Project, Library of Congress.

13. Carl Edwin Anderson (The HistoryMakers A2003.278), interview by Larry Crowe, November 19, 2003, The HistoryMakers Digital Archive, session 1, tape 3, story 7.

14. Carl Edwin Anderson, interview.

15. As Geri Augusto later reflected, "The defining moments of my consciousness," came when she "decided doing things as a student was not enough." Geri Augusto, Toward a Black University, Internationalism: Pan-Africanism, SNCC Digital Gateway, SNCC Legacy Project and Duke University.

16. Phil Hutchings, "Let Us Build One Massive Protest," *The Hilltop*, March 20, 1964.

17. On "truth" in Gandhian nonviolence, see Dennis Dalton, *Mahatma Gandhi: Nonviolent Power in Action* (New York: Columbia University Press, 1993), 10, 11, 34, and 44. Nico Slate translates *satyagraha* as "truth" and "holding firm." Slate, *Colored Cosmopolitanism: The Shared Struggle for Freedom in the United States and India* (Cambridge, MA: Harvard University Press, 2012).

18. Wesley Hogan, *Many Minds, One Heart: SNCC's Dream for a New America* (Chapel Hill: University of North Carolina Press, 2007), 20.

19. "Nonviolence and the Achievement of Desegregation," pamphlet, box 71, folder 15; SNCC meetings, October 14–16, 1960, Atlanta Conference, Highlander Research and Education Center Records, 1917–2005, part 1 (MSS, 265), Wisconsin Historical Society (hereafter, WHS).

20. "Disregard That Question," *The Hilltop*, November 15, 1963.

21. "Demonstrators State Their Position on Rally."

22. "Demonstrators State Their Position on Rally."

23. "Demonstrators State Their Position on Rally."

24. Ed Brown, "A Philosophy of Activism: An Escape from Apathetic Responses," *The Hilltop*, November 19, 1962.

25. "A Philosophy of Activism: An Escape from Apathetic Responses."

26. "Hilltop Position on Student Social Action," *The Hilltop*, March 1, 1963.

27. "Hilltop Position on Student Social Action."

28. "Hilltop Position on Student Social Action."

29. "Hilltop Position on Student Social Action."

30. "Hilltop Position on Student Social Action."

31. Ella Baker, "Bigger Than a Hamburger," *The Southern Patriot*, May 1960.

32. "Our Stories Your Legacy: A Dialogue with SNCC Veterans," March 9, 2016, SNCC Digital Gateway, SNCC Legacy Project and Duke University.

33. For more on Baker and her political vision, see Barbara Ransby, *Ella Baker and the Black Freedom Movement: A Radical Democratic Vision* (Chapel Hill: University of North Carolina Press, 2003), 95, 329, 263.

34. Baker, "Bigger Than a Hamburger."

35. "Cleveland Sellers Oral History Interview Conducted by John Dittmer in Denmark, South Carolina," March 21, 2013, video, US Civil Rights History Project, https://www.loc.gov/item/2015669180/.

36. Programs included a "self-help" project in Ruleville where local women made quilts and a syrup-making enterprise in Amite County.

37. "COFO Workshop," November 11–17, 1963, Greenville, Mississippi, Highlander Records, (MSS, 265), box 41, folder 5, WHS; Minutes of the SNCC Executive Committee meeting, December 27–31, 1963, Highlander Records (MSS, 265), box 71, folder 18, SNCC, WHS.

38. "In-Service Education Program for Civil Rights Workers in the South," June 17–22, 1964 box 72, folder 1, Highlander Research and Education Center Records, 1917–2005, part 1 (MSS, 265), WHS.

39. "In-Service Education Program for Civil Rights Workers in the South."

40. SNCC pamphlet, box 47, Social Action Vertical Files, WHS.

41. Bill Mahoney to Muriel Tillinghast, November 1, 1963, SNCC Conference on Jobs and Food, Subgroup C, Washington Office, 1960–1968, SNCC Papers.

42. Ed Brown to the dean of Howard Law School, October 17, 1963, SNCC Conference on Jobs and Food, Subgroup C, Washington Office, 1960–1968, SNCC Papers.

43. "Workshop Leader," SNCC Conference on Jobs and Food, Subgroup C, Washington Office, 1960–1968, SNCC Papers.

44. William Mahoney to Dean Evan Crawford, December 9, 1963, SNCC Conference on Jobs and Food, Subgroup C, Washington Office, 1960–1968, SNCC Papers.

45. "SNCC Conference: 'Jobs and Food' Report of the Washington Office," Subgroup C, Washington Office, 1960–1968, Series I, Administrative Files, 1960–1968, SNCC Papers.

46. Gilbert A. Lowe Jr., "Howard University Students and the Community Service Project," *Journal of Negro Education* 36, no. 4 (Autumn 1967): 368–369.

47. When Nelson sent him his 1958 article, "Satyagraha: Gandhian Principles of Non-Violent Non-Cooperation," King wrote back that it was "one of the best and most balanced analyses of the Gandhian principles of nonviolent, noncooperation that I have read." Martin Luther King Jr. to William Stuart Nelson, August 18, 1957, Martin Luther King Jr. Papers, 1954–1968, Boston University, Boston, MA. Nelson, "Satyagraha: Gandhian Principles of Non-Violent Non-Cooperation," *Journal of Religious Thought* (Fall 1957/Winter 1958): 15–24.

48. "Dr. King Commends Clergy Voter Registration Drive," *The Hilltop*, April 17, 1964.

49. For an overview of service programs developed by the Black Panther Party, see David Hilliard, *The Black Panther Party: Service to the People Programs* (Albuquerque: University of New Mexico Press, 2008).

50. "1967 Student Leadership Conference," Student Assembly, 1967 Resolutions, Howard University Assembly Department Files, box 69, Office of Student Life/Activities—HUSA—Conference Files 1968, Howard University Archives.

51. "What Happened at Howard University: The Chronology of Crisis," Howard University Assembly Department Files, box 69, Office of Student Life/Activities—HUSA—Conference Files 1968, Howard University Archives.

52. Janet Knight, "Notes from Key Note Addresses at the Towards a Black University Conference," November 13–17, 1968, Howard University Assembly Department Files, box 69, Office of Student Life/Activities—HUSA—Conference Files 1968, Howard University Archives.

53. Knight, "Notes from Key Note Addresses at the Towards a Black University Conference."

54. "SEI Challenges Idea of Black University," *The Hilltop*, October 11, 1968.

55. "NET Journal; Color Us Black. Part 1," September 14, 1970, Library of Congress, American Archive of Public Broadcasting (GBH and the Library of Congress), Boston, MA, and Washington, DC, accessed September 8, 2023, http://americanarchive.org/catalog/cpb-aacip-512-f47gq6rz2w.

56. Michael Harris, student president, "Howard University Student Association Taking a New Direction: The Washington, D.C. Project," 1969–1970, Howard University Assembly Department Files, box 69, Office of Student Life/Activities—HUSA—HUSA Project Files, 1969–1970, Howard University Archives.

57. Harris, "Howard University Student Association Taking a New Direction." The tutoring program was tied to a research effort that focused on approaches in the school, in particular the Clark Reading Plan, which prioritized team teaching as a solution to raise student reading scores. Studying the new effort, Howard students and tutoring participants questioned the plan and presented their findings to the DC Board of Education.

58. Harris, "Howard University Student Association Taking a New Direction."

59. Reginald Hildebrand, "Law Students to 'Liberators,'" *The Hilltop*, September 25, 1970.

60. "Law Students Go Into Community," *The Hilltop*, March 20, 1970.

61. "Students Journey to Miami to Help NWRO," *HUSA News*, June 29, 1972.

62. Theoia Miller, "Intern Program Offers Service to Area," *The Hilltop*, December 18, 1970.

63. James E. Cheek, "To Seek a New Direction," *Close Up: Howard University Magazine* (Summer 1970).

64. Brenda Goss, "Billingsley 'Faces the People,'" *The Hilltop*, October 16, 1970.

65. Iris Holiday, "Project Voice Seeks Volunteer Aids," *The Hilltop*, October 22, 1971. Hall believed that "as an educational institution we must take the lead in bringing about change for the betterment of our community." Holiday, "Volunteer Bureau Seeks Active Support," *The Hilltop*, November 5, 1971.

66. "Volunteer Assistance Bureau Involves Howard," *The Hilltop*, September 14, 1973.

67. D.C. Project Staff to *The Hilltop*, "Lack of Academic Credit, Funds Hamper D.C. Project," *The Hilltop*, February 4, 1972.

68. "HUSA's Evaluation of D.C. Project," *The HUSA Herald*, March 1975, Howard University Assembly Department files, box 69, Office of Student Life/Activities—HUSA—HUSA Publications, Howard University Archives.

69. Anthony "Mawu" Straker, "D.C. Project: Daring to Struggle, Daring to Win," *The Hilltop*, August 30, 1974. Mawu's efforts to resurrect the D.C. Project were not unique. Other students in the mid- to late 1970s also called for a greater university commitment to "educational opportunities through working with members of the community." Many argued that "community service efforts at Howard have often times been sporadic." "Community Involvement a Must," *The Hilltop*, September 16, 1977.

70. "Community Inspires, Aids Protest," *The Hilltop*, October 7, 1977.

71. "D.C. Survival Conference Begins Today," *The Hilltop*, February 9, 1979.

72. "Negro Students Seek Relevance," *New York Times*, November 18, 1968.

73. "QT Jackson Defines HUSA's Goals for Making Howard Truly Black," *The Hilltop*, September 27, 1968.

74. "Community Inspires, Aids Protest."

2. Michigan State University

1. Char Jolles, "John A. Hannah on Education," *The Paper*, November 17, 1966, MSU Paper Archives, http://msupaper.org/issues/The_Paper_1966-11-17.pdf.

2. Ivanhoe Donaldson, interview by Rachel Reinhard, September 20, 2003, Center for Oral History and Cultural Heritage, University of Southern Mississippi.

3. "Human Rights," *State News*, March 9, 1960.

4. Interview with Maxie Jackson, conducted by author, December 18, 2018.

5. "Why We Sat In," *State News*, May 28, 1965.

6. Kenneth J. Heineman, *Campus Wars: The Peace Movement at American State Universities in the Vietnam Era* (New York: New York University Press, 1994), 24. The regulatory response was an extension of John Hannah's institutional politics. In the

mid-1950s, Hannah shaped an institution culture at MSU that defined certain activities and political beliefs outside the realm of a good civic education. In 1954, he threatened to fire any faculty who pleaded the Fifth when called before the House Unamerican Activities Committee.

7. "'The Movement' Bucks the System," *State News*, June 3, 1965.

8. "'Real' Education?," *State News*, June 7, 1965.

9. "Hannah Addresses Seniors," *State News*, June 8, 1965.

10. "Rights in Our Own Backyard," *State News*, May 26, 1965.

11. "Rights in Our Own Backyard."

12. Heineman, *Campus Wars*, 24.

13. Interview with Mary Ann Shupenko Ehinger, June 2, 2006, and October 23, 2006, in "The Whole Story: The 1960s Collaboration between MSU and Rust College and the Challenge of Dr. King's Legacy," Personal Archives of John S. Duley. Interview with Mary Ann Shupenko, box 5468, folder 46, UA 17.371, John Duley Papers, MSU Archives.

14. Freedom Schools, folder 1, Pamela P. Allen Papers, 1967–1974 (M85-013), Wisconsin Historical Society (hereafter, WHS).

15. Liz Fusco to Elizabeth Moos, December 21, 1964, reel 67, SNCC Papers.

16. Staughton Lynd to Bob Moses, reel 68, microfilm, SNCC Papers. Mary Rothschild, *A Case of Black and White* (Westport, CT: Praeger, 1982), 403.

17. Mary Varela to Lois Chaffee, October 5, 1964, "Reports and Letters from the Field," Civil Rights Movement Veterans website, Tougaloo College; Lois Chaffee to Ernest T. Smith, October 5, 1964, "Reports and Letters from the Field," Civil Rights Movement Veterans website, Tougaloo College.

18. "A Movement Changes and So Does a Man," *State News*.

19. "King Fires Out Three Challenges in Speech before 4,000 Students," *State News*, February 12, 1965.

20. John Duley, "Marginality as Lifestyle," box 5468, folder 9, UA 17.371, John Duley Papers, MSU Archives.

21. Student Educational Program, box 2470, folder 23, Associated Students MSU Records, 12.1.1, MSU Archives.

22. "STEP Summer, 1966," Wayne Albertson, Fall 1966, box 5468, folder 44, UA 17.371, John Duley Papers, MSU Archives.

23. Memo to STEP Volunteers, box 1, folder 11, MSS 290, Special Collections, MSU Archives.

24. Interview with Kathy Wolterink, box 5468, folder 50, UA 17.371, John Duley Papers, MSU Archives.

25. "The Summer of the Work-In," *State News*, June 24, 1965; "No Martyrs from MSU," *State News*, August 17, 1965.

26. Jim Krathwohl, "Short History of STEP," box 1, folder 16, MSS 290, Special Collections, MSU Archives.

27. Sargent Shriver to John Hannah, June 1, 1961, folder 66, box 67, John A. Hannah Papers, UA 2.1.12, MSU Archives.

28. Sargent Shriver, "Report to the President on the Peace Corps," February 22, 1961, 18. John F. Kennedy Digital Library, http://www.jfklibrary.org/Asset-Viewer/Archives/JFKPOF-085-014.aspx, 6–7, accessed May 1, 2024.

29. Michigan State Youth Corps Proposal, March 16, 1961, folder 56, box 205, University of Nigeria Program Records, MSU Archives.

30. Case Studies 4, 9, folder 56, box 205, University of Nigeria Program Records, MSU Archives.

31. David Schickele, "When the Right Hand Washes the Left," *Peace Corps Volunteer* 3, no. 4 (February 1965): 17.

32. Schickele, "Draft of the Education Task Force," December 30, 1965, box 23, Subject Files of the Office of the Director, 1961–1966, Records of the Peace Corps, RG 490, US National Archives and Records Administration (hereafter: NARA).

33. Eugene Jacobson to Sargent Shriver, January 14, 1965, box 67, folder 66, John A. Hannah Papers, UA 2.1.12, MSU Archives.

34. George Axin to John Simons, January 10, 1962, box 205, folder 71, University of Nigeria Program Records, MSU Archives.

35. "Who'll Greet Peace Corps," *State News*, August 9, 1961.

36. Training Evaluation Report, Michigan State University, box 2, Training Evaluation Reports, 1964–1969, NARA.

37. "A Discussion of Returned Peace Corps Volunteers," March 3, 1965, Returned Volunteers Conference, box 5, Personal Papers Gerald Bush, John F. Kennedy Library, Boston, MA.

38. "A Discussion of Returned Peace Corps Volunteers."

39. Roger Harrison and Richard L. Hopkins, "The Design of Cross-Cultural Training: An Alternative to the University Model," *Journal of Applied Behavioral Sciences* 3, no. 4 (December 1967): 438–439.

40. "Justin Morrill College Field Study Program," Michigan State University, pamphlet, folder 6, Justin Morrill College Records UA 12.12, MSU Archives.

41. Duley became a key figure of the "experiential learning" movement in the 1970s, playing a vital role in the establishment of the National Society for Experiential Education.

42. Frank Blanco and Robin Ruhf, "Student Education Corps Year-End Report," box 65, folder 77, John Hannah Papers UA 2.1.12, MSU Archives.

43. Blanco and Ruhf, "Student Education Corps Year-End Report."

44. Blanco and Ruhf, "Student Education Corps Year-End Report."

45. Blanco and Ruhf, "Student Education Corps Year-End Report."

46. Vietnam Summer Organizers' Manual, box 6, Vietnam Summer Records, DG067, Peace Collection, Swarthmore College Special Collections.

47. "Hannah Defends Dissent," *State News*, April 26, 1965.

48. Response by Hannah to 1966 Ramparts Article on MSU involvement in Vietnam, box 2727, Center for Latin American Studies, UA 2.9.3.9, MSU Archives.

49. Stu Dowty, "The Academic Quagmire," box 49, Social Action Vertical File, WHS.

50. Linda Knibbs, "'U' Committee Demands Abolishment of ROTC," *State News*, April 28, 1970; Helen Clegg and Ginger Sharp, "Protesters Deaf to Wharton," *Lansing State Journal*, May 11, 1972; "Statement from Anti-War Protestors," May 11, 1972, Media Communication Records, UA 8.1.1, MSU Archives.

51. James Tanck, "The Volunteer Action Effort at Michigan State University: A Report on the Initial Effort of the M.S.U. Office of Volunteer Programs," 1968, folder 6, Center for Service Learning Records, UA 7.15, MSU Archives.

52. Tanck, "The Volunteer Action Effort at Michigan State University."

53. "Wharton Urges Unity to Make a Better World," *State News*, April 29, 1970.

54. "Mrs. Nixon Skips 'U' to Go Where Action Is," *State News*, March 4, 1970.

55. "HEW Secretary Asks for New 'Volunteerism,'" *State News*, January 4, 1973.

56. Some administrators were aware of the efforts to use the office to deflect other forms of activism. Mary Edens, the associate director of the office in the 1970s, noted that Michigan State University officials "milked the publicity it got from students' doing good in the community." Timothy K. Stanton, Dwight E. Giles, Jr., and Nadinne I. Cruz, *Service-Learning: A Movement's Pioneers Reflect on Its Origins, Practice, and Future* (San Francisco: Jossey-Bass, 1999), 75.

57. Proposal for an All-University Committee to investigate the role of academic field placement and its relationship to the Offices of Volunteer Programs, Center for Service Learning Records, UA.7.15, MSU Archives.

58. "Educational Tokenism at MSU," *State News*, January 9, 1968.

59. For more on "organized research units," see Ethan Schrum, *The Instrumental University: Education in Service of the National Agenda after World War II* (Ithaca, NY: Cornell University Press, 2019).

60. Robert L. Green and Lawrence W. Lezotte, "Unresolved Issues in Community-Based Research," *Journal of Non-white Concerns* (April 1973).

61. Robert Green, "Philosophy of C.U.A. and E.O.P., Draft," September 17, 1969, box 5744, College of Urban Develop / Urban Affairs Program records, UA 15.20, MSU Archives.

62. "Colleges Should Act on Poverty—Wharton," *State News*, January 23, 1970.

63. "Service Learning Program Guidelines," box 5744, College of Urban Develop / Urban Affairs Program records, UA 15.20, MSU Archives.

64. Green, *At the Crossroads*.

65. "White Investigating CUA Finances, Actions," *State News*, March 3, 1970.

66. "Advisor Council Working Paper on Community Outreach and College Structure," February 2, 1972, box 5772, Faculty Meeting Minutes, College of Urban Develop / Urban Affairs Program records, UA 15.20, MSU Archives.

67. "Urban Service Programs," box 5774, College of Urban Develop / Urban Affairs Program records, UA 15.20, MSU Archives.

68. "Demonstrators Can Represent the Cheapest Form of Involvement for Some Picketers," *State News*, May 27, 1965.

69. "Students Still Care, but in a Realistic Way," *State News*, October 25, 1975.

3. San Francisco State College

1. Herbert Wilner, "Zen Basketball, etc.," in *Academics on the Line: The Faculty Strike at San Francisco State* (San Francisco: Jossey-Bass, 1970), 18.

2. "Official Statement Position Paper," folder 19:163, SFSU Strike Collection, University Archives, J. Paul Leonard Library.

3. "A Proposal for a Center For Educational Innovation at San Francisco State College," box 6, folder 51, SFSU Strike Collection, University Archives, J. Paul Leonard Library.

4. For more on Black power and education, see Russell Rickford, *We Are an African People: Independent Education, Black Power, and the Radical Imagination* (Oxford, UK: Oxford University Press, 2016).

5. This is *not* Supreme Court Justice Clarence Thomas.

6. Martha Biondi, *The Black Revolution on Campus* (Berkeley: University of California Press, 2014), 57.

7. Karen Duncan, "Progress Report on Community Action Curriculum Project," October 15, 1967, box 121, US Student Association Records, 1946–1971, WHS.

8. Elizabeth Sutherland, ed., *Letters from Mississippi* (New York: McGraw-Hill, 1965), 228.

9. "Conversation on Community Education Program, SFS," July 30, 1965, box 2, Jo Ann Ooiman Robinson Papers, 1960–1965, MSS 191, WHS.

10. "Conversation on Community Education Program, SFS."

11. Reel 21, SNCC Papers; Daniel Peter Hinman-Smith, "Does the Word Freedom Have a Meaning? The Mississippi Freedom Schools, the Berkeley Free Speech Movement, and the Search for Freedom through Education" (PhD diss., UNC, 1993), 121.

12. Duncan, "A Place to Start From," June 13, 1966, Experimental College Collection, box 1, folder 14, University Archives, J. Paul Leonard Library.

13. "A Proposal for a Center for Educational Innovation at San Francisco State College," box 6, folder 51, SFSU Strike Collection, University Archives, J. Paul Leonard Library.

14. Jimmy Garrett and Fred Thalheimer, "Center for Educational Innovation," box 6, folder 51, SFSU Strike Collection, University Archives, J. Paul Leonard Library.

15. John Summerskill, *President Seven* (New York: World Publishing Company, 1971), 103.

16. Summerskill, *President Seven*, 23.

17. Sharon Gold, Community Service Institute in the Center for Educational Innovation, box 6, folder 51, SFSU Strike Collection, University Archives, J. Paul Leonard Library.

18. Gold, Community Service Institute.

19. "Rationale for a Bachelor of Arts Program in Community Service," draft, Equal Opportunity Program Archive, box 1, folder 2, University Archives, J. Paul Leonard Library. In its initial proposal, it was called the Community Involvement Program.

20. Wendy Alfsen, interview with the author, Ann Arbor, MI, December 18, 2018.

21. For more on the election of Reagan and the broader grassroots conservative movement in California, see Lisa McGirr, *Suburban Warriors: The Origins of the New American Right* (Princeton, NJ: Princeton University Press, 2001).

22. Students were also concerned because the program had also helped combat the effects of California's 1960 Master Plan of Education. The plan implemented a tracking system in its three tiers of higher education. Although this opened access to the university, Black students were overwhelmingly relegated to junior colleges. The plan reduced the percentage of those admitted to state colleges from the top 70 percent of high school graduates to the top 33 percent. San Francisco State had larger numbers of Black students before the master plan and the introduction of standardized entrance tests in 1965. In just four years, Black student enrollment plunged from 10 to 4 percent of the student body.

23. Minutes of a Meeting with College President Robert Smith, October 29, 1968, Administration Files, President Hayakawa, Associated Students, University Archives, J. Paul Leonard Library.

24. "Back to 'in loco parentis,'" November 6, folder 121, SFSU Strike Collection, University Archives, J. Paul Leonard Library.

25. Summerskill, *President Seven*, 26.

26. Summerskill, *President Seven*, 198.

27. Minutes of a Meeting with College President Robert Smith.

28. Minutes of a Meeting with College President Robert Smith.

29. "Who's Being Violent," box 11, folder 102, SFSU Strike Collection, University Archives, J. Paul Leonard Library.

30. "Press Statement: S.F.S.C. Student Programs," box 7, folder 8, SFSU Strike Collection, University Archives, J. Paul Leonard Library.

31. Arlene Kaplan Daniels, "From Lecture Hall to Picket Line," in *Academics on the Line*, 43.

32. Theodore Kroeber, "Confronting Irreconcilable Issues," in *Academics on the Line*, 120.

33. Kroeber, "Confronting Irreconcilable Issues," 121.

34. David West, "Educational Opportunity Program," box 1, folder 3, EOP Archive, University Archives, J. Paul Leonard Library.

35. Robert Smith, "Why I Resigned," in *By Any Means Necessary* (San Francisco: Jossey-Bass, 1970), 187.

36. Daniels, "From Lecture Hall to Picket Line," in *Academics on the Line*, 46.

37. Summerskill, *President Seven*, 68.

38. Smith, "Why I Resigned," 193.

39. S. I. Hayakawa, "The F.S.M. Demonstrations," December 8, 1964, Administration Files, box 5, University Archives, J. Paul Leonard Library.

40. "Public Statement by President S.I. Hayakawa," November 30, 1968, box 15, folder 15, SFSU Strike Collection, University Archives, J. Paul Leonard Library.

41. "The State of the College," January 20, 1969, a statement from the Academic Senate Ad Hoc Committee, box 2, folder 1, SFSU Strike Collection, University Archives, J. Paul Leonard Library.

42. "The State of the College."

43. "Letter," box 11, folder 102, SFSU Strike Collection, University Archives, J. Paul Leonard Library.

44. "Testimony Given by Dr. S.I. Hayakawa Before Senate Permanent Subcommittee on Investigations," May 13, 1969, box 16, folder 137, SFSU Strike Collection, University Archives, J. Paul Leonard Library.

45. "Testimony Given by Dr. S.I. Hayakawa."

46. "Welcome to San Francisco State University," Daniel Feder Papers, folder 3, University Archives, J. Paul Leonard Library.

47. "Community Service Fund," Administration Files (Hayakawa), box 2, University Archives, J. Paul Leonard Library.

48. "The Death of the Experimental College," Administration Files, box 4, University Archives, J. Paul Leonard Library.

49. Statement on Plans and Policies, March 21, 1969, *On the Record*, box 16, folder 137, SFSU Strike Collection, University Archives, J. Paul Leonard Library.

50. Glen Elsasser, "Compulsory National Youth Service for Youth Urged," *Chicago Tribune*, July 16, 1970.

51. Timothy K. Stanton, Dwight E. Giles Jr., and Nadinne I. Cruz, *Service-Learning: A Movement's Pioneers Reflect on Its Origins, Practice, and Future* (San Francisco: Jossey-Bass, 1999), 58.

52. "Associated Students Handbook, '73–'74," J. Paul Leonard Library.

53. Morley Safer, *60 Minutes Report on SFSC*, transcript, Daniel Feder Papers, folder 3, University Archives, J. Paul Leonard Library.

54. "Summer Volunteers Sought," *Zenger's*, May 7, 1975.

55. "Volunteer Bureau Works," *Zenger's*, December 4, 1974.

56. Nathan Hare, "The Battle for Black Studies," *Black Scholar* 3, no. 9 (May 1972): 33–34.

57. "Community Work Stressed in Urban Indian Program," *Zenger's*, September 11, 1974.

58. Nancy McDermid, "Strike Settlement," in *Academics on the Line*, 230.

59. "Community Work Stressed in Urban Indian Program."

60. Safer, *60 Minutes Report on SFSC*.

61. "Hayakawa Blasts Black Studies," *Daily Gater*, November 4, 1969.

62. "Conversation on Community Education Program, SFS."

4. Harvard University–Radcliffe College

1. Harvard University Committee, *General Education in a Free Society, Report of the Harvard Committee*, with an introduction by James Bryant Conant (Cambridge, MA: Harvard University Press), 50.

2. *i.e., The Cambridge Review*, no. 1–5 (1956): 15; 98; 9–22.

3. Bob Moses, interview with Clayborne Carson, March 29,1982; Laura Visser-Maessen, *Robert Parris Moses: A Life in Civil Rights and Leadership at the Grassroots* (Chapel Hill: University of North Carolina Press, 2016), 22–23.

4. Debbie Louis, *And We Are Not Yet Saved: A History of the Movement As People* (Garden City, NY: Doubleday, 1970), 57.

5. "General Letter, 1965," Series: Subgroup C, Washington office, 1960–1968, Series II, Subject Files, 1963–1968, SNCC Papers, WHS.

6. Moses to Phillip Stern, July 15, 1963, Series: Subgroup A, Atlanta office, Series X, Education Department, 1960–1967, SNCC Papers.

7. Moses, "Letter from Magnolia," *Harvard Crimson*, January 22, 1962; "Bob Moses to Speak on Situation in Miss.," *Harvard Crimson*, December 1, 1964.

8. "Program Outline for Campus Friends of SNCC Groups," Lucile Montgomery Papers, 1963–1967; Historical Society Library Microforms Room, micro 44, reel 3, segment 48.

9. "Program Outline for Campus Friends of SNCC Groups."

10. "You Can Help: Support Programs for SNCC," n.d., Civil Rights Movement Veterans website, Tougaloo College.

11. "Friends of SNCC Sending Supplies to Help Mississippi Sharecroppers," *Harvard Crimson*, February 7, 1964.

12. Open Letter from Aaron Henry, Robert Moses, and David Dennis introducing Mississippi Summer Project Prospectus, April 8, 1964, CORE—Mississippi Summer Project (COFO, SNCC, CORE)—memoranda and reports, 1964, Congress of Racial Equality, Mississippi 4th Congressional District records, 1961–1966, micro 793, reel 3, segment 72.

13. "SNCC Faculty Fund," n.d., Civil Rights Movement Veterans website, Tougaloo College.

14. Gail Falk, letter, September 1964, box 16, folder 7, SAVF–Council of Federated Organizations (COFO) papers, Social Action vertical file, circa 1930–2002, archives main stacks, Mss 577, WHS.

15. Ellen Lake to parents, August 12, 1964, SC 3057, folder 1, Ellen Lake Papers, WHS.

16. Elizabeth Sutherland, ed., *Letters from Mississippi*, (New York: McGraw-Hill, 1965), 229.

17. Paul Cowan, *The Making of an Un-American: A Dialogue with Experience* (New York: Viking, 1967), 10.

18. Cowan, *The Making of an Un-American*, 25.

19. Cowan, *The Making of an Un-American*, 15.

20. Cowan, *The Making of an Un-American*, 24.

21. Philadelphia Tutorial Project, December 1962 to April 1963 (SNCC files); "Guidelines for Social Change: The Tutorial Project," box 11, folder 3, City Projects Files, Northern Student Movement Records, Schomburg Center.

22. "Tutorials: To Be Or Not To Be," Philadelphia Summer Tutorials 1962, box 6, folder 1, Central Office Files, Northern Student Movement Records, Schomburg Center.

23. William Strickland, NSM, n.d., SNCC Files on the Northern Student Movement, Subgroup A. Atlanta Office, Series IX. Northern Coordination Department, Correspondence with Other Organizations, 1963–1966, SNCC Papers, Black Freedom Struggle in the 20th Century: Organizational Records and Personal Papers, Part 2, ProQuest History Vault.

24. "College Does Not Plan to Act in Perdew Case; Monro Asks Fund Drive," *Harvard Crimson*, October 7, 1963.

25. "Harvard's Responsibility to Mississippi," box 16, folder 11, CORE Southern Regional Office—Student Nonviolent Coordinating Committee, May 1964–August 1965, Congress of Racial Equality, Southern Regional Office records, 1954–1966, Mss 85, WHS.

26. "College Does Not Plan to Act in Perdew Case; Monro Asks Fund Drive."

27. Mary I. Bunting to Lyndon B. Johnson, January 17, 1966, box 30, folder 469, records of Radcliffe College President Mary Ingraham Bunting-Smith, 1960–1972, RG II, series 4, Schlesinger Library, Radcliffe Institute.

28. J. Dennis Huckabay to Mary I. Bunting, July 22, 1968, box 41, folder 601, records of Radcliffe College President Mary Ingraham Bunting-Smith, 1960–1972, RG II, series 4, Schlesinger Library, Radcliffe Institute.

29. James P. Dixon, "The Peace Corps in an Educating Society," excerpts from a discussion at the Brookings Institute, July 22, 1965.

30. Roger Landrum to Mary Bunting, September 19, 1966, records of Radcliffe College President Mary Ingraham Bunting-Smith, 1960–1972, RG II, series 4, box 34, folder 522–523, Schlesinger Library, Radcliffe Institute.

31. Dixon, "The Peace Corps in an Educating Society," 7.

32. E4A Report, 1969, box 44, folder 669, records of Radcliffe College Education for Action, 1966–2000, RG XXVII, Schlesinger Library, Radcliffe Institute.

33. "Report on the First Year of E4A," August 1967, box 37, folder 580, records of Radcliffe College Education for Action, 1966–2000, RG XXVII, Schlesinger Library, Radcliffe Institute.

34. "Report on the First Year of E4A."

35. Radcliffe College Education for Action Records, 1966–2000; "Ford Foundation Application," 1966, box 1, folder 6, records of Radcliffe College Education for Action, 1966–2000, RG XXVII, Radcliffe College archives, Schlesinger Library, Radcliffe Institute.

36. Maria Montamat, letter, July 19, 1968, box 41, folder 635, records of Radcliffe College President Mary Ingraham Bunting-Smith, 1960–1972, RG II, series 4, Schlesinger Library, Radcliffe Institute.

37. "Evaluation of the Political Nature of Social Service: Implications for the Volunteer," box 8, folders 63–77, records of Radcliffe College Education for Action, 1966–2000, RG XXVII, misc., Schlesinger Library, Radcliffe Institute.

38. "Evaluation of the Political Nature of Social Service."

39. "Evaluation of the Political Nature of Social Service."

40. "Evaluation of the Political Nature of Social Service."

41. Stefan M. Bradley, "Black Studies the Hard Way: Fair Harvard Makes Curricular Changes," in *Upending the Ivory Tower: Civil Rights, Black Power, and the Ivy League* (New York: New York University Press, 2018).

42. E4A Meeting with Charles Whitlock, May 11, 1972, records of Radcliffe College Education for Action, 1966–2000, RG XXVII, box 1, folder 20, Schlesinger Library, Radcliffe Institute.

43. Laurie Oliver, "Comments on the Student Center," October 10, 1972, carton 1, records of Radcliffe College Education for Action, 1966–2000, RG XXVII, R2002-CR19, Schlesinger Library, Radcliffe Institute.

44. David Riesman was a prominent advocate of the Peace Corps and the ideas of education that emerged from the agency in the 1960s. He participated in the 1965 Returned Peace Corps Conference and the Brookings Institution Conference where Bunting first began to formulate the E4A program. In its first couple years of operation, Riesman was on the Board of E4A. Riesman saw volunteerism as a means to combat the "other-directed" character that he identified in *The Lonely Crowd*. Riesman participated in the Peace Corps discussions that created the Great Books training program at St. John's. He believed that the Peace Corps represented a "great educative experience" because a "volunteer is faced with impossible tasks which he discovers are not quite impossible." Notes on UYA, box 8, 70, records of Radcliffe College Education for Action, 1966–2000, Schlesinger Library, Radcliffe Institute.

45. Funding in 1976 came from Vinmont Foundation and individual donors like Bunting. The total budget was $2,910. Annual Report 1976–1977, carton 1, records of Radcliffe College Education for Action, 1966–2000, RG XXVII, R2002-CR19, annual reports, 1970–1978, Schlesinger Library, Radcliffe Institute.

46. "Application for the Student Board," box 1, 19, records of Radcliffe College Education for Action, 1966–2000, student board, 1971–1972, Schlesinger Library, Radcliffe Institute.

47. "Education for Action Annual Report, 1972–3," carton 1, records of Radcliffe College Education for Action, 1966–2000, RG XXVII, R2002-CR19, annual reports, 1970–1978, Schlesinger Library, Radcliffe Institute.

48. In the academic year 1975–1976, the fourteen-member board was 50 percent women and 50 percent minority students. Report 1975–1976, carton 1, records of Radcliffe College Education for Action, 1966–2000, RG XXVII, R2002-CR19, annual reports, 1970–1978, Schlesinger Library, Radcliffe Institute.

49. "Education for Action: Philosophy of Funding," carton 1, records of Radcliffe College Education for Action, 1966–2000, RG XXVII, R2002-CR19, Schlesinger Library, Radcliffe Institute.

50. "A New Style for Student Social Action," *Harvard Crimson*, March 31, 1971.

51. Annual Report, 1976–1977, carton 1, records of Radcliffe College Education for Action, 1966–2000, RG XXVII, R2002-CR19, annual reports, 1970–1978, Schlesinger Library, Radcliffe Institute.

52. "Education for Action: Not PBH, Not Vista, Not the School of Hard Knocks, It Struggles to Do Its Own Thing," *Harvard Bulletin* 75, no. 2 (October 1972).

53. "Education for Action."

54. "Thanks but No Thanks," *Harvard Crimson*, January 26, 1976.

55. Eddie Quiñonez, "What is E4A? Why E4A? Etc.," February 5, 1977, carton 1, records of Radcliffe College Education for Action, 1966–2000, RG XXVII, R2002-CR19, 1978 including Agassiz struggle, 1980, and move, Schlesinger Library, Radcliffe Institute.

56. Quiñonez, "What is E4A?"

57. Bunting to Howard Dressner, box 44, 699, papers of President Bunting, Schlesinger Library, Radcliffe Institute.

5. Stanford University

1. "Truth and Service," Stanford University Board of Trustees, meeting records, 1898–2015 (SC1010), Stanford University Archives.

2. Letter to George E. Crothers, October 17, 1907, Stanford University Board of Trustees, meeting records, 1898–2015 (SC1010), Stanford University Archives.

3. "A Night in Milpitas," *Stanford Daily*, May 11, 1977.

4. Chris Hables Gray, representative, Stanford Committee for Responsible Investments, "Letter to Board of Trustees," May 5, 1977, carton 8, SC0315 1983-177, Donald Kennedy Presidential Papers, Stanford University Archives.

5. Keith Archuletta, interview with the author, April 17, 2019.

6. "Guidelines for Research at Stanford," A3M, Stanford University, Historical Archive, https://dynamics.org/Altenberg/ARCHIVES/STANFORD/A3M/.

7. "What is SWOPSI?," pamphlet, Stanford Student Demonstrations Collection, 1970, SC0376, Stanford University Archives.

8. Lawrence Litvak, Robert DeGrasse, and Kathleen McTigue, *South Africa: Foreign Investment and Apartheid* (Washington, DC: Institute for Policy Studies, 1978).

9. "President Lyman to the Faculty Senate," *Campus Report*, May 18, 1977.

10. Stanford Committee for a Responsible Investment Policy (SCRIP), "The University As Institutional Investor," carton 8, SC0315 1983-177, Donald Kennedy Presidential Papers, Stanford University Archives.

11. Joann Lublin, "Stanford's Recipe for Relevance," *Change* 3, no. 6 (October 1971): 13–15.

12. "President Lyman to the Faculty Senate."

13. Ad Hoc Faculty Committee, "Letter and Memo to the Board of Trustees," November 15, 1977, carton 4, SC0315 1994-132, Donald Kennedy Presidential Papers, Stanford University Archives.

14. Rodney Adams, "Social Responsibility and Investment," *Campus Report*, July 26, 1978, carton 4, SC0315 1994-132, Donald Kennedy Presidential Papers, Stanford University Archives.

15. Mark Funk, "A Night in Milpitas," *Stanford Daily*, May 11, 1977.

16. Samuel was the chairperson of a council of South African students studying under the International Institute of Education and Aurora scholarship programs. Mary Yuh, "Groups to Rally for Divesture," *Stanford Daily*, May 9, 1986.

17. Stephen Kasierski, "Panel Clashes Over Divestment," *Stanford Daily*, March 6, 1985.

18. Stanford African Students Association, "Statement on Azania," box 22, folder 318, South African Apartheid Collection, Manuscripts and Archives, Yale University Archives.

19. "Revolution Is the Only Solution," *Stanford Daily*, February 10, 1983.

20. Stanford African Students Association, "Statement on Azania," box 22, folder 318, South African Apartheid Collection, Manuscripts and Archives, Yale University Archives.

21. "Noon Rally Decries Apartheid," *Stanford Daily*, January 18, 1985.

22. Phillip J. Ivanhoe to Donald Kennedy, May 28, 1987, carton 24, Sullivan Prin. / Corresp. w / Board G 5.3 9 / 86-8 / 1987, SC0315 1992-179, Donald Kennedy Presidential Papers, Stanford University Archives.

23. "Up Close in South Africa," *Stanford Daily*, May 1, 1986.

24. Marcus Marby, "BSU Leader Carries Big Ideals and Captivates Crowds," *Stanford Daily*, February 18, 1987.

25. Stanford Out of South Africa, "A Stanford Divestment Primer," pamphlet, box 22, folder 318, South African Apartheid Collection, Manuscripts and Archives, Yale University Archives.

26. "Statement by President Donald Kennedy," April 17, 1985, carton 25, SC0315 1989-267, Donald Kennedy Presidential Papers, Special Collections and University Archives, Stanford University.

27. Technology from both Hewlett-Packard and IBM was used widely by the South African government.

28. "South Africa Conference, Notes," August 27, 1985, carton 25, Special SC0315 1989-267, Donald Kennedy Presidential Papers, Collections and University Archives, Stanford University.

29. "Statement by President Donald Kennedy."

30. "Statement by President Donald Kennedy."

31. "Stanford and South Africa," booklet, box 22, folder 318, South African Apartheid Collection, Manuscripts and Archives, Yale University Archives.

32. "'Stanford and South Africa' Book Not Objective," *The Stanford Daily*, October 9, 1985.

33. "Panel Pummels Booklet," *Stanford Daily*, October 16, 1985.

34. "Kennedy Coloured?," *Stanford Daily*, n.d.

35. "Revised Proposal for Student Examination of Congressional Anti-Apartheid Legislation—Summer 1985," carton 24, South Africa G 5.3 9 / 87-8 / 88, SC0315 1992-179, Donald Kennedy Presidential Papers, Stanford University Archives.

36. "Divestment Still Solution to Liberate South Africa," *Stanford Daily*, October 3, 1985.

37. Bill King and Amanda Kemp to Donald Kennedy, October 26, 1987, box 24, SC015-1992-179, Donald Kennedy Presidential Papers, Special Collections and University Archives, Stanford University.

38. "1988 Guide to Public Service at Stanford University," carton 18, SC0315 1991-141, Donald Kennedy Presidential Papers, Special Collections and University Archives, Stanford University.

39. "University Needs to Act," *Stanford Daily*, February 24, 1986.

40. Ibid.

41. "Make a Difference, Not Just Noise," *Stanford Daily*, March 5, 1986.

42. "'Noise' Needed to Implement Change," *Stanford Daily*, March 7, 1986.

43. "Rockefeller Foundation Seminar on Public Service," October 18–19, 1990, SC541, box 4, HASS Center for Public Service, Series: Volunteer Coordinator, Special Collections and University Archives, Stanford University.

44. "Rockefeller Foundation Seminar on Public Service."

45. Jonathan Jensen, interview with the author, October 23, 2018.

46. Jensen, interview with the author, October 23, 2018. Jensen expanded on the notion of "two faces" in his book *Knowledge and Power in South Africa: Critical Perspectives Across the Disciplines* (Johannesburg: Skotaville, 1991).

6. Brown University

1. "From a Poor College to a Hot College Brown," *Brown Daily Herald*, August 30, 1985.

2. Brown Trustees Release Proxy Issues Votes, April 17, 1978, box 41, S.A. Investment Policy, S.A. General, 1.OF-1C-15 Swearer, Howard R., Files, Dates: 1977–1990 OC15A (hereafter Swearer Papers), Brown University Archives.

3. "UCS Endorses U. Divestiture of Holdings Tied to S. Africa," *Brown Daily Herald*, April 14, 1978.

4. In 1978 alone, IBM's South African sales jumped 250 percent, with total annual sales amounting to approximately $300 million in 1982.

5. IBM technology played a critical role in South Africa. The IBM computer was vital to South African's population registry, which was used to print passes, transmit fingerprints, and monitor the movements of Black citizens. For more on the history of computer technology in South Africa, see NARMIC/America Friends Service Committee, *Automating Apartheid—U.S. Computer Exports to South Africa and the Arms Embargo* (Philadelphia: Omega Press, 1982).

6. "Statement on Investment Policy," 1971, box 41, S.A. Investment Policy, S.A. General, Swearer Papers, Brown University Archives.

7. "Statement on Investment Policy: The Advisory and Executive Committee," box 41, S.A. Investment Policy, S.A. General, Swearer Papers, Brown University Archives.

8. "Statement on Investment Policy: The Advisory and Executive Committee."

9. "Statement on Investment Policy: The Advisory and Executive Committee."

10. Walter Freiberger to Swearer, May 5, 1978, box 41, S.A. Investment Policy, S.A. General, Swearer Papers, Brown University Archives.

11. David Buchdahl to Swearer, May 1, 1978, box 41, S.A. Investment Policy, S.A. General, Swearer Papers, Brown University Archives.

12. Monica Ladd to Swearer, May 8, 1978, box 41, S.A. Investment Policy, S.A. General, Swearer Papers, Brown University Archives. Other alumni went a step further and refused financial pledges to Brown. In a letter to Swearer, Elizabeth Sweeney wrote, "In support of the campus divestiture campaign, I am withholding my pledge to the Brown fund. . . . I support their efforts, and urge you, the President of the College, and the members of the Corporation to consider concrete and responsible policies which will end Brown University's complicity in the apartheid regime." Sweeney to Swearer, June 1, 1978, box 41, S.A. Investment Policy, S.A. General, Swearer Papers, Brown University Archives.

13. Dean E. McHenry to the Advisory Committee on Corporate Responsibility in Investments, December 10, 1980, Southern Africa Collection, Michigan State University Libraries Special Collections.

14. Text of Remarks by Swearer, April 17, 1978, box 41, S.A. Investment Policy, S.A. General, Swearer Papers, Brown University Archives.

15. Swearer to South African Solidarity Committee, May 11, 1978, box 41, S.A. Investment Policy, S.A. General, Swearer Papers, Brown University Archives.

16. "Students Call for U. Divestiture at Rally," *Brown Daily Herald*, April 18, 1978.

17. "Students Call for U. Divestiture at Rally."

18. "SASC Denies Swearer Chance to Address Protesting Ugrads," *Brown Daily Herald*, April 18, 1978.

19. "Unfair Tactics," *Brown Daily Herald*, April 18, 1978.

20. Brown University memo, from Richard A. Marker to Swearer, "Re, South Africa Business," April 5, 1978, box 41, S.A. Investment Policy, S.A. General, Swearer Papers, Brown University Archives.

21. "Council Grants Ad Hoc Status to Group Opposing Disinvestment," *Brown Daily Herald*, April 18, 1978.

22. Julie A. Shapiro to Swearer, April 20, 1978, box 41, S.A. Investment Policy, S.A. General, Swearer Papers, Brown University Archives.

23. Brown University memo, from Swearer to Shaun Brown and Ruben Cordova, April 25, 1978, box 41, S.A. Investment Policy, S.A. General, Swearer Papers, Brown University Archives.

24. "SASC Denies Swearer Chance to Address Protesting Ugrads."

25. "SASC Denies Swearer Chance to Address Protesting Ugrads."

26. "Guidelines for the Use of University Resources for Political Activity on the Brown University Campus," box 37, Swearer Papers, Brown University Archives.

27. Swearer to Pedro Noguera, December 14, 1979, box 41, S.A. Investment Policy, S.A. General, Swearer Papers, Brown University Archives.

28. "Guidelines for the Use of University Resources for Political Activity on the Brown University Campus."

29. Swearer to Noguera, December 19, 1979, box 41, S.A. Investment Policy, S.A. General, Swearer Papers, Brown University Archives.

30. Cordova, Sharon Smith, and Ahmed Sehrawy to Swearer, December 6, 1978, box 41, S.A. Investment Policy, S.A. General, Swearer Papers, Brown University Archives.

31. James Forman Jr., phone interview with the author, Ann Arbor, MI, November 6, 2018.

32. "Exploring Names and Faces Behind Pro-Divest," *Brown Daily Herald*, November 14, 1985.

33. "Students Strike, Sit-In to Support TWC," *Brown Daily Herald*, April 15, 1985.

34. "Stressing Education," *Brown Daily Herald*, October 24, 1985.

35. "Swearer on Divestment," *Brown Daily Herald*, September 19, 1985.

36. Eric Widmer to members of the Free Southern Africa Coalition, February 25, 1986, South Africa—1985–86, file 2, from March 1, 1986, VI.79, box 98, Swearer Papers, Brown University Archives.

37. "Students Rally for End of Apartheid," *Brown Daily Herald*, April 8, 1985.

38. "Brown Divest Refutes Bray," *Brown Daily Herald*, October 28, 1985.

39. "Political Role of Endowment," *Brown Daily Herald*, November 6, 1985.

40. Advisory Committee on Corporate Responsibility in Investment, meeting minutes, October 9, 1980, box 49, Swearer Papers, Brown University Archives.

41. "Brown Corporation Votes for Limited, Phased Divesture of U.S. Companies in South Africa," *Brown News Bureau*, February 15, 1986.

42. "W. Duncan MacMillan, 'Trustee Speaks Out,'" *Brown Daily Herald*, February 12, 1986.

43. "Finger-Wagging Stirs Outrage," *Brown Daily Herald*, February 13, 1986.

44. "Finger-Wagging Stirs Outrage."

45. "A Visit With A South African Student," *Brown Daily Herald*, August 28, 1985.

46. "Brown Corporation Votes for Limited, Phased Divestiture of U.S. Companies in South Africa," February 15, 1986, box 98, South Africa—1985–86, file 2, from March 1, 1986, VI.79, Swearer Papers, Brown University Archives; "Excerpts from the Minutes of the Corporation Meeting," February 15, 1986, box 99, South Africa—1985–86, file 1, to February 28, 1986, VI.80, Swearer Papers, Brown University Archives.

47. STARR National Service Fellowship at Brown University, box 58, Swearer Papers, Brown University Archives.

48. "We Are Involved, James," *Brown Daily Herald*, November 11, 1987.

49. "On Political Action," *Brown Daily Herald*, September 23, 1986.

50. "A Semester of Change for Divest Coalition," *Brown Daily Herald*, May 8, 1986.

51. "A Semester of Change for Divest Coalition." In response to the decision by the Brown University Corporation, Paul Zimmerman and two other members fasted, a technique originally employed by students at Stanford University in the late 1970s. University officials threatened expulsion. Widmer, the dean of students, stated: "Unless you are promptly admitted to the care and supervision of a licensed physician in an appropriate setting, I must . . . reassess your continued eligibility for enrollment at Brown. We cannot continue to be responsible for your well-being in an environment over which we have no control." Andi Feron responded: "They're not morally concerned with our health, they're legally concerned with our health." "Widmer Tells Fasters Disenrollment Possible," *Brown Daily Herald*, March 6, 1986.

52. "Swearer to Award 9 Starr Fellowships," *Brown Daily Herald*, September 9, 1986.

53. Swearer, "The Academy and Public Service," March 13, 1987, box 106, Center for Public Service, Swearer Papers, Brown University Archives.

54. Susan Stroud, "Report to the Education Commission of the States and Campus Compact," March 12, 1987, box 106, Center for Public Service, 1986–88, VII.28, Swearer Papers, Brown University Archives.

7. Georgetown University

1. Leslie M. Harris, James T. Campbell, and Alfred L. Brophy, eds., *Slavery and the University: Histories and Legacies* (Athens: University of Georgia Press, 2019); and

Rachel L. Swarms, *The 272: The Families Who Were Enslaved and Sold to Build the American Catholic Church* (New York: Penguin Random House, 2023).

2. Franklin J. Pearl, "Timothy S. Healy, 69, Dies; President of Public Library," *New York Times*, January 1, 1993.

3. "Does Anyone Care About Apathy?," *Georgetown Voice*, December 1, 1981.

4. "The University Seen from the Top," *Georgetown Voice*, December 1, 1981.

5. Transcripts of Proceedings, First Meeting of the Coalition of College Presidents for Civic Responsibility, Washington, DC, January 16, 1986, Campus Compact Library, Boston, MA.

6. "The University Seen from the Top."

7. "Meet the Less Fortunate," *Hoya*, August 30, 1980.

8. Lisa Ferdette, "The New Activism," *Georgetown Voice*, September 10, 1985.

9. "Where Did the Activism Go?," *Georgetown Voice*, November 9, 1982.

10. "'You Had to Be There,'" *Georgetown Voice Magazine*, April 1973.

11. "Where Have the Activists Gone?," *Georgetown Today*, September 1976.

12. "Protesting '80s-Style," *Georgetown Voice*, February 2, 1985.

13. "The Establishment Protesting Itself," *Georgetown Voice*, February 12, 1985.

14. "South Africa Liberation Week Planned," *Hoya*, January 26, 1979.

15. "Stu-Senate Wants Discussion of 'Questionable' Investments," *Hoya*, February 3, 1978.

16. Richard McSorely, "South African Investments," *Hoya*, February 3, 1978.

17. "Anti-Apartheid at GU," *Georgetown Voice*, April 3, 1984.

18. "Students Call on the University to Divest," *Hoya*, April 11, 1986.

19. "Report of the Policy and Budget Subcommittee to the Board of Trustees," October 19, 1985.

20. "Report on the Committee on Investments and Social Responsibility," Georgetown University and South Africa, n.d., box 2, folder 26, Secretary (Board Minutes), Georgetown University Archives.

21. Suzy Gallager, "Law Center Boycott Succeeds; Marriot Signs Sullivan Code," September 29, 1981, Unknown, Reference File 1, Georgetown University Archives.

22. "Richard McSorely, South African Investments," *Hoya*, February 3, 1978.

23. In the early meetings, older members of the Black-nationalist All African Peoples' Revolutionary Party talked a lot about the importance of Black students needing to lead the coalition. Marty Ellington wrote in the constitution of SCAR that the organization must be led by students of color.

24. SCAR, "Why American Youth and Students Should Oppose Apartheid and Fight for the Total Isolation of South Africa," February 1, 1985, Kathleen McShea Erville Papers, African Activist Archive, Michigan State University.

25. "The Need for Change . . .," *Georgetown Voice*, April 3, 1984.

26. "Rally Highlights South Africa Issue," *Georgetown Voice*, April 16, 1985.

27. "With an Eye to the Future, GU Grads Teach in Africa," *Hoya*, n.d.

28. "With an Eye to the Future, GU Grads Teach in Africa"; "Georgetown Volunteers Await South African Visas," *Hoya*, August 28, 1987.

29. "A Report On: The Harvard University South African Internship Program," box 21, folder 310, South African Apartheid Collection, Manuscripts and Archives, Yale University Archives.

30. Interview; "Volunteering in DC Schools for the Love of the Children" (Cesie, Jesuit Service Mission); "Service: A Bargain at Twice the Price," *Hoya*, September 1, 1989.

31. "DC SCAR Plans Protest of Barriers to Education," *Hoya*, October 11, 1988.

32. "Corporate Actions Cloud Jesuit Identity," *Hoya*, n.d.

33. "Report on the Committee on Investments and Social Responsibility."

34. Rob Nau, "SCAR, PSU Rally Against University," *Hoya*, April 18, 1986.

35. "SCAR, PSU Rally Against University."

36. Phillip Inglima to William C. Schuerman, May 2, 1985, box 35, folder 27, President's Office (O'Donovan), Georgetown University Archives.

37. "DeGioia Orders Student Arrests," *Hoya*, May 2, 1986.

38. "DeGioia Orders Student Arrests."

39. "Shanty Raid Shatters Ideal," *Hoya*, May 2, 1986.

40. Statement to the Adjudication Board, May 2, 1986, box 14, folder 25, President's Office (Healy), Georgetown University Archives.

41. "University Shuts Down Freedom College Protest," *Hoya*, May 2, 1986.

42. "Resolutions Passed at the Faculty Meeting," May 14, 1986, box 2, folder 25, Secretary (Board Minutes), Georgetown University Archives. Although it was not cited in the meeting, Seidman likely was referring to the Edwards v. South Carolina case, 372 U.S. 229 (1963).

43. "Resolutions Passed at the Faculty Meeting."

44. John Pfordresher to Timothy Healy, April 30, 1986, box 14, folder 24, Papers of the President's Office (Healy), Georgetown University Archives.

45. John Glavin to Father Healy, April 25, 1986, box 14, folder 24, President's Office (Healy), Georgetown University Archives.

46. "Freedom to Dissent: The University As a Public Forum," *Hoya*, May 27, 1983.

47. "Resolutions Passed at the Faculty Meeting."

48. Open Letter, Rev. Robert J. Rokusek, Rev. Dr. Bruce G. Epperly, Rev. Joseph Currie, S.J., Rev. Dr. Katherine G. Epperly, Rabbi Harold S. White, Sr. Dorinda Young, Sr. Mary Himens, May 2, 1986, box 14, folder 25, President's Office (Healy), Georgetown University Archives.

49. "Catholic Group to Shed South African Investments," *Washington Post*, June 6, 1987.

50. "250 Held in Rallies Against Apartheid," Associated Press, May 3, 1985.

51. "A U.S Policy Toward South Africa: The Report of the Secretary of State's Advisory Committee on South Africa," January 1987, 891110, box 176, South Africa, President's Office (Healy), Georgetown University Archives.

52. Twiggs Xiphu to Father Healy, April 21, 1986, box 14, folder 23, President's Office (Healy), Georgetown University Archives.

53. "SCAR Disciplining Actions Dropped," *Hoya*, August 29, 1986.

54. "DeGioia Discusses Student Service in DC Area," *Hoya*, October 24, 1988.

55. "New Committee Proposes Speech and Protest Guidelines," *Hoya*, September 18, 1987.

56. "DeGioia Bungles Protest Policy," *Hoya*, September 18, 1987.

57. Maria R. Rodriguez and Beth Knight, "Freedom College Revisited," *Georgetown Voice*, September 30, 1986.

Conclusion

1. Student Leadership Seminar Prospectus, box 109, US Student Association Records (hereafter USNSA Records), 1946–1971 (M70-277), WHS; "Report: USNSA Civil Rights Leadership Institute," Interdenominational Theological Center, Atlanta, GA, July 15–August 12, 1963, box 109, USNSA Records (M70-277), WHS.

2. "A Statement by Paul Potter . . . submitted for the consideration of the SDS 1964 National Convention in Pine Hill," Richard Flacks Papers, Department of Special Collections, UC Santa Barbara Library, University of California, Santa Barbara.

3. Paul Potter, letter to Rennie Davis, June 3, 1965, reel 11, SDS Papers.

4. Southern Regional Education Board, "Atlanta Service-Learning Conference Report" (1970), Conference Proceedings, 2.

5. Paul Lauter and Florence Howe, *The Conspiracy of the Young* (Cleveland: World Publishing, 1970), 10.

6. Lauter and Howe, *The Conspiracy of the Young*, 13.

7. Lauter and Howe, *The Conspiracy of the Young*, 5.

8. *The Report of the President's Commission on Campus Unrest* (Washington, DC: US Government Printing Office, 1970), 193.

9. National Student Volunteer Program, *Directory of College Student Volunteer Programs, Academic Year 1972–1973* (Washington, DC: US Government Printing Office, 1973).

10. Frank Newman, William Cannon, Stanley Cavell, Audrey Cohen, Russel Edgerton, James Gibbons, Martin Kramer, Joseph Rhodes, and Robert Singleton, *Report on Higher Education* (Washington, DC: US Government Printing Office, 1971), 21.

11. Newman, *Higher Education and the American Resurgence* (Princeton, NJ: Carnegie Foundation, 1985).

12. "Transcripts of Proceedings, First Meeting of the Coalition of College Presidents for Civic Responsibility," January 16, 1986, Washington, DC, Campus Compact Library, Boston, MA.

13. "Public Service by Students Is Promoted," *Boston Globe*, October 17, 1985.

14. During his opening address, Newman encouraged everyone to read the COOL resource book as a model for the Campus Compact. Wayne Meisel, Robert Hackett, and COOL, *Building A Movement: A Resource Book for Students in Community Service* (St. Paul, MN: Cool Press, 1986).

15. "The Durham Statement," from the participants of the Campus Outreach Opportunity League's Summit, Duke University, August 12, 1987, carton 14, Donald Kennedy Presidential Papers, SC0315 1989-267, Stanford University Archives.

16. William F. Buckley Jr., "Common Service," *Universal Press Syndicate*, January 28, 1986. Buckley also supported calls for national service and volunteerism. See Buckley, *Gratitude: Reflections on What We Owe to Our Country* (New York: Random House, 1990).

17. James S. Coleman, "Social Capital in the Creation of Human Capital," *American Journal of Sociology* 94 (1988), supplement S95–S120; Robert D. Putnam, "Bowling Alone: America's Decline Social Capital," *Journal of Democracy* 6 (1995): 65–78.

18. Carole Levine, "Campus Compact, Members' Report, 1988–89," Campus Compact Library, Boston, MA.

19. Martha Prescod Noonan, "Experiencing the Sixties at the Intersection of SDS and SNCC," in *A New Insurgency: The Port Huron Statement and Its Times*, ed. Howard Brick and Gregory Parker (Ann Arbor: Maize Books, Michigan Publishing, 2015).

20. Edward Zlotkowski, "Linking Service-Learning and the Academy," *Change* 28 (January/February 1996): 20–27.

21. John W. Eby, "Why Service-Learning Is Bad." *Service Learning, General* (1998): 27.

22. Timothy K. Stanton, Dwight E. Giles, Jr., and Nadinne I. Cruz, *Service-Learning: A Movement's Pioneers Reflect on Its Origins, Practice, and Future* (San Francisco: Jossey-Bass, 1999), 171–172.

23. Kathryn Forbes, Linda Garber, Loretta Kensinger, and Janet Trapp Slagter, "Punishing Pedagogy: The Failings of Forced Volunteerism," *Women's Studies Quarterly* 27, no. 3/4 (Fall/Winter 1999): 158–168.

24. Italics in original quote. Harry C. Boyte, "Community Service and Civic Education," *Phi Delta Kappan* (June 1991): 766. Boyte has become a strong advocate for "civic politics" in higher education. See Boyte, Stephen Elkin, Peter Levine, Jane Mansbridge, Elinor Ostrom, Karol Soltan, Rogers Smith, "The New Civic Politics: Civic Theory and Practice for the Future," *Good Society* 23, no. 2 (2014): 206–211.

25. Tania D. Mitchell, "Traditional vs. Critical Service-Learning: Engaging the Literature to Differentiate Two Models," *Michigan Journal of Community Service Learning* (Spring 2008): 50–65. Sociologist Randy Stoecker also developed a similar "ideal type" framework in his discussion on community based research, an extension of service learning. Stoecker, "Community-Based Research: From Practice to Theory and Back Again," *Michigan Journal of Community Service Learning* (Spring 2003): 35–46.

26. Anne Colby, Elizabeth Beaumont, Thomas Ehrlich, and Josh Corngold, *Educating for Democracy: Preparing Undergraduates for Responsible Political Engagement* (San Francisco: Jossey-Bass, 2007). As other political scientists have noted, this is part of a broader trend in American public life. On the relationship between shifting economic policy and volunteerism, see Nina Eliasoph, *The Politics of Volunteering* (Cambridge, UK: Polity, 2013).

27. Despite the fact that many service learning pioneers cite the influence of mass student politics in the 1960s on the emergence of service learning, students have been notably absent in histories of service learning. Most histories of service learning focus on either foundational ideas or the policy frameworks that enabled its growth in American higher education. On the pioneers, see Timothy K. Stanton, Dwight E. Giles, and Nadinne Cruz, *Service-Learning: A Movement's Pioneers Reflect on Its Origins, Practice and Future* (San Francisco: Jossey-Bass, 1999). The historian David Scobey, in making his argument for the 2000s as a "Copernican Moment" for civics, claims that the beginning of the civic education movement started in the 1980s with the Campus Compact. See Donald W. Harward, ed., *Civic Provocations* (Washington, DC: Bringing Theory to Practice, 2012). Scholars have started to look at alternative roots of service learning. See Matthew Countryman and Timothy K. Eatman, "Connecting Civil Rights and Community Engagement," in *The Cambridge Handbook of Service Learning and Community Engagement*, ed. Corey Dolgon, Tania D. Mitchell, and Timothy K. Eatman (Cambridge, UK: Cambridge University Press, 2017); Nicholas Longo, "The Highlander Folk School," in *Why Community Matters: Connecting Education with Civic Life* (Albany: State University of New York Press, 2007);

and Kecia Hayes, "Critical Service-Learning and the Black Freedom Movement," in *Critical Service Learning as a Revolutionary Pedagogy: An International Project of Student Agency in Practice*, ed. Brad J. Portfillio and Heather Hickman (Charlotte, NC: Information Age, 2011). Interestingly, some service learning scholars, academic leaders, and policy makers have returned to the frameworks of the Truman Commission. See National Task Force on Civic Learning and Democratic Engagement, *A Crucible Moment: College Learning and Democracy's Future* (Washington, DC: Association of American Colleges and Universities, 2012).

28. Although not focused on the university per se, the scholarship of Wesley Hogan is a rare exception. See "Who's the Expert? An Essay on Evidence and Authority," in *On the Freedom Side: How Five Decades of Youth Activists Have Remixed American History* (Chapel Hill: University of North Carolina Press, 2019).

29. On free speech, see "Report of the Committee on Freedom of Expression," accessed August 2014, https://provost.uchicago.edu/sites/default/files/documents/reports/FOECommitteeReport.pdf. On justice as antithetical to the pursuit of truth and the psychology of contemporary student activism, see Greg Lukianoff and Jonathan Haidt, *The Coddling of the American Mind: How Good Intentions and Bad Ideas Are Setting Up a Generation for Failure* (New York: Penguin Press, 2008). For a more balanced overview of the central issues, see Jonathan Zimmerman, *Campus Politics: What Everyone Needs to Know* (New York: Oxford University Press, 2016). Peter Levine, "Another Time for Freedom? Lessons from the Civil Rights Era for Today's Campus," *Liberal Education* 105, no. 1 (Winter 2019).

30. "Kalven Committee: Report on the University's Role in Political and Social Action, Report of a faculty committee, under the chairmanship of Harry Kalven, Jr. Committee appointed by President George W. Beadle," *Record* I, no. 1 (November 11, 1967), https://provost.uchicago.edu/sites/default/files/documents/reports/KalvenRprt_0.pdf.

31. Foundation for Individual Rights and Expression, "The Wisdom of the University of Chicago's 'Kalven Report,'" October 12, 2023, https://www.thefire.org/news/wisdom-university-chicagos-kalven-report; Board of Trustees of the University of North Carolina at Chapel Hill, "Resolution on the Affirmation of Academic Freedom and Freedom of Speech," July 27, 2022. https://bot.unc.edu/wp-content/uploads/sites/160/2022/07/Meeting-Book-University-Affairs-Committee_Strategic-Initiatives-Committee-July-27-PUBLIC.pdf; Daniel Diermier, "The Need For Institutional Neutrality At Universities," *Forbes*, December 20, 2023. For a broader discussion of the uses of the Kalven report, see Jennifer Ruther, "The Uses and Abuses of the Kalven Report," *Chronicle of Higher Education*, October 23, 2023. For a critique, see Robert Post, "The Kalven Report, Institutional Neutrality, and Academic Freedom," July 20, 2023, in *Revisiting The Kalven Report: The University's Role In Social And Political Action*, ed. Keith E. Whittington and John Tomasi (Johns Hopkins Press, forthcoming), Yale Law School, Public Law Research Paper, available at https://ssrn.com/abstract=4516235.

32. Mario Savio, "Response to Assistant Dean Thomas Barnes," September 30, 1964, in *The Essential Mario Savio: Speeches and Writings That Changed America*, ed. Robert Cohen (Berkeley: University of California Press, 2014), 119.

Index

www.ingramcontent.com/pod-product-compliance
Lightning Source LLC
Chambersburg PA
CBHW020443100426
42812CB00036B/3434/J